What Can I Do Now?

Nursing

Second Edition

Books in the
What Can I Do Now? Series

Art
Computers
Engineering, Second Edition
Fashion
Health Care
Music
Nursing, Second Edition
Radio and Television, Second Edition
Safety and Security, Second Edition
Sports, Second Edition

What Can I Do Now?

Nursing

Second Edition

Ferguson

An imprint of Infobase Publishing

What Can I Do Now? Nursing, Second Edition

Copyright ©2007 by Infobase Publishing

Ferguson
An imprint of Infobase Publishing
132 West 31st Street
New York NY 10001

ISBN-10: 0-8160-6028-2
ISBN-13: 978-0-8160-6028-3

Library of Congress Cataloging-in-Publication Data

What can I do now? Nursing. — 2nd ed.
    p. cm.
  Rev. ed. of: Chicago, Ill. Preparing for a career in nursing. c1998.
  Includes index.
  ISBN 0-8160-6028-2 (hc : alk. paper)
  1. Nursing—Vocational guidance—Juvenile literature. [1. Nursing—Vocational guidance. 2. Vocational guidance.] I. J.G. Ferguson Publishing Company. Preparing for a career in nursing. II. J.G. Ferguson Publishing Company.
  RT82.P74 2007
  610.7306'9—dc22   2006031215

Ferguson books are available at special discounts when purchased in bulk quantities for businesses, associations, institutions, or sales promotions. Please call our Special Sales Department in New York at (212) 967-8800 or (800) 322-8755.

You can find Ferguson on the World Wide Web at http://www.fergpubco.com

Text design by Kerry Casey
Cover design by Takeshi Takahashi

Printed in the United States of America

VB Hermitage 10 9 8 7 6 5 4 3 2 1

This book is printed on acid-free paper.

All links and Web addresses were checked and verified to be correct at the time of publication. Because of the dynamic nature of the Web, some addresses and links may have changed since publication and may no longer be valid.

Contents

Introduction

There are more than 3 million nurses working in the United States today. Most work in hospitals, but more and more are working in less mainstream settings—public health centers, corporations, schools, private homes. Just as the focus of their service can be vastly different, the opportunities available to them as health care professionals can be quite diverse. If you are considering a career in nursing—which presumably you are since you're reading this book—you must realize that the better informed you are from the start, the better your chances of having a successful, satisfying career.

There is absolutely no reason to wait until you get out of high school to "get serious" about a career. That doesn't mean you have to make a firm, undying commitment right now. Indeed, one of the biggest fears most people face at some point (sometimes more than once) is choosing the right career. Frankly, many people don't "choose" at all. They take a job because they need one, and all of a sudden 10 years have gone by and they wonder why they're stuck doing something they hate. Don't be one of those people! You have the opportunity right now—while you're still in high school and still relatively unencumbered with major adult responsibilities—to explore, to experience, to try out a work path. Or several paths if you're one of those overachieving types. Wouldn't you really rather find out sooner than later that you're not cut out to be a nurse after all, that you'd actually prefer to be doctor? Or an occupational therapist? Or a health care facility administrator?

There are many ways to explore the health care industry in general and nursing in particular. What we've tried to do in this book is give you an idea of some of your options. Section 1, What Do I Need to Know? will give you an overview of the field of nursing—a little history, where it's at today, and promises of the future; as well as a breakdown of its structure (how it's organized) and a glimpse of some of its many career options.

Section 2, Careers, includes 10 chapters, each describing in detail a specific nursing specialty: legal nurse consultant, licensed practical nurse, neonatal nurse, nurse anesthetist, nurse assistant, nurse-midwife, nurse practitioner, nursing instructor, registered nurse, and surgical nurse. The educational requirements for these specialties range from high school diploma to Ph.D. These chapters rely heavily on first-hand accounts from real people on the job. They'll tell you what skills you need, what personal qualities you have to have, what the ups and downs of the jobs are. You'll also find out about educational requirements—including specific high school and college classes—

1

advancement possibilities, related jobs, salary ranges, and the future outlook.

In keeping with the secondary theme of this book (the primary theme being "You can do something now"), Section 3, Do It Yourself, urges you to take charge and start your own programs and activities where none exist—school, community, or the nation.

The real meat of the book is in Section 4, What Can I Do Right Now? This is where you get busy and *do something*. The chapter "Get Involved" tells you about volunteer and intern positions as well as summer camps, summer college study and summer college courses, high school nursing programs, and student health care organizations.

The best way to explore nursing is to jump right in and start doing it, but there are plenty of other ways to get into the nursing mind-set. "Surf the Web" offers you a short annotated list of nursing Web sites where you can explore everything from job listings (start getting an idea of what employers are looking for now) to educational and certification requirements to on-the-job accounts to nurse jokes. (Yes, nurses are funny, too.)

"Read a Book" is an annotated bibliography of books (some new, some old) and periodicals. If you're even remotely considering a career in nursing, reading a few books and checking out a few magazines is the easiest thing you can do. Don't stop with our list. Ask your librarian to point you to more nursing materials.

"Ask for Money" is a sampling of nursing scholarships. You need to be familiar with these because you're going to need money for school. You have to actively pursue scholarships; no one is going to come up to you in the hall one day and present you with a check because you're such a wonderful student. Applying for scholarships is work. It takes effort. And it must be done right and often a year in advance of when you need the money.

"Look to the Pros" is the final chapter. It's a list of professional organizations that you can turn to for more information about accredited schools, education requirements, career descriptions, salary information, job listings, scholarships, and much more. Once you become a nursing student, you'll be able to join many of these. Time after time, professionals say that membership and active participation in a professional organization is one of the best ways to network (make valuable contacts) and gain recognition in your field.

High school can be a lot of fun. You may be involved in many social and extracurricular activities, or maybe you are just biding your time until you graduate. Whoever you are, take a minute and try to imagine your life five years from now. Ten years from now. Where will you be? What will you be doing? Whether you realize it or not, how you choose to spend your time now—studying, playing, watching TV, working at a fast-food restaurant, hanging out, whatever—will have an impact on your future. Take a look at how you're spending your time now and ask yourself, "Where is this getting me?" If you can't come up with an answer, it's probably "nowhere." The choice is yours. No one is going to take you by the hand and lead you in the "right" direction. It's up to you. It's your life. You can do something about it right now!

SECTION 1

What Do I Need to Know About the Nursing Industry?

Let's face it. Visiting the doctor and going to the hospital aren't on most people's top 10 lists of favorite things to do. However, millions of people all over the country do just that every day and enjoy it! They want to be there—most have even worked hard to get there. No, they're not members of some weird group that likes to eat hospital food and wear paper clothing—they're nurses. Nurses that make your doctor's appointment or hospital stay quicker, easier, and less painful. If you think about it, when you go to the doctor, you spend the majority of your time interacting with nurses—whether in the waiting room, at the main desk, or in the treatment room.

GENERAL INFORMATION

The demand for nurses has skyrocketed over the past decade. More importantly for you, this growth is expected to remain steady through 2012, according to the U.S. Department of Labor. That's great news whether you're a high school student or still in junior high. Nursing has become a highly respected career. Unfortunately, nursing didn't start out that way. The nurses of today—possibly you in the future—have several founding heroines to thank for the nursing industry's current high standards.

In the United States, hospitals developed slowly in colonial times. When someone became sick, relatives and friends usually took care of them. This was true of the upper and middle classes, at least. If you were poor and sick . . . well, that was a different story. Many poor people who became sick were sent to poorhouses because they had no nonworking family or friends to care for them. Medical care in these poorhouses was often little more than threadbare bandages and infrequent medications. Because these poorhouses were run with public money, medical care and supplies were lacking. There was a vast difference in the quality of medical care given to those with money and those without. The care we often take for granted today was out of reach for many poor colonials.

The first hospital in the United States—The Pennsylvania Hospital—opened in 1751, but conditions were very crude. Although called "nurses," the staff were actually just untrained servant women. Obviously, changes were necessary, and the establishment of the American Medical Association in 1847 was a step in the right direction. However, it was not until 1911 that medical reform and nursing standards were addressed and upgraded.

At about the same time, Florence Nightingale, the founder of modern nursing, was helping thousands of wounded soldiers in the Crimean War. She tended four miles of beds all day long, caring for around 10,000 soldiers during her time there. In the years after the war, Nightingale began to structure nursing into an

> While our soldiers stand and fight, I can stand and feed and nurse them.
> —Clara Barton, founder of the Red Cross

orderly, trained workforce. In 1860 she established the first school of nursing at St. Thomas Hospital in London. The school trained hospital nurses and nurses to serve the poor in remote and inner-city areas. Nurses were also trained to teach other nurses to spread nursing practices and expertise as quickly as possible. Graduates from the Nightingale Training School traveled to many parts of the world and continued to train others in nursing techniques. The first U.S. school of nursing was established in 1872 at the New England Hospital for Women and Children in Boston. By 1898 there were schools of nursing in New York City and New Haven, Connecticut. Nightingale's work influenced nursing practices in countries throughout the world.

Along with Nightingale's contributions, the early American spirit of giving played a large role in the further growth of the nursing field. Volunteerism, especially by women, formed a foundation for organized nursing in America. At the beginning of the Civil War, Ladies Aid Societies included nurses who traveled to the front lines to treat wounded soldiers. More than 2,000 women from both the North and the South served in military hospitals, hospital ships, trains, and wagons. In fact, though better known for her accomplishments with the Underground Railroad, Harriet Tubman served as a nurse during the Civil War. Her special homemade water lily brew helped treat hundreds of Union soldiers.

After the Civil War, interest in nursing grew and, along with the teaching of Nightingale, led to the opening of several

Lingo to Learn

American Nurses Association This organization represents the nation's more than 3 million registered nurses.

anesthetic Substance used to keep the patient from feeling pain during surgery.

defibrillation The application of an electric current to the heart of a patient to treat irregular heart rhythms.

dressings Another name for bandages used to cover wounds.

health maintenance organization A system of health care with physicians and professional staff providing care within certain limitations to people who pay to be a part of the health care system.

managed care A philosophy of health care that tries to keep medical costs down through education and preventive medicine.

patient history A record of past illnesses, injuries, and treatments given to a patient; usually taken when the patient is admitted to a care facility.

preferred provider organization A health insurance plan that contracts with doctors, hospitals, and other providers to obtain discounts for medical care. The providers agree on a predetermined list of fees for all services. It is a form of managed care.

vital signs Information such as blood pressure, respiration, pulse, and temperature that tell how the vital processes of the body are functioning.

nursing schools. The most popular method of training nurses was through hands-on work in teaching hospitals, which led to a hospital diploma for the nursing students. Today, this educational pathway is still available to you and others interested in a nursing career.

The increased focus on educating nurses also led to the appeal for nursing standards and regulations. You may wonder why nurses were interested in setting standards and creating regulations that they would have to follow and be judged by. There were two main reasons for this. First, nurses wanted to be certain the patients they were serving were given the correct care at all times. Remember, the concern for the welfare of others is now, and was then, at the core of nursing. Secondly, these standards and regulations would help give nursing the professional status it deserved. In other words, nurses hoped that the adoption of regulations and certification requirements would cause others in medical careers to stop looking down on nurses as unskilled and unprofessional. Although nurses would continue doing the same work, with the same level of commitment as before the regulations, it was hoped that standards and regulations would bring the profession of nursing into the forefront of the medical community as a respected occupation.

To answer this demand, nurses established the first national nursing association—the American Society of Superintendents of Training Schools for Nurses. This eventually led to the formation of the American Nurses Association, which remains today in service to the nursing field.

Other state regulations helped support the effort for standardized nursing. In New York, nurses had to be graduates of training schools approved by the leaders of the state university to obtain a license to work in the nursing field. Still, laws were inconsistent within and between states. Most states required training but did not specify the quality of training required. Nurses with the same number of years of training often had vastly different skill and knowledge levels.

Like the Crimean War and the Civil War, World War II greatly affected the nursing field. More nurses were recruited during this war than at any other time in history. Thousands signed up for the Cadet Nurse Corps. What a perfect time to graduate with a nursing degree! Again, nurses played a vital role in the treatment and care of thousands of soldiers.

Because of the enormous response of these Cadet Nurses, nursing became a popular field of study for women and men. Prior to this time, women made up almost the entire nursing field. (Although women continue to outnumber men in this field even today, more and more men are finding satisfying careers in nursing.) With greater numbers pursuing this line of work, more pressure was applied to have a consistent set of guidelines and regulations for the nursing profession.

In 1970, New York revised its Nursing Practice Act and acknowledged nursing as its own separate profession with its own licensing and educational requirements, regulations, and standards. Other

> We must be learning all our lives . . . every year we know more of the great secrets of nursing.
> —*Florence Nightingale*

states soon followed. More than 100 nursing organizations sprang up to meet the needs of that growing population of nursing and nursing-related professionals. As needs for specific medical treatments arose, nurses began to specialize in different medical areas, such as cardiology (treatment of the heart) and gerontology (treatment of elderly patients).Today, registered nurses alone make up 28 percent of the entire health care industry. That's staggering considering that the health care industry includes doctors, lab workers, physician assistants, orderlies, attendants, optometrists, podiatrists, chiropractors, dermatologists, dentists, clinical chemists, radiological technicians, respiratory therapists, physical therapists, speech therapists, and many more professionals.

One of the major developments in nursing today is the shift in where nurses work. In the past, most nurses found jobs in hospitals, but in recent years, there has been a shift to community health nursing (or public health nursing). Nurses in public health settings concentrate on preventing disease and sickness through educating the public, promoting healthy living, and working to make health care accessible to those who may otherwise

not be able to get it. These are also goals of nurses in hospitals and doctors' offices, but they are more focused on the treatment and care of a patient after the disease or sickness has occurred. Public health nurses try to curb the numbers of sick and diseased people by increasing awareness of the different threats to good health and helping to prevent the spread of illnesses.

You'll find community health nurses in clinics, labor camps, rural areas, schools, outpatient clinics, and other public institutions. Unique settings and people with various ethnic, economic, and social backgrounds await the services of the community health nurse. These opportunities are increasing and pulling many nurses away from traditional hospital roles.

Hospitals are losing their nursing staff to other areas as well. Home health care agencies continue to have unfilled openings for nurses. Home health care allows patients to spend less time in a hospital and more time in their homes recuperating. Many nurses are turning to home health care for the opportunity to become more involved on a long-term, one-on-one basis with a patient and his or her family. Also, these nurses work independently in most cases, so they are free to make their own decisions about general nursing care without answering to other medical staff.

Finally, from the early days of the Florence Nightingale Training School to the present, nursing has been about learning. Advances in technology are one of the things that make the medical industry, and nursing in particular, ever-changing and exciting. Medical machinery quickly becomes outdated. Nurses who specialize in certain areas and keep abreast of technological advances and enhancements are in high demand. Nurses must be continually seeking information about new technology and new ways of treating patients.

STRUCTURE OF THE INDUSTRY

Today, most nurses (about 60 percent) still work in hospitals. Other nurses work in community health settings, ambulatory care, nursing homes, home health care, clinics, HMOs, research, rehabilitation centers, schools, corporate health departments, and shared practices.

The trend in hospitals today is cost cutting. One of the ways hospitals achieve this is to shorten hospital stays and perform more procedures on an outpatient basis. This policy reduces the number of nurses needed. As a result, many nurses are making their way to long-term care, home health care, school clinics, and community nursing.

Another method hospitals use to cut costs is to merge several hospitals together to become one larger entity with several campuses. Mergers allow different hospitals to share technology, knowledge, programs, and activities.

Despite often drastic cost-cutting methods, hundreds of hospitals have closed because a lack of funds prevents them from keeping up with new technology. Of the 6,000 hospitals in the United States today, one-fifth are teaching hospitals. These teaching hospitals offer accredited medical residency programs and clinical learning sites for nursing students. Large medical centers (called academic health centers) often combine teaching and research facilities.

Hospitals vary in physical size and in the number of patients that can be treated at any one time. Small hospitals may have as few as 25 beds and large hospitals as many as 2,000. The two major kinds of facilities are short-term general hospitals (approximately 160 beds) and long-term hospitals (approximately 900 beds).

There are also government hospitals, with the Veterans Administration Hospital being the largest centrally directed hospital and clinic system. States, cities, and counties have their own hospitals, and there are also many hospitals that provide specific care to specific patients, such as women's hospitals, rehabilitation hospitals, and psychiatric hospitals. All hospitals are licensed by the state in which they reside and must maintain certain state and federal standards.

The internal organization varies from hospital to hospital, but some general practices are usually found everywhere. Most hospitals have nursing units that are composed of many different nursing areas. The nursing department in most hospitals is the largest individual department, with many levels of general nurses and specialized nurses. Registered nurses (RNs) direct and supervise licensed practical nurses (LPNs) and unlicensed nursing staff members.

The hierarchy of the nursing department usually follows this order: chief nurse, nurse manager, staff nurse. The *chief nurse* (or *executive nurse*) is in charge of the nursing unit and makes all work assignments and instructs the nurse manager and staff nurses. The *nurse manager* carries out administrative duties and helps supervise staff nurses. *Staff nurses* complement the doctor's treatment with hands-on care. These are usually the duties and order of positions, but each hospital may be somewhat different.

Primary nursing style is fairly common in most hospitals. The *primary nurse* is completely responsible for all aspects of a patient's care, although other nurses will treat the patient under the primary nurse's instruction. The primary nurse (usually an RN) consults other members of the medical staff on the overall treatment of the patient.

Matrix-style nursing units are fairly new and involve grouping nurses and other medical staff around special projects. The difference between matrix-style and traditional nursing styles is that the matrix-style nurse works directly with a team on a project-by-project basis. Instead of being just one step in the whole method of treatment, the nurse is involved in the entire process from beginning to end.

Functional nursing is a less common nursing style. This style calls for several different nurses to care for the same patient but with different focuses. For example, John Doe may have a nurse who checks his vital signs and takes care of administering medicines, another nurse who is responsible for making sure the medical machinery is working properly, and another who takes care of his comfort needs.

The style of nursing used by a hospital is dependent on several things. The number of nurses compared to the number of patients, the administration's understanding of the nursing needs, the level of training of the nurses, and the management style of head nurses may all be factors contributing to the style of nursing for individual hospitals.

The hospital leadership is usually the administrator, president, or corporate executive officer. This leadership position usually reports to a governing board of trustees.

If you've ever walked through a hospital, you know that it's made up of a lot of different sections, or units. The physical structure of most hospitals includes clinical units, operating rooms, recovery suites, emergency rooms, intensive care units, treatment units, laboratories, radiology departments, pharmacies, social services, doctors' offices, and so on. Nurses can usually be found in almost all hospital

> Nursing is the art and science dedicated to compassionate concern for health, preventing illness, and caring for and rehabilitating the members of our society.
> —*A registered nurse describing nursing today*

units where care and treatment are being administered.

Nursing homes offer another structure of work that may differ from facility to facility. Nursing homes usually have more regular tasks, so there may be no middle nursing manager. A chief nurse and a group of staff nurses make up the nursing team.

Home health situations offer a vastly different structure. One-on-one, long-term care means that the nurse is independent of other staff members. He or she will be making decisions and judgments concerning care without constant supervisory instruction. The nurse is usually given complete control over the care of the patient, along with medication instructions from a physician.

Similar to the home health care nurse, community health care nurses are independent also. No supervisor accompanies these nurses to homes that they visit to offer nursing services. They are employed by public health departments and visiting nurse associations.

School nurses and occupational health nurses are unique in that they are supervised by nonmedical management personnel.

Fast Facts

Neonatal nurses (newborn baby care) are now able to help save more than 80 percent of all infants born up to two months premature.

CAREERS

The two nursing career titles you may have heard of before you began researching the nursing field—registered nurse and licensed practical nurse—are the heart of the nursing field. Licensed practical nurses provide basic care to patients, often under the supervision of a registered nurse, and registered nurses can be found in areas from anesthetist nurses to emergency room nurses. You can aspire even further than registered nursing and become an advanced-practice nurse. These nurses perform many of the duties normally restricted to doctors. Nursing assistants also make up a large part of the nursing personnel in most hospitals; this is a job that you can start during your summer vacations during high school or right after graduation.

Nursing assistants help the registered nurses and licensed practical nurses with routine daily care of patients. Depending on where they are employed, nursing assistants may focus mainly on the physical needs of patients, such as helping them in and out of bed, admitting their paperwork, pushing their wheelchairs, and helping them walk. Some facilities also have nursing assistants who take and record blood pressure, pulse, temperature, and other vital signs.

Licensed practical nurses (*LPNs*), or *licensed vocational nurses*, give bedside care to sick, recovering, and injured patients in hospitals, clinics, nursing homes, and various other institutions. LPNs are required to have technical knowledge allowing them to perform tasks such as giving some medications, preparing and administering injections, and monitoring the patient's condition. They also record the patient's vital signs, assist the patient, and give general care in the form of wound dressing, compresses, and injections.

Registered nurses can work in a variety of settings. The workplace often defines the nature of the work for RNs. The following list explains specific nursing careers that RNs can choose.

- *Community health nurses*, sometimes known as *public health nurses*, work in clinics, schools, and patients' homes to provide preventive health care, immunizations, health education, and nursing treatments prescribed by a physician.
- *Critical care nurses* are specialized nurses who provide highly skilled direct patient care to critically ill patients needing intense medical treatment. Contrary to previously held beliefs that critical care nurses work only in intensive care units or cardiac care units of hospitals, today's critical care nurses work in the emergency departments, post-anesthesia recovery units, pediatric intensive care units, burn units, and neonatal intensive care units of medical facilities, as well as in other units that treat critically ill patients.
- *Dermatology nurses* treat patients with diseases and ailments of the skin, hair, mucous membranes, nails, and related tissues or structures.
- *Emergency nurses* provide highly skilled direct patient care to people who need emergency treatment for an illness or injury. Emergency nurses incorporate all the specialties of nursing. They care for infant, pediatric, adult, and elderly patients with a broad spectrum of medical needs.
- *Forensic nurses* examine victims of crimes such as sexual assault, domestic abuse, child abuse, or elder abuse. They gather evidence and information for law enforcement officials. They may also gather evidence at crime scenes or in other settings.
- *Geriatric nurses* provide direct patient care to elderly people in their homes, or in hospitals, nursing homes, and clinics. The term "geriatrics" refers to the clinical aspects of aging and the overall health care of the aging population. Since older people tend to have different reactions to illness and disease than younger people, treating them has become a specialty, and because the population is aging, the geriatric nurse is a promising nursing specialty.
- *Home health care nurses*, also called *visiting nurses*, provide home-based health care under the direction of a physician. They care for persons who may be recovering from an accident, illness, surgery, cancer, or childbirth. They may work for a community organization or a private health care provider, or they may be independent nurses who work on a contract basis.
- *Hospice nurses* care for people who are in the final stages of a terminal

illness. Typically, a hospice patient has less than six months to live. Hospice nurses provide medical and emotional support to the patients and their families and friends. Hospice care usually takes place in the patient's home, but patients may also receive hospice care in a hospital room, a nursing home, or a relative's home.

- *Hospital nurses* follow the medical care instructions provided by the physician to care for the needs of the patients. This includes giving medications and treatments. Nurses also maintain patient records. RNs in this setting also instruct and supervise nursing staff in the bedside care of patients.

- *Neonatal nurses* provide direct patient care to newborns in hospitals for the first month after birth. The babies they care for may be normal, they may be born prematurely, or they may be suffering from an illness or birth defect. Some of the babies require highly technical care such as surgery or the use of ventilators, incubators, or intravenous feedings.

- *Occupational health nurses* work in businesses, government facilities, and factories to provide treatment for minor, on-the-job illnesses and injuries. Nurses also give physical examinations and provide educational sessions about workplace safety and health.

- *Office nurses* assist doctors by preparing patients for examinations, performing laboratory testing, and overseeing administrative duties. These nurses may also work for dental surgeons, dentists, nurse practitioners, and nurse-midwives.

- *Oncological nurses* specialize in the treatment and care of cancer patients. While many oncological nurses care directly for cancer patients, some may be involved in patient or community education, cancer prevention, or cancer research. They may work in specific areas of cancer nursing, such as pediatrics, cancer rehabilitation, chemotherapy, biotherapy, hospice, or pain management.

- *Psychiatric nurses* focus on mental health. This includes the prevention of mental illness and the maintenance of good mental health, as well as the diagnosis and treatment of mental disorders. They care for pediatric, teen, adult, and elderly patients who may have a broad spectrum of mentally and emotionally related medical needs. In addition to providing individualized nursing care, psychiatric nurses serve as consultants, conduct research, and work in management and administrative positions in institutions and corporations.

- *School nurses* give physical examinations to students; provide yearly visual, audio, and scoliosis screenings; and educate students, staff, and parents on child wellness issues.

- *Surgical nurses* care for patients who are undergoing surgery. They include *floor nurses* (who work on surgical units) and *perioperative nurses.* There are several kinds of perioperative nurses. *Day surgery preop nurses* check patients in and get them ready for the day's surgery. *Scrub nurses* select and organize supplies and medical instruments that will be used during the surgery. The *circulating nurse* is a non-sterile member of the surgical team. Scrub and circulating nurses are also called *intra-op nurses. Post-anesthesia care unit nurses* take over from the intra-op nurses once the surgery is completed. They assess the patient for pain, breathing, bleeding, and general vital signs. They are also known as *postop nurses* and *recovery room nurses*. Additionally, *RN first assistants* are a relatively new type of surgical nurse who work directly with surgeons in the operating room and in office settings seeing preop and postop patients. They may also check on preop and postop patients, but they are not floor nurses.

While RNs, LPNs, and nursing assistants make up the greatest percentage of the nursing field, *advanced-practice nurses* have greater training requirements and more responsibility. Nurse anesthetists, nurse-midwives, nurse practitioners, and clinical nurse specialists are examples of advanced-practice nurses. These advanced-practice nurses have enough training and skill to do many of the tasks that are normally reserved for physicians.

- *Clinical nurse specialists* have higher training levels that are focused on a particular area, such as transplant nursing, critical care nursing, and cardiovascular nursing. Duties for these nurses vary depending on their specialty.

- *Nurse anesthetists* are among the highest paid in the nursing field. They administer anesthetics to patients prior to treatment or surgery.

- *Nurse-midwives* take care of newborn babies and their mothers. The nurse-midwife spends much of the workday talking to and instructing new, or soon-to-be, fathers and mothers.

- *Nurse practitioners* take on many of the responsibilities of a general physician. Nurse practitioners examine patients, take their histories, and diagnose and treat common medical illnesses and conditions.

Additionally, *nursing instructors* are needed to teach patient care to nursing students in classroom and clinical settings. They demonstrate care methods and monitor hands-on learning by their students. They instruct students in the principles and applications of biological and psychological subjects related to

Fast Facts

Known as the "Nurses on Horseback," Mary Breckinridge and her team of nurses traveled the dusty roads of the Midwest to provide complete health care 24 hours a day to rural areas for the first time in 1928.

nursing. Some nursing instructors specialize in teaching specific areas of nursing such as surgical or oncological nursing.

EMPLOYMENT OPPORTUNITIES

When looking for a job in nursing, the first places to check into (and the biggest employers of nurses nationwide) are hospitals. Larger hospitals that are equipped to handle hundreds and sometimes thousands of patients are the best bet, although smaller hospitals usually have fewer doctors and need the services of many nurses. Approximately 60 percent of all registered nurses work in hospitals today. Even though hospitals remain the major source of jobs for nurses, they are beginning to cut back in the hiring of nurses because of mergers and pressure to cut costs.

If the hospital scene isn't what you're after, there are plenty of other employers of nurses. Nursing homes and long-term health care facilities are expected to grow rapidly and employ more and more nurses to take care of the aging population. Doctors' offices, community health clinics, home health care, schools, health maintenance organizations, colleges and universities, prisons and correctional facilities, and disaster relief organizations are just a sampling of the wide variety of organizations that employ nurses today. Some nurses work as legal consultants, and others work as forensic nurses in law enforcement settings.

And let's not forget the government. The Department of Veterans Affairs runs 154 medical centers, 875 ambulatory care and community-based outpatient clinics, 136 nursing homes, 43 residential rehabilitation treatment programs, 206 veterans centers, and 88 comprehensive home care programs. The Department of Health and Human Services, Indian Health Service (IHS), and the National Institutes of Health (NIH) employ thousands of nurses at all levels of education and specialty areas.

INDUSTRY OUTLOOK

Better health benefits everyone—especially nurses! More and more people are living longer and requiring nursing care during the latter stages of their lives. The number of nursing homes and extended-care facilities is expected to increase steadily in the next decade, causing geriatric nurses (LPNs or RNs who specialize in caring for the elderly) to be in high demand. Home health care for the elderly should see the fastest growth in employment.

The current changes in hospital care and structure are also affecting the nursing industry. While there will continue to be a need for nurses in hospitals, many hospitals are being forced to cut back on their nursing staff to save money and to reallocate resources. What is contributing to these changes in hospitals? HMOs and other health care facilities are growing and providing strong competition. Also, hospitals are releasing patients after much shorter stays than in the past, lessening the need for nursing care. Nurse practitioners, however, should be in high

Interview: Lisa Rosenberg

Lisa Rosenberg, Ph.D., R.N., is the Associate Dean of Students at Rush University College of Nursing in Chicago, Illinois. She was kind enough to discuss nursing education and careers with the editors of What Can I Do Now?: Nursing.

Q. Rush University College of Nursing has an excellent reputation for preparing students for nursing careers. How can high school students who are interested in attending Rush and other nursing programs prepare effectively for postsecondary study?

A. Our best prepared students have a strong science background, that is, they like science, are curious about it, and have done well academically. In addition, strength in math and English is important. We also recommend that students get some experience being in a hospital either as a certified nursing assistant or through volunteer experience. Prospective students should have a strong sense that they find caring for sick people intrinsically rewarding.

Q. What personal qualities do students in your program need to be successful in their studies and in their careers?

A. Students should be empathetic; have good communication skills, the ability to control anxiety in stressful situations, and a strong ability to apply scientific knowledge in clinical situations; be curious and persevering; and truly care about the human condition.

Q. What advice would you offer nursing majors as they graduate and look for jobs?

A. Do what you love. Nursing fits 51 flavors, you can make a career doing just one thing or 10 different things in nursing. Continue your education; it is never a mistake to get a graduate degree in nursing. There is great deal of flexibility that comes with a master's or doctoral degree in nursing.

Q. How is the current job market for nursing grads?

A. The current job market is excellent. Our students usually have several job offers upon graduation. Critical care, operating room, neurosurgery, and orthopedics are particularly promising in terms of open positions. Nursing educators will continue to be in demand.

demand as hospitals replace some highly paid physicians with not-as-highly-paid nurse practitioners.

Technological advances in medicine have also made outpatient surgery a common occurrence today. While this means fewer nursing opportunities in hospitals, it greatly increases the demand for nurses in HMOs, outpatient facilities, and ambulatory surgery centers.

Most nurses entering the field today meet the challenges of new technology head-on by acquiring more education and specific training. As medical technology continues to improve, nurses are challenged to upgrade their training and are rapidly moving toward specialized areas. Unprecedented opportunities await nurses who are highly trained in medical technology and advanced medical practices.

Employment for LPNs is expected to increase much faster than average at nursing homes and long-term-care facilities, but is expected to remain about the same at hospitals. Again, the shift toward outpatient care leaves fewer inpatients who require the care of an LPN. Not only are there more outpatients to care for, but

federal and state legislation has also forced nursing homes to hire LPNs to care for patients instead of other health workers with minimal training.

The health care industry overall is expected to grow by 27 percent through 2014—or 13 percent more than the average for all industries in the United States. Within the health care arena, nursing continues to grow even as more and more nurses enter the field. Where hospitals are slowing down as the main avenue for nurses entering the field, outpatient and long-term-care facilities are picking up the slack.

SECTION 2

Careers

Legal Nurse Consultants

SUMMARY

Definition
Legal nurse consultants are experienced nurses who assist litigation teams with cases.

Alternative Job Titles
None

Salary Range
$30,000 to $45,000 to $100,000+

Educational Requirements
Some postsecondary training

Certification or Licensing
Voluntary (certification)
Required (licensing as a nurse)

Employment Outlook
Much faster than the average

High School Subjects
Anatomy and physiology
Biology
Chemistry
English (writing/literature)
Health
Law
Mathematics

Personal Interests
Current events
Helping people: physical health/medicine
Law

If you love nursing, enjoy research, and have a bit of detective in you, you might be interested in a career as a legal nurse consultant.

Barbara Levin, a legal nurse consultant since 1988, used all of these talents on a case that involved the review of medical records regarding a 31-year-old woman who was in a motor vehicle accident. The woman had sustained numerous orthopedic injuries, including right femur fracture, left tibia/fibula fracture, left humerus fracture, right radial fracture, and pelvic fracture. She underwent several surgeries to repair her fractures and was sent home from the hospital. Seven days later, she died of massive blood clots that broke off from her leg and lodged in her lung.

"I was hired by the plaintiff attorney and was asked to comment about the nursing care delivered to this woman in the hospital," Barbara recalls. "While reviewing the woman's medical records, I found a 'needle in the haystack'. She was at high risk for developing deep vein thrombosis and had initially been placed on a blood thinner medication for only three days instead of her entire hospitalization and recuperation. In addition, she never worked with physical therapy and was sent home via an ambulance to stay in a hospital bed. Both parents needed to care for her and there were no home services arranged to assist the family with the care." The prolonged immobility, lack of physical therapy, and other factors placed this woman at high risk for developing blood clots. "This woman was not a candidate to be discharged home." Barbara says, "Instead, she should have been transferred to a rehabilitation facility and continued on the blood thinner medication. This would have helped protect her against the development of blood clots."

Barbara testified on many aspects of this case regarding standards of nursing practice. "As a result of my testimony," Barbara says, "the case settled out of court for an undisclosed amount of money."

WHAT DOES A LEGAL NURSE CONSULTANT DO?

Legal nurse consultants are members of a litigation team that deal with medical malpractice, personal injury, and product liability lawsuits as well as other medically related legal cases. They may be employed independently on a contract or retainer basis; or they may be employed by law firms, insurance companies, corporations, government agencies, or as part of a risk management department in hospitals. Legal nurse consultants are trained nurses who have thorough understanding of medical issues and trends. They utilize their clin-

The History of Legal Nurse Consulting

Nurses have served as expert witnesses in nursing malpractice cases for many years. But it was not until the early 1970s, according to the American Association of Legal Nurse Consultants (AALNC), that nurses began to receive compensation for providing this much-needed expertise to the legal community. As nursing and medical malpractice litigation increased in the 1980s, more nurses were needed to serve as expert witnesses in legal proceedings. During this time, according to the AALNC, nurses also began assisting lawyers with understanding medical records and literature, hospital policies and procedures, and medical testimony. Law firms quickly realized that legal nurse consultants were a knowledgeable, cost-effective alternative to physician consultants and began to hire these professionals to assist them with not only nursing and medical malpractice issues, but also personal injury and criminal cases.

The American Association of Legal Nurse Consultants was founded in 1989 to serve the professional needs of legal nurse consultants.

ical experiences, knowledge of health care standards, and medical resources to assist litigation teams and to act as liaisons between the legal and health care communities. Their primary roles are to evaluate, analyze, and render informed opinions regarding health care. They practice in both plaintiff and defense capacities in collaboration with attorneys and others involved in legal processes.

Legal nurse consultants' job responsibilities vary depending on the case and their medical implications. When working on cases, they may conduct client interviews, which involve talking to people who feel they have legal claims against medical facilities, physicians, or nurses. They may research past medical cases and treatments. They often advise attorneys regarding medical facts, treatments, and other medical issues that are relevant to the cases. Legal nurse consultants obtain and organize medical records and locate and procure evidence. They may identify, interview, and retain expert witnesses. Assisting with depositions and trials, as well as developing and preparing exhibits for jury or judge trials, is also an aspect of this role.

As part of legal teams, legal nurse consultants are often required to do considerable research and paperwork. They must gather information and write reports.

Independent legal nurse consultants must also be responsible for getting their work done within strict deadlines. They often work under a contract and must produce the records, information, and reports within a specified time frame. In addition, they must generate their own clients. This requires that they be entrepreneurial nurses with a business mindset as well. Independent legal nurse consultants need to learn and practice business skills such as marketing, sales, and record keeping.

WHAT IS IT LIKE TO BE A LEGAL NURSE CONSULTANT?

Barbara Levin is a former president of the American Association of Legal Nurse Consultants and she is also the advanced clinician of the Orthopaedic Trauma Unit at Massachusetts General Hospital in Boston, Massachusetts. "I started in the field," she explains, "when an attorney contacted me to review medical records regarding a pedestrian who was struck by a motor vehicle and sustained numerous orthopedic injuries. My role was to explain the injuries and long-term/short-term goals for the person's future health."

Barbara works on a variety of cases with clients all around the United States. "Every day brings new beginnings," she says. "Some days I review medical records exclusively, while other days I participate in conference calls with attorneys and at times their clients to educate them on the variety of issues. Much of my time is spent researching various data for cases including research studies. I also serve as an expert witness by testifying on standards of care issues." Barbara also attends Independent Medical Examinations (IMEs) and writes detailed reports. Her practice includes participation in a variety of practice areas including: personal injury, medical malpractice, mediation/arbitration, IMEs, and limited criminal-related work. "Several years ago I expanded my practice to include participation at court mediations," she says. "This is a wonderful opportunity to serve as the educator on the various health issues to both parties as well as the mediator or judge."

To Be a Successful Legal Nurse Consultant, You Should . . .

- have strong organizational and writing skills
- be able to explain medical issues and procedures to people with nonmedical backgrounds
- be able to handle deadline pressure
- be able to work well with many types of people

DO I HAVE WHAT IT TAKES TO BE A LEGAL NURSE CONSULTANT?

To be a successful legal nurse consultant, you should enjoy organizing information, writing reports, explaining medical issues and procedures to people with nonmedical backgrounds, and be skilled to handle multiple tasks under deadline pressure. You should also have strong reasoning skills, self-motivation, and the ability to work well with many types of people.

If you practice as a nurse, you should enjoy working with people and be able to give directions as well as follow instructions and work as part of a health care team. "Anyone interested in becoming a legal nurse consultant should have a fascination and a strong desire to continue learning because new tests, procedures, and technologies are continually being developed," states Barbara Levin.

HOW DO I BECOME A LEGAL NURSE CONSULTANT?

Education

High School

While in high school, take mathematics and science courses, including biology, chemistry, and physics. Health courses will also be helpful. English and speech courses should not be neglected because you must be able to communicate well with attorneys and other legal professionals. Business and accounting classes can provide you with the basic tools necessary to run a business.

Postsecondary Training

Legal nurse consultants must first become registered nurses. There are three ways to become a registered nurse—a two-year associate's degree program at a junior or community college, a two- or three-year diploma program at a hospital, or a bachelor's degree program at a college or university. All the programs include supervised hands-on training in a hospital setting.

All legal nurse consultants must have clinical nursing experience. They draw on this work experience to present cases and testify. It is imperative that they have up-to-date medical knowledge that they can utilize. Legal nurse consultants should have work experience in critical care areas such as hospital emergency rooms, intensive care units, and obstetrics, since these are the areas that are most likely to be involved in litigation.

There are a variety of ways one would obtain the education necessary to become a legal nurse consultant. Legal education is not a prerequisite, although many legal nurse consultants acquire knowledge of the legal system by consulting with attorneys, taking classes, and attending seminars. You must evaluate your preferred method of learning—do you prefer a classroom setting, online courses, or textbooks? Barbara recommends that you first join the American Association of Legal Nurse Consultants and then follow by joining the local chapter. This association will help support all levels of legal nurses ranging from the beginner to the most advanced. The AALNC is the professional organization recognized by the American Nurses Association and will soon be offering an online course for beginner legal nurses.

While some independent legal nurse consultants maintain their clinical practices, other may depart from this arena and work exclusively as legal nurse consultants. It is important for legal nurse consultants to maintain up-to-date knowledge of the current practices in the health care fields. "Remaining abreast of the current health care literature is really integral to the success of my business," Barbara says. "Much time is devoted to reading clinical nursing, legal nursing, medical journals, and books. In addition, I attend a variety of conferences yearly and participate on many committees."

Certification and Licensing

You must pass a licensing exam to become a nurse. Licensing is required in all 50 states, and license renewal or continuing education credits are also required periodically. In some cases, licensing in one state will automatically grant licensing in reciprocal states. For further information, contact your state's nursing board. (See the National Council of State Boards of Nursing Web site at http://www.ncsbn.org for contact information.)

The legal nurse consultant certified (LNCC) program is the only certification in legal nurse consulting recognized by the American Association of Legal Nurse Consultants. Administered by the American Legal Nurse Consultant Certification Board (ALNCCB), the LNCC program promotes the recognition of legal nurse consulting as a specialty practice of nursing. The certification is renewed every five years through continuing education or reexamination and continued practice in the specialty.

Internships and Volunteerships

As part of your basic nursing program, you will be required to complete several nursing internships, or clinical rotations. Usually these rotations are set up through the college or university to be completed at a hospital or other health care facility.

WHO WILL HIRE ME?

The only way to become a registered nurse is through completion of one of the three kinds of educational programs and successful performance on the licensing examination. Registered nurses may apply for employment directly to hospitals, nursing homes, and companies and government agencies that hire nurses. They can also sometimes obtain jobs through school career services offices, by signing up with employment agencies specializing in placement of nursing personnel, or through the state employment office. Other sources of jobs include nurses' associations, professional journals, and newspaper want ads.

Barbara landed her first job as a legal nurse consultant through networking. "Since then," she says, "I have taken many opportunities to network with my colleagues, nursing staff, and attorneys, and this is how I receive my work. In addition, I have had opposing counsel as well as judges contact me to later work on their cases."

Nurses who are interested in becoming legal nurse consultants should plan their transition into the field carefully. "You really need to have a firm nursing foundation of about five years with a clinical nursing position before venturing into legal nursing. Joining the American Association of Legal Nurse Consultants will assist you in many ways including education, networking, and business development. When you decide to enter this field, do not quit your regular job until you have enough work to sustain you.

"There are numerous legal practice specialties within legal nursing," Barbara says. "To quote from the *Scope and Standards of Legal Nurse Consulting*, 'the legal nurse consultant practices in a variety of settings including law firms, government offices, insurance companies, hospital risk management departments, forensic environments, and as self employed practitioners. They serve as a liaison between the legal and health care communities and between the consumer and health care or legal communities. Legal nurse consultants provide consultation and education to legal, health care professionals and others in litigation related to illness or injury including areas such as personal injury, product liability, medical malpractice, workers' compensation, toxic torts, risk management, medical professional licensure investigation, and criminal law.'" Other responsibilities include legal writing, medical record analysis, literature research, report preparation, and locating and working with expert witnesses.

WHERE CAN I GO FROM HERE?

Administrative and supervisory positions in the nursing field go to nurses who have earned at least the bachelor of science in nursing (BSN). Nurses with many years of experience who are graduates of the diploma program may achieve supervisory positions, but requirements for such promotions have become more difficult in recent years and in many cases require at least the BSN.

Legal nurse consultants with considerable experience may advance to supervisory positions or move on to open their own consulting companies. Barbara feels that serving as the president of the American Association of Legal Nurse Consultants gave her many opportunities for professional and personal growth. "I also want to continue growing my independent practice of legal nurse consulting," she says, "as well as [to] continue advancing

Related Jobs

- advanced-practice nurses
- clinical nurse specialists
- critical care nurses
- emergency nurses
- geriatric nurses
- home health care and hospice nurses
- lawyers
- legal secretaries
- licensed practical nurses
- neonatal nurses
- nurse anesthetists
- nurse assistants
- nurse managers
- nurse-midwives
- nurse practitioners
- occupational health nurses
- oncological nurses
- paralegals
- psychiatric nurses
- registered nurses

my clinical skills and [to] seek advancement within my clinical position."

WHAT ARE THE SALARY RANGES?

According to several sources, independent legal nurse consultants may be paid on an hourly basis that can range from $60 to $250 per hour. The fee depends on the type of services they are performing, such as testifying, reviewing records, or doing medical research, and also reflects their experience and reputation. In addition, fees vary in different parts of the country. Some legal nurse consultants may work on a retainer basis with one or more clients.

Many legal nurse consultants who work for law firms and other businesses and institutions are employed full or part time. Their salaries vary by experience, geographic location, and areas of expertise. The full-time salary range, according to various sources, is from under $30,000 to a small percentage making more than $100,000. Some litigation situations may require that consultants work overtime.

General employment benefits such as health and life insurance, vacation time, and sick leave may be offered to full-time legal nurse consultants.

WHAT IS THE JOB OUTLOOK?

Nursing specialties will be in great demand in the future. The U.S. Department of Labor reports that the career of registered nurse will grow much faster than the average for all occupations through 2014. As long as there is litigation involving medical issues, one can expect the specialty nursing field to continue to grow.

Licensed Practical Nurses

SUMMARY

Definition
Licensed practical nurses (LPNs) provide direct patient care under the supervision of physicians or registered nurses in hospitals, clinics, private homes, schools, and other similar settings.

Alternative Job Titles
Home health nurses
Licensed vocational nurses

Salary Range
$23,000 to $33,000 to $45,000+

Educational Requirements
High school diploma; completion of state-approved practical nursing program (12 months)

Certification or Licensing
Voluntary (certification)
Required (licensing)

Employment Outlook
About as fast as the average

High School Subjects
Anatomy and physiology
Biology
Chemistry
Health
Mathematics
Science

Personal Interests
Helping people: emotionally
Helping people: physical health/medicine
Science

It was Friday, August 13, 2004, and Hurricane Charley was bearing down on central Florida. Terry Bucher, a licensed practical nurse working in hospice care, was ready for action.

"Our 12-bed unit was well secured and prepared for the storm," she recalls. "We had gathered water and checked backup generators and oxygen supplies." When the 100- to 120-mph storm crossed into Terry's county at 7 P.M., she and her colleagues activated their emergency plan. "We moved all the patients and their family members into the hallways to offer additional protection from the winds and the possibility of windows shattering. Each of us maintained the appropriate schedules for our patients' medications and care, offered encouragement, answered questions to settle fears and, in general, created an atmosphere where everyone felt safe and secure."

In addition to handling the regular care and needs of her patients and families, Terry was on constant lookout for any damages. "We toweled all windowsills

25

where water collected through the window seams," she says, "told stories of other weather crises that had been faced successfully, and kept everyone comfortable in a situation that was [unlike any] other central Florida had seen."

It took about three hours for the hurricane to pass through Terry's county—uprooting trees, downing power lines, and flooding many areas in its wake. "The damage was massive, yet the experience of working as an LPN in health care during this crisis is one that I will long remember," Terry says. "The teamwork involved in proper preparations and the teamwork that assured everyone in the unit—patients, family members, and staff—that their needs could and would be met is one that will long remain with me."

WHAT DOES A LICENSED PRACTICAL NURSE DO?

Licensed practical nurses (LPNs) provide quality, cost-effective nursing care wherever patient care is needed. They work in hospitals, nursing homes and long-term-care facilities, hospice settings, rehabilitation facilities, doctors' offices, health maintenance organizations (HMOs), clinics, schools, private homes, and in all military branches. Their duties vary according to each state's Nurse Practice Act and the place of employment, but generally involve basic patient care. Licensed practical nurses provide for the emotional and physical comfort of their patients. They observe, record, and report to the appropriate people any changes in the patient's status. Licensed practical nurses also perform more specialized nursing functions, such as administering medications and therapeutic treatments, as well as assisting with rehabilitation. Licensed practical nurses might also participate in the planning, implementation, and evaluation of nursing care.

In the hospital setting, licensed practical nurses usually work under the supervision of registered nurses (RNs), performing many basic nursing duties of bedside care, particularly those that are routine or performed regularly. They take vital signs such as temperature, pulse, and blood pressure; prepare and administer prescribed medicines to patients (in most states); help prepare patients for examinations and operations; collect samples from patients for testing; and perform routine laboratory procedures, such as urinalysis. They also observe patients and report any adverse reactions to medications or treatments. One of a licensed practical nurse's main functions is to ensure that patients are comfortable and that their personal hygiene needs are met. They give alcohol rubs or massages, if necessary, and help patients bathe or brush their teeth. They respond to patient calls and answer their questions.

The licensed practical nurse may work in any unit of the hospital, including intensive care, recovery, pediatrics, medical-surgical, and maternity, with varying duties according to the demands of the department. For instance, in the obstetrics department, a licensed practical nurse helps in the delivery room and may feed and bathe newborns, as well as give basic care to recovering new mothers. Some licensed practical nurses direct nursing aides and orderlies and may also have clerical duties. Barb Liebe is an LPN who works as a surgical scrub nurse at Resurrection Medical Center in Chicago, Illinois. She has been a LPN for 22 years. "I am responsible for preparing the operating room for surgery," Barb explains. "I prepare the instruments, sutures, and anything else that the doctor needs to perform the surgery. I am also responsible for the sterile field. I scrub in and gown and glove every professional in the operating room who is part of the sterile field and maintain this field during the procedure." Barb says that the best part of her job is being relied on as part of a team that is responsible for the critical care of patients.

In nursing or retirement homes, licensed practical nurses often serve as *charge nurses*, taking over many of the responsibilities that registered nurses would have in a hospital setting. Because much of the care provided in nursing homes is of the routine variety, licensed practical nurses are used extensively and are often in charge of an entire floor, with responsibility for the hands-on care of many patients. In addition to providing routine bedside care, licensed practical nurses in nursing homes—fast becoming the largest employer of LPNs after hospitals—may also help to evaluate residents' needs, develop care treatment plans, and supervise nursing aides. In addition, they are charged with contacting doctors when necessary, completing any associated paperwork, and reporting to doctors or

registered nurses on patients' status. Doctors and registered nurses often depend on detailed reporting from LPNs to accurately maintain patient records and treatment course. Licensed practical nurses frequently act as supervisors of nursing assistants in nursing homes.

Licensed practical nurses who work in hospice settings care for people who are

Lingo to Learn

anatomy The science of the structure of the body and its organs.

catheter A rubber, plastic, or glass tube used to insert into the bladder in order to withdraw urine; or a tube for passage into a structure for the purpose of injecting or withdrawing a fluid into or out of the body.

clinical rotation Time spent working on a floor or unit of a health care facility, usually as part of required training for medical health care professionals.

geriatrics A branch of medicine that deals with the problems and diseases of old age and aging people.

inpatient A hospital patient who receives lodging and food as well as treatment.

IV Abbreviation for intravenous—going into a vein.

long-term care Care administered over a long period of time, usually for chronically ill or incapacitated patients, such as those in nursing homes.

nasal gastric tube Flexible tubing placed up the patient's nose and down the throat to provide an airway and feeding passage for patients who are unconscious.

in the final stages of a terminal illness. Typically, a hospice patient has less than six months to live. Hospice nurses provide medical and emotional support to the patients and their families and friends. Hospice care usually takes place in the patient's home, but patients may also receive hospice care in a hospital room, a nursing home, or a relative's home.

Licensed practical nurses working in clinics for physicians and dentists, including HMOs, help prepare patients for examination and even help the physician conduct the exam. They apply dressings, explain prescribed treatments or health measures, schedule appointments, keep records, and perform other clerical duties. Licensed practical nurses who work in home health care as private duty nurses prepare meals for their patients, keep rooms orderly, and teach family members simple nursing tasks as part of patient care.

WHAT IS IT LIKE TO BE A LICENSED PRACTICAL NURSE?

Terry Bucher has been a licensed practical nurse for 40 years. "I strongly recommend this career to anyone who enjoys offering service to other people—in a very personal way and in a very professional way," she says. "If you're interested in research, working in a doctor's office, hospital nursing, working with the elderly, helping new mothers and infants, working in schools, or in specialties, there are just hundreds of opportunities available."

Licensed practical nurses work in a variety of settings. Terry works in a 12-bed hospice care center on an as-needed basis. "Hospice is one of the most wonderful things in the world for individuals and families for the last stages of life," Terry explains. "When an individual comes under our care, their condition very frequently improves and they have some real quality family time before the disease turns and progresses again. Hospice care provides a great relief from stress for every-

---

More Lingo to Learn

obstetrics The branch of medicine dealing with childbirth.

occupational health nurse A nurse working, usually on-site, in a workplace setting, providing nursing services to employees there.

outpatient A person who is not a patient at a hospital, but who visits a clinic or dispensary connected with it for diagnosis or treatment.

pediatrics The branch of medicine dealing with the development, care, and diseases of children.

physiology The science dealing with the study of the function of tissues or organs.

psychiatric nursing A nursing specialty that deals with psychiatry; that is, mental, emotional, or behavioral disorders in patients.

public health nurse A nurse working for a community or government health organization stressing preventive medicine and social science.

body involved. A lot of the anxiety is taken away because there is someone to ask questions, someone there to help you, and patients know that they're not alone."

Terry's daily tasks as an LPN working in hospice focus on the primary care of patients. "We care for two different types of hospice patients," she explains. "The first type of patient requires symptom management. In other words, there has been a change in their condition for which they need close monitoring because that may be hard to do in the home. The disease has progressed to a point where their needs change, and they need help with pain management. Our second type of patient is an individual who does not have a primary care giver that would allow them to stay at home. If they meet the requirements of the hospice residential unit, they can come in and stay in our home-like atmosphere and be cared for in that manner."

Terry's duties include bathing, feeding, offering measures of comfort, changing dressings, administering IVs (a task LPNs in Florida can only do if they have taken and passed an extended IV therapy course), administering medications, documenting her work, and speaking with families. "A lot of our hospice work is education with families and spending time with our patients and explaining anything they have a need to know," Terry says. "It's very holistic as far as not just meeting their physical needs, but also meeting their emotional and spiritual needs at the same time."

Licensed practical nurses need physical stamina, as they spend much of the working day on their feet, performing tasks that can be strenuous. The bedside care LPNs provide—helping patients bathe, sit up, get out of bed, stand, or walk—requires a fair share of reaching, bending, and stretching, which can sometimes subject them to back injuries. "Students who are interested in getting into nursing have to really like people and be service oriented because the job of nursing can be both physically and emotionally demanding," Terry says. "When you are dealing one-on-one with patients who are not in the best of health, you are not dealing with an ideal situation. In the business community, you might expect to deal with people at their very best. When you're dealing with the sick and infirm, that's not always true. You're dealing with individuals who are very vulnerable."

Most licensed practical nurses working in nursing homes or hospitals work a 40-hour week on a variety of shifts, including nights, weekends, and holidays. Licensed practical nurses working as private duty nurses can usually set their own work hours.

Along with the many rewards that licensed practical nurses experience in helping patients and medical staff with their care, some professional hazards do exist that include both physical and psychological stresses. The hands-on care that LPNs provide brings them very close to their patients, many of whom are very sick, in pain, or dying. They must sometimes deal with the demands of patients who are confused, agitated, or uncooperative. In addition to experiencing the emotional stress that this close contact may bring, LPNs, particularly in hospitals, must also be mindful of potential exposure to caustic chemicals, radiation, and infectious diseases such as AIDS and hepatitis. Licensed practical nurses who provide in-home services often work long days and have a considerable adjustment period when moving to different homes to work with new patients, as each move requires adapting to new surroundings, patients, families, and physicians.

DO I HAVE WHAT IT TAKES TO BE AN LPN?

Licensed practical nurses—and virtually anyone opting for a career in patient care—should possess physical and mental stamina, patience, and endurance. While LPNs should possess a compassionate nature, they sometimes need to be thick-skinned when it comes to occasional unkind treatment from others. Doctors, nurses, and others who supervise licensed practical nurses, particularly in a hospital setting, are often under a lot of pressure and may take their frustrations out on those standing shoulder to shoulder with them in providing patient care. In any case, all would agree that focusing on the higher goal of contributing to the health and well-being of people can counter the stresses of being on your feet all day or receiving unkind remarks from anguished patients or overburdened and frustrated doctors or supervisors. These qualities, along with good communication skills and the ability to follow directions, will help licensed practical nurses achieve a workable balance in their chosen field.

FYI

Approximately 40 percent of licensed practical nurses use their practical nursing license as a stepping-stone to other health occupations with greater pay and more responsibilities.

HOW DO I BECOME A LICENSED PRACTICAL NURSE?

Education

High School

To become a licensed practical nurse, you must first complete an approved practical nursing program in your state. Nearly all states require a high school degree to enroll in the program. Several states in the country, however, require that applicants complete only one or two years of high school. And some high schools even offer a practical nursing program that is approved by a state board of nursing or other regulatory body.

Generally, if you have a broad educational background and wide-ranging interests, you'll be prepared for the academic work and clinical practice required for the licensed practical nurse training program. Although many practical nursing schools do not require specific high school courses for admission, course offerings in science and mathematics—especially biology, chemistry, and physics—will give you a leg up when it comes time to start your advanced training.

Because communication skills are critical to effective nursing, English and speech courses are also a good idea. But perhaps most importantly, you will need to have a caring, sympathetic nature, a sincere desire to contribute to the health and well-being of people, and the ability to follow oral and written directions.

Postsecondary Training

To be eligible to take the examination required for licensing, you must graduate from an approved school of practical nursing. (A correspondence course in practical nursing does not qualify you to take the state licensing examination.) The length of this program varies from state to state, depending on the individual state's admission requirements. Most programs last 12 months, although some are as long as 18 months, and a few are less than a year. (Terry Bucher attended a one-year, nationally accredited training program at St. Joseph Hospital School of Practical Nursing in Lorain, Ohio.) The trend now is toward an 18-month or two-year program leading to an associate's degree. The trend of expanded education speaks to the growing need for all nurses to have a broader base of knowledge. More complex technologies and the desire to minimize liability risks are two reasons for this. Many nursing students, too, are opting for a four-year degree because of the accompanying increase in job status and opportunities.

Licensed practical nurse programs are generally offered through two-year colleges and vocational and technical schools. Some programs are offered in high schools, hospitals, and colleges and universities. You must be 18 years of age or older to apply; some programs actually have an upper age limit. Once enrolled, you will attend school five days a week, for six to eight hours a day. Participation in a practical nursing program is a full-time commitment. If you must work a part-time job while enrolled, be sure to consult the program director in advance to work out an arrangement. Any LPN program involves a lot of studying, referencing of notes, and staying in touch with professional resources after you finish the program.

Although practical nursing programs are no longer strictly hospital-based and contain more theory than clinical practice, they are generally affiliated with a hospital and include a clinical rotation along with classroom instruction. Classroom study covers basic nursing concepts, anatomy, physiology, medical-surgical nursing, pediatrics, obstetrics, psychiatric nursing, nutrition, first aid, and the administration of drugs. They also participate in clinical opportunities where they learn about nursing via hands-on training. After successfully completing the program, students receive a diploma or certificate and may then take the board licensing exam in the state where they plan to work.

Some schools have waiting lists for their practical nursing education programs. It is wise to plan early by obtaining and completing all application forms and beginning this process approximately one year ahead of intended enrollment. Contact several schools in your desired area and ask for their brochures, financial aid

To Be a Successful Licensed Practical Nurse, You Should . . .

- be mature, alert, and tactful, displaying patience and emotional stability

- maintain an objective point of view

- be able to follow detailed instructions and take correct action, particularly in a crisis

- have a caring, sympathetic nature and the flexibility to adapt to diverse situations

- possess good communication skills and the ability to assume responsibility

- be in good health and have physical stamina

information, and application forms. Make sure the practical nursing program you select is approved by your state's board of nursing.

Certification or Licensing

After graduating from an approved school of practical nursing, you will need to pass an examination to become licensed. All states and Washington, D.C., require practical nurses to be licensed and to renew that license every two years. The state board of nursing issues the practical nursing license (or the vocational nursing license in California and Texas) once a candidate has passed the written National Council Licensure Examination for Prac-

tical Nurses. Legal minimum requirements for the license are set by each state through its board of nursing, so these may vary from state to state. Licensed practical nurses in one state wishing to practice nursing in another state must apply to the board of nursing in that state. Although requirements vary slightly, it is generally not difficult to obtain another license and may not even require a written examination. Licensed practical nurses can identify themselves by putting the initials "LPN" or "LVN" (in Texas and California) after their names.

Terry is a certified hospice palliative licensed nurse. This voluntary national certification program is offered by the National Hospice and Palliative Care Association. "I studied very hard for the test and took some preparatory classes," she says, "and I am very happy to say that I was in the first group of approximately 200 LPNs in the nation who received national certification."

In addition to working as an LPN, Terry is the President of the Florida Association of Nurse Assistants. She highly recommends membership in a professional nursing association as a means to network and stay up to date with trends and certification requirements. "Regardless of your level in the profession," she says, "membership in professional associations allows you access to those individuals who are doing the same kind of work, and you can network with them and gain support. Professional organizations also keep their members updated about new rules and regulations that pertain to their profession. Most professional organizations also offer specific services for their members. For example, we offer members and non-members alike programs of home in-service, a 14-hour leadership course, and an annual convention."

Internships and Volunteerships

Clinical rotations usually take place in a supervised hospital setting, but may include other settings as well. Students practice nursing techniques on mannequins before moving on to human patients. Clinical practice usually involves a series of rotations where LPNs are exposed to a variety of health care areas, such as orthopedics, oncology, or pediatrics.

Terry Bucher suggests that students interested in preparing for health care careers volunteer as candy stripers at a local hospital. "If you feel that you have a love for the elderly, you should also visit nursing homes and assisted-living facilities in your area to experience firsthand some of the joys and challenges of those professions," she advises. "Get involved in activities that meet the needs of developmentally challenged individuals or disabled youth. By exposing yourself to these type of things, you will be able to decide if this is a career path that you want to pursue."

WHO WILL HIRE ME?

New licensed practical nurses frequently step into part-time or full-time jobs with the hospitals where they did their training. Networking with staff may also uncover other job leads worth exploring.

While veterans hospitals still employ a large number of licensed practical nurses, growth for LPNs working in hospitals generally is not expected to continue. This is due largely to the decreasing number of inpatients, which is related to cost concerns: it has become too costly for hospitals to care for patients for a prolonged recovery period.

Although the latest available statistics show the major employer of practical nurses still to be hospitals (27 percent), nursing care facilities now employ nearly as many LPNs as do hospitals (25 percent). Employment in nursing care facilities will remain steady as the number of aged and disabled persons in need of long-term care rises rapidly with the aging baby-boomer population. Nursing facilities will also be called on to care for the increasing number of convalescing patients who have been released from hospitals but are not recovered enough to go home. Home health care services will provide the most new jobs for licensed practical nurses as the older population grows and preferences for care in the home increases.

There are many ways to find a job in this field. You may consider trying local employment agencies, although newspaper want ads may be the best avenue. Openings for licensed practical nurses are usually advertised in the classified section of the paper under headings such as "Nurses," "Licensed Practical Nurses," "LPNs," "Health Care," "Hospitals," "Private Duty," or "Temporary Nursing." You can also apply directly to hospitals, public health agencies, or nursing homes. Targeting a major hospital with acute care facilities may offer greater growth potential, and veterans hospitals in particular use a large number of licensed practical nurses to meet their ongoing need for basic, hands-on patient care. Applicants can send their résumés, with a short cover letter, directly to the personnel directors of health care facilities. Nurses associations and professional journals sometimes offer job leads and should be contacted individually.

Advancement Possibilities

Charge nurses oversee a particular floor or unit of a hospital, nursing home, or other health care setting.

Nurse anesthetists are registered nurses who administer an anesthetic agent to patients before and during surgery to desensitize them to pain. They also work with pain management and respiratory management of patients.

Nurse practitioners are registered nurses who have advanced training and education. This training enables them to carry out many of the responsibilities traditionally handled by physicians.

Physician assistants provide health care services to patients under the direction and responsibility of a physician and may perform comprehensive physical examinations, compile patient medical data, administer or order diagnostic tests, and interpret test results.

Registered nurses have received advanced training in nursing and have been licensed by a state authority after qualifying for registration.

Rapid growth for licensed practical nurse employment is also expected in such residential care facilities as board and care homes and group homes for people with mental disabilities.

Again, newspaper want ads are a good place to begin the job search, along with employment agencies. Large cities generally have employment agencies that specialize in jobs in the health care industry.

WHERE CAN I GO FROM HERE?

It is still true that licensed practical nurses can advance to higher-paying careers as medical technicians and registered nurses, and many do. Forty percent, in fact, use their licensed practical nurse designation as a stepping-stone to greater pay and more responsibilities. "Licensed practical nurses have a very good base foundation if they decide to advance to a higher degree within the nursing profession or health care field," Terry Bucher says. "I personally have not chosen to do that. I've been very satisfied in my career, but I have also had a very diverse career. I haven't done all of my nursing at the bedside. I've also spent a lot of time in organizational work."

There are several ways for a licensed practical nurse to climb the career ladder. One is to locate similar positions in larger or more prestigious facilities where higher salaries are offered. It is also possible, by accumulating experience, to obtain supervisory duties overseeing nurse assistants and nurse's aides. Another way to advance is to complete the additional education (usually two years at a community college) necessary to become a registered nurse.

But regardless of specialty or career ambition, licensed practical nurses must keep their skills current; participation in ongoing self-education is critical to job performance and advancement.

Participating in continuing education courses is a good way to stay current with the technological advances and growing complexity of patient care techniques and procedures. Some states even require a minimum number of continuing education hours before they will renew the practical nursing license every two years. Continuing education programs may be sponsored by a variety of organizations, including community colleges, government agencies, vocational-technical institutes, private educational firms, and local, state, and national health associations. Licensed practical nurses must assess the educational opportunities available in their communities and determine which are the most relevant for maintaining their skills.

Another method of improving skills and growing in the field is to take advantage of in-service educational programs that more and more employers are offering. These may include seminars, workshops, and clinical sessions on relevant work topics. Taking advantage of these in-house opportunities will help the LPN accumulate additional skills and may even lead to more specialized and higher-paying careers. Some hospitals offer programs that teach licensed practical nurses to do kidney dialysis or to work with patients in cardiac or intensive care units, which may lead to more specialized job titles.

WHAT ARE THE SALARY RANGES?

The salary range for licensed practical nurses varies considerably between geographic locations and between institutions, and depends on many factors, including experience and responsibilities. According to the U.S. Department of Labor, LPNs earned a median annual salary of $35,230 in 2005. Ten percent earned less than $25,340, and 10 percent earned more than $48,510. Nursing facilities and home health care services tend to pay a little more than hospitals.

For accurate information on wage scales for licensed practical nurses in the community where you want to work, call a hospital in the area, ask for the personnel department, and inquire about salaries for newly licensed practical nurses. Other sources include registries, long-term care facilities, or the visiting nurse associations, which can provide specific details on licensed practical nurse wage scales.

Licensed practical nurses also usually receive fringe benefits, such as paid sick, holiday, and vacation time, medical coverage, 401(k) plans, and other perks determined by the employer.

WHAT IS THE JOB OUTLOOK?

The job outlook is good for licensed practical nurses. "Right now, there is a

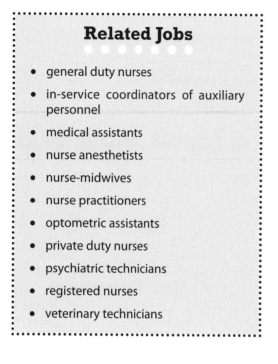

Related Jobs

- general duty nurses
- in-service coordinators of auxiliary personnel
- medical assistants
- nurse anesthetists
- nurse-midwives
- nurse practitioners
- optometric assistants
- private duty nurses
- psychiatric technicians
- registered nurses
- veterinary technicians

great nursing shortage," Terry Bucher says. "Many of the nurses and nursing instructors are nearing retirement age, and within a five-year period, you are going to have a lot of retirees. There are so many opportunities for young people today. If you go back in time, the job field was not geared toward many possibilities for women. There were secretarial, clerical, teaching, and nursing positions, but most young women in my youth weren't looking to the workplace for a career. It's very different now. Young people have taken advantage of the variety of opportunities open to them in non–health care careers, and this has created a real shortage of workers to meet the needs of the health care community."

The general growth in health care and the long-term health care needs of an aging population help ensure the continued need for licensed practical nurses and other health care professionals over the next 10 years. In fact, employment of LPNs is expected to increase about as fast as the average for all occupations through 2014 in response to the needs of a rapidly growing older population and to the cost constraints hospitals experience relative to providing long-term patient care. As in most other occupations, replacement needs will be the main source of job openings.

As mentioned previously, most new jobs for licensed practical nurses will be in nursing care facilities and home health care services that cater to the growing aging population. Faster-than-average employment growth is predicted for LPNs in these settings. Nursing facilities will also house recovering patients released from hospitals but not yet well enough to return home. State and federal regulations on nursing homes are requiring them to hire more licensed practical nurses in lieu of other so-called "health aides," who may be given minimal training, are unlicensed, and are often under-qualified to administer patient care.

The increasing number of people age 65 and over and technological innovations that allow for more treatments at home will create much-faster-than-average employment opportunities for LPNs who work in home health care services. Rapid growth is expected in board and care homes and group homes for people with mental disabilities as well.

Neonatal Nurses

SUMMARY

Definition
Neonatal nurses provide direct patient care to newborns in hospitals for the first month after birth. The babies they care for may be normal, they may be born prematurely, or they may be suffering from an illness or birth defect. Some of the babies require highly technical care such as surgery or the use of ventilators, incubators, or intravenous feedings.

Alternative Job Titles
None

Salary Range
$38,660 to $54,670 to $79,460+

Educational Requirements
Nursing degree; on-the-job training

Certification or Licensing
Voluntary (certification)
Required (licensing)

Employment Outlook
Much faster than the average

High School Subjects
Anatomy and physiology
Biology
Chemistry
Health
Mathematics

Personal Interests
Helping people: emotionally
Helping people: physical health/medicine
Science

An urgent announcement blares through the hospital's speakers: *A neonatal intensive care unit (NICU) nurse is needed in Labor and Delivery Room #8 STAT for a 30-week gestation gastroschesis!* (a condition where some or all of the newborn's abdominal contents will be on the outside of its body).

Although she feels her heart quicken, NICU nurse Allison Cole calmly gathers the supplies for intubation (there is a strong possibility that the infant's immature lungs will not be able to function without help), the nurse medication box from the counter, as well as sterile gauze wraps and a bottle of sterile normal saline (which she will use to wrap the external abdominal contents to keep them clean and safe from injury until surgery can be performed).

As she walks into Labor and Delivery, Allison sees the mother on the operating table. The surgeon is performing a cesarean section to try to prevent injury to the infant. Allison, a respiratory therapist (RT), and a physician gather near an open warmer bed that the infant will be placed on once he is born.

As the surgeon makes his final cut, he reaches for the infant. The infant is pulled out of the mother's abdomen, and Allison and her colleagues can tell that quite a bit of his abdominal contents are on the outside. The entire bottom half of the infant's body, including the misplaced abdominal contents, is placed in a sterile bag, and the bag is pulled closed up near his armpits. This sterile bag keeps the organs clean until she and her colleagues can wrap them.

The infant is brought to the warmer bed. He is making no effort to breathe on his own. Allison listens to his heart rate and lets the doctor know that it is low. A breathing tube is placed and secured to the infant's face, and Allison listens for breath sounds as the RT bags the baby. The heart rate increases to a normal rate. The infant is now stable, and everyone breathes a sigh of relief.

Allison and her colleagues carefully remove the sterile bag from the infant. A large portion of his intestines, as well as the bladder, are outside of his body. As Allison looks closer, she can even see part of the liver. The medical team gazes in amazement as they silently wrap the contents with saline-soaked gauze. Once all the abdominal contents are safely wrapped and secured, they place a smaller sterile bag over the wrapped contents to keep them moist and clean. The infant is then placed in a warm isolette, and Allison and her colleagues take him back to the NICU. Thanks to their quick work and professionalism, another baby has been saved and has a chance to live a normal life.

WHAT DOES A NEONATAL NURSE DO?

Neonatal nurses care for newborn babies in hospitals. Depending on the size of the hospital, their duties may vary. Some neonatal nurses may be in the delivery room and, as soon as the baby is born, they are responsible for cleaning up the baby, visually assessing it, and drawing blood by pricking the newborn's heel. This blood sample is sent to the laboratory, where a number of screening tests are performed as required by the state. These assessments help the staff and doctor determine if the baby is normal or needs additional testing, a special diet, or intensive care.

Babies who are born without complications are usually placed in a Level I nursery (some hospitals may have different names for these various care levels) or in the mother's room with her. However, because of today's short hospital stays for mother and child, many hospitals no longer have Level I, or healthy baby, nurseries. *Neonatal* or *general staff nurses* help the new mothers care for their newborns in their hospital rooms.

Level II is a special care nursery for babies who have been born prematurely or who may have an illness, disease, or birth defect. These babies are also cared for by a neonatal nurse, or a staff nurse with more advanced training in caring for newborns. These babies may need oxygen, intravenous therapies, special feedings, or because of underdevelopment, they may simply need more time to mature.

Specialized neonatal nurses or more advanced degree nurses care for babies placed in the Level III neonatal intensive care unit. This unit admits all babies who cannot be treated in either of the other two nurseries. These at-risk babies require high-tech care such as ventilators, incubators, or surgery. Level III units are generally found in larger hospitals or may be part of a children's hospital.

Neonatal nurses can expect to work in a hospital environment that is clean and well lighted. Inner-city hospitals may be in a less than desirable location, and safety may be an issue. Generally, neonatal nurses who wish to advance in their careers will find themselves working in larger hospitals in major cities.

WHAT IS IT LIKE TO BE A NEONATAL NURSE?

Allison Cole is a neonatal intensive care nurse at Jackson Memorial Hospital in Miami, Florida. Her neonatal intensive care unit (NICU) is large—about 70 beds—and split into two units. Neo A has about 28 beds and contains the most critical patients. When full, it can overflow into Neo B, which normally contains more stable patients who may still need additional care. Her hospital also has an Intermediate Nursery, which contains babies too sick to go to the normal newborn nursery, but not sick enough to go to the NICU. "I love my job," Allison says, "and I look forward to going to work every day. Neonatalolgy is a highly research-based area of medicine, so there are always learning opportunities—a new technique, a new med, a new procedure, and new equipment. We are constantly making discoveries that allow us to save more babies and provide better outcomes."

Newborns under Allison's care have a variety of serious conditions and illnesses, but in the following paragraphs Allison describes one recent 12-hour shift that left her tired, but feeling proud that she was able to provide the best care to her patients.

"One patient was in critical condition," Allison recalls. "She was a premature infant born at 23-weeks gestation (40 weeks = full-term infant). She weighed

A Brief History of Neonatal Nursing

Neonatal care in some basic form has been around since the dawn of time. But the specialized field of neonatal nursing did not develop until the 1960s as advancements in medical care and technology allowed for the improved treatment of premature babies. According to the March of Dimes, one of every 13 babies born in the United States annually suffers from low birth weight. Low birth weight is a factor in 65 percent of infant deaths. Neonatal nurses play a very important role in providing care for these infants, those born with birth defects or illness, and healthy babies.

only one pound and one ounce. She was thin and fragile, with skin so thin that I could easily see her veins on her arms and legs and forehead." Allison says that the infant was so ill that she needed to be intubated, placed on a special kind of ventilator designed especially for preemies, given almost 100 percent oxygen from the ventilator to keep her oxygen levels in her blood at a safe level, and fitted with IVs that administered medications to keep her blood pressure and heart rate at acceptable levels. "As I assessed her," Allison explains, "I observed her color and activity level. I listened to her breath sounds, heart sounds, and bowel sounds. I checked her pulses, felt the fontanels on her head, and checked her IV sites. I carefully changed her tiny diaper. As I assessed her, I looked for signs of distress, sepsis, and irritability." With additional medications and care from Allison, the infant eventually stabilized.

While her first patient was relatively stable, Allison went to the other infant's bedside and assessed its condition. "My second patient was on what is called nasal CPAP," she explains, "which essentially is short tubes that go just inside the infant's nostrils, supplying a constant flow of air to help keep the infant's lung air sacks open." This patient was also born premature (born at 28-weeks gestation), but was now three weeks old. "He had an IV in his right arm that supplied his IV fluids," Allison says, "but he was eating as well. Because he was still premature, he was unable to suck a bottle like a normal baby. He had a tube in his mouth that went to

his stomach. He would receive his milk through this tube until he was old enough and coordinated enough to eat on his own."

Allison stayed busy the rest of her shift. "My first patient required constant attention and documented assessments at least every hour," she says, "but more often when she had her bad episodes." Allison's second patient, although less critical, still required a great deal of attention. "I fed him and documented assessments at least every two hours," she recalls. "Both patients had IV antibiotics and other medications that had to be given. My first patient required a blood transfusion as well as lab draws to follow up on therapies used."

In addition to nursing care, Allison also dealt with families coming in and out to visit their babies and ask questions. "As you can imagine," she says, "when these infants are born and placed in our unit, parents experience a rush of emotions, questions, and concerns. I enjoy serving as a resource to these parents, helping them to understand and hopefully cope with what is happening to their child, and they certainly appreciate me."

Nurses usually spend much of the day on their feet, either walking or standing. Many hospital nurses work 10- or 12-hour shifts, which can be tiring and stressful. "The NICU is generally a noisy, busy, stressful area," Allison says. "Our patients are in critical condition, and, sadly, death is an aspect of the job we deal with often. Sometimes, despite all our efforts, a patient is just too sick to survive. There have been some tearful days at work, but

To Be a Successful Neonatal Nurse, You Should . . .

- enjoy working with mothers, newborns, and families
- have compassion and patience
- have strong communication skills
- be able to work long hours under sometimes stressful conditions
- be decisive and able to act quickly in emergencies

the joyful, hopeful, fulfilling days vastly outnumber the bad."

Long hours and intense nursing demands can create burnout for some nurses, meaning that they often become dissatisfied with their jobs. Fortunately, there are many areas in which nurses can use their skills, so sometimes trying a different type of nursing may be the answer.

DO I HAVE WHAT IT TAKES TO BE A NEONATAL NURSE?

Neonatal nurses should like working with mothers, newborns, and families. This is a very intense nursing field, especially when caring for the high-risk infant, so the neonatal nurse should be compassionate, patient, and able to handle stress and make decisions. The nurse should also be able to communicate well with patients' families. Families of an at-risk newborn are often frightened and very worried about their infant. Because of their fears, family members may be difficult to deal with, and the nurse must display patience, understanding, and composure during these emotional times. The nurse must be able to communicate with the family and explain medical terminology and procedures to them so they understand what is being done for their baby and why.

Neonatal nurses should also be able to work as members of a team. "One of my favorite things about neonatal nursing," says Robin Garcia, a neonatal nurse in the Special Care Nursery at Saint Joseph Hospital in Chicago, Illinois, "is that the work environment is small and confined, which allows the team to work closely together. No one needs to go searching down long hallways to find help. All you need to do is turn your head and say, 'Could someone help me?' Neonatal nursing really fosters great teamwork."

HOW DO I BECOME A NEONATAL NURSE?
Education
High School

In order to become a neonatal nurse, you must first train to be a registered nurse. To prepare for a career as a registered nurse, you should take high school mathematics and science courses, including biology, chemistry, and physics. Health courses will also be helpful. English and speech courses should not be neglected because you must be able to communicate well with patients.

In addition to high school classes, there are a lot of activities you can do to learn more about this field while in high school. Kristin VandenBranden, a neonatal nurse in a Level II Special Care Nursery at St. Francis Hospital in Evanston, Illinois, offers the following advice to young people interested in learning more about neonatal nursing: "Try to arrange a visit to a hospital neonatal unit and talk with the staff there. Read about neonatology and labor and delivery. This career may be right for you if you like being around new life, if you like teaching, if you love a challenge, and if you never want to stop learning."

Allison Cole advises students to volunteer in a neonatal unit. "We often utilize volunteers to help us feed, bathe, and console some of our more stable babies," she says.

Finally, you can also learn more about nursing by becoming involved in clubs related to the field, such as Health Occupation Students of America (http://www.hosa.org).

Postsecondary Training

There is no special program for neonatal nursing in basic RN education; however, some nursing programs have an elective course in neonatal nursing. Entry-level requirements to become a neonatal nurse depend on the institution, its size, and the availability of nurses in that specialty and geographical region. Some institutions may require neonatal nurses to demonstrate their ability to administer medications, suctioning, cardiopulmonary resuscitation, and ventilator care; to perform necessary math calculations; and to

carry out other newborn care duties. Nurses who wish to focus on caring for premature babies or sick newborns may choose to attend graduate school to become a neonatal nurse practitioner or clinical nurse specialist.

Allison Cole has a bachelor of science in nursing from Baylor University School of Nursing. "My undergraduate studies were not too difficult, but nursing school was a bit more challenging," she recalls. "Baylor Nursing School has always been known for creating well-trained nurses, so the curriculum was set up to maintain that reputation. Nursing school included lecture-type studies as well as clinical rotations. The curriculum exposed us to all types of nursing including med/surg, psych, specialty, and community nursing for adults and children." Allison says that her most difficult class was pharmacology since it involved learning about so many medications, their actions, side effects, and compatibilities. "The 30 or so of us who graduated nursing school together became very close," she says. "We survived by leaning on each other, creating study groups, and hanging out together on the weekends. Receiving that diploma and nursing pin made all the hard work worth it. Graduation day was one of the most rewarding days of my life."

Robin Garcia received her training to become a nurse at Union Memorial School of Nursing in Baltimore, Maryland. "My training was a mix as far as difficulty," she says. "Some subjects were much harder, such as pediatrics and psychiatry, and others, such as intensive care and oncology, were easy for me. I took

The Pros of Being a Neonatal Nurse

We asked Robin Garcia, Team Leader in the Special Care Nursery at Saint Joseph Hospital in Chicago, Illinois, what she liked best about being a neonatal nurse and nursing in general. The following are her answers, in her own words:

- **Job flexibility.** Nursing offers a lot of flexibility; there are not many jobs where you can change specialties so easily. If you become tired of your current position, you can switch units and try something else for a while. As a registered nurse, you also can choose the population you want to care for, such as older/geriatric patients, general medical-surgical patients, pediatric patients, or, my favorite, neonatal.

- **Convenient hours/flexible schedules.** As a single mother, I find that nursing is a wonderfully flexible and rewarding career. You can choose to work nights and weekends or only one day a month. At Saint Joseph Hospital, we have a choice of working 4-, 6-, 8-, 10-, 12-, or 16-hour shifts. For those who have children or plan on having a family, nursing also offers convenient hours and flexible schedules.

- **A rewarding experience.** In the past 14 years, I have found neonatal nursing to be extremely rewarding because I help parents have the greatest experience of their life—even when the baby is sick, it is rewarding to know that I made their time here as meaningful and enjoyable as possible. I am privileged to see new life being born and the first breath being taken. I learn something from each and every delivery because it is always a different and new experience. Taking care of a baby for 120 "roller coaster" days and seeing them go home healthy at the end is something so moving that words cannot adequately describe the feeling.

eight clinical rotations, including Intensive Care Unit, Psychiatry, and Labor and Delivery."

Certification and Licensing

Neonatal nurses who work in critical care may become certified in neonatal critical care nursing by the AACN Certification Corporation, a subsidiary of the American Association of Critical Care Nurses (AACN). Applicants must have a minimum of 1,750 hours within the two years preceding application (with 875 hours in the year previous to application), pay an application fee, and take and pass a three-hour exam. The AACN Certification Corporation also offers cardiac medicine and cardiac surgery subspecialty certifications.

In addition to obtaining voluntary certification from the AACN Certification Corporation, neonatal nurses should also be certified in neonatal resuscitation protocol (NRP). "NRP is the national standard of resuscitating infants, including techniques used on admission (in labor and delivery) and during 'code' situations," Allison Cole explains. "NRP gives specific information on when and how to do respiratory care (intubating, bagging), compressions (number, depth), and emergency med administration (meds, doses, methods). It also includes information on specific disorders and problems that could alter the care provided." The American Academy of Pediatrics developed the protocol and offers training materials at its Web site, http://www.aap.org/nrp/nrpmain.html.

Some neonatal nurses also complete a course in lactation consultation and became board-certified lactation consultants. "The course I completed," says Kristin VandenBranden, "provided me with many skills to help mothers and babies get off to a good start with breastfeeding."

All states and Washington, D.C., require nurses to have a license to practice nursing. To obtain a license, graduates of approved nursing schools must pass a national examination. Nurses may be licensed by more than one state. In some states, continuing education is a condition for license renewal. For further information, contact your state's nursing board. (See the National Council of State Boards of Nursing Web site at http://www.ncsbn.org for contact information.)

Internships and Volunteerships

Nursing students are required to complete several nursing internships, or clinical rotations, as part of their post-secondary training. Depending on your educational program, your school may offer these opportunities on-site or have agreements with nearby hospitals and medical centers.

Robin Garcia participated in what some might consider an untraditional internship while in college. "My nursing program allowed students...to work as technicians at the area hospital," she explains. "In my first year, I worked as an EKG technician in cardiology. My second year I was assigned to work on a medical-surgical floor with a high oncology patient population. During my third and final year, I worked on a CCU [critical care unit] step-down unit."

WHO WILL HIRE ME?

Neonatal nurses are employed primarily by hospitals. Jobs can also be obtained through school career services offices, by signing up with employment agencies specializing in placement of nursing personnel, or through the state employment office. Other sources of jobs include nurses' associations, professional journals, and newspaper want ads.

Allison Cole's first job as a neonatal nurse was in the NICU at Baylor University Medical Center. "This hospital was certainly not the best-paying," she says, "but I chose it because of the experience I hoped to gain while working there. Baylor's NICU was well organized and provided an exceptional learning experience for me as a new nurse. I enjoyed the challenges and triumphs this job provided."

WHERE CAN I GO FROM HERE?

Neonatal nurses seeking career advancement, but who would like to continue to care for babies, might consider becoming a neonatal nurse practitioner or clinical nurse specialist. They can do this by gaining at least two years of experience in a neonatal intensive care unit (recommended by the National Association of Neonatal Nurses) and then completing graduate school training in their desired specialty.

Allison Cole doesn't see herself ever leaving the NICU setting. "Since working as a nurse new to the NICU generally requires a short internship-type training, I could see myself serving as an educator," she says. "On several occasions, I have served as a preceptor (trainer) for new nurses, working with them for the first month or so, and thoroughly enjoyed the experience. I could see myself continuing to do so on a larger scale, maybe as director of new nurse education for the NICU."

WHAT ARE THE SALARY RANGES?

Salary is determined by many factors, including nursing specialty, education, and place of employment, shift worked, geographic location, and work experience. According to the U.S. Department of Labor, registered nurses had a median annual income of $54,670 in 2005. The lowest paid 10 percent of all registered nurses earned less than $38,660 per year. The highest paid 10 percent made more than $79,460. However, neonatal specialty nurses can generally expect to earn more, especially when advancing to administrative positions. According to the National Association of Neonatal Nurses, nurses just starting out in

this field may have starting salaries in the upper $30,000s to mid-$40,000s. Given these high beginning salaries, it is logical to expect a neonatal nurse with some experience to earn more than the national median for all registered nurses.

Flexible schedules and part-time employment opportunities are available for most nurses. Employers usually provide health and life insurance, and some

Related Jobs

- clinical nurse specialists
- community health nurses
- critical care nurses
- emergency nurses
- geriatric nurses
- home health care and hospice nurses
- legal nurse consultants
- licensed practical nurses
- nurse anesthetists
- nurse assistants
- nurse managers
- nurse-midwives
- nurse practitioners
- nursing instructors
- occupational health nurses
- oncological nurses
- psychiatric nurses
- registered nurses
- school nurses
- transplant coordinators

offer educational reimbursements and year-end bonuses to their full-time staff.

WHAT IS THE JOB OUTLOOK?

The U.S. Department of Labor predicts that employment for all registered nurses will grow much faster than the average through 2014. In addition, nursing specialties should be in great demand in the future. The outlook for neonatal nurses is very good, especially for those with master's degrees or higher. According to the National Association of Neonatal Nurses, positions should be available due to downsizing in previous years. These cutbacks have led to a decrease in the number of nurses choosing advanced-practice education. Also, the average neonatal nurse today is middle-aged, and some may be choosing to move into less stressful areas of nursing after years of service in this field.

Nurse Anesthetists

SUMMARY

Definition
Nurse anesthetists are registered nurses (RNs) with advanced education in anesthesiology. They are responsible for administering, supervising, and monitoring anesthesia-related care for patients undergoing surgical procedures.

Alternative Job Titles
Advanced-practice nurses
Certified registered nurse anesthetists

Salary Range
$60,000 to $120,000 to $150,000+

Educational Requirements
Master's degree

Certification or Licensing
Required

Employment Outlook
Faster than the average

High School Subjects
Anatomy and physiology
Biology
Chemistry
Health
Mathematics

Personal Interests
Helping people: emotionally
Helping people: physical health/medicine
Science

One late fall evening Juan Quintana, a certified registered nurse anesthetist, found himself in one of those situations in which you say to yourself, "How did I end up here?"

One of the secretaries from the hospital where he worked called saying a child needed his immediate attention. Juan jumped into his car and made the 15-minute trip in 10 minutes flat. "Initially," he recalls, "I went to the surgery area expecting to have a surgical patient awaiting my services. I looked around and realized everything in the OR was locked up tight."

Juan ventured to the hospital floor and saw a flurry of activity near a room down the hall. "I was drawn to the commotion like a moth to a bright light," he says.

In the room, a pediatrician and a surgeon were providing resuscitative breathing and attempting to start an intravenous infusion on an approximately two-month-old baby girl. "She was pasty and a sickly bluish color," Juan remembers. "As if by remote control the physician providing the resuscitative breathing said a big, 'thank God' and handed me the ambu-bag. I immediately went into action. I inserted a breathing

47

Lingo to Learn

analgesic Pain-relieving medication.

epidural Local anesthesia administered by injection into the space just outside the dural sac that surrounds the spinal cord.

holding room Room just outside the operating room where the patient is prepared for surgery.

infiltration Local anesthesia administered by injection directly into the surgical area.

IV Intravenous. Refers to anesthetics or any other substance administered through a vein.

nerve block Local anesthesia administered by injection near the nerves that control sensation in the surgical area.

spinal Local anesthesia administered by injection into the dural sac that surrounds the spinal cord, resulting in loss of sensation in the entire body below that point in the spinal cord.

tertiary health care The high-tech specialized diagnosis and treatment available only at large research and teaching hospitals.

topical Local anesthesia administered by applying a drug to the surface of a mucous membrane that absorbs it; a method often used for surgery on the eye, nose, or throat.

tube in the child's airway and provided 100 percent oxygen. Her color changed to pasty pink, but at least she wasn't blue."

Juan and the physicians then placed intravenous lines in the child to provide medications until she could be trans-

ported by helicopter to a pediatric facility for further evaluation. "Though only 20 to 30 minutes transpired," Juan says, "it felt like a lifetime. Every minute was crucial, every second the hollow in the pit of my stomach deepened."

Later that evening, the child underwent open heart surgery at a pediatric hospital for Transposition of the Great Vessels, a congenital condition in which the blood vessels coming out the heart are somewhat transposed causing poor to very little oxygen availability to the body.

"Today," Juan reports, "she is a beautiful three-year-old with a bright smile and mischievous laugh. I wasn't working in the operating room, I wasn't providing anesthesia, and I wasn't sure how I ended up getting called to assist, but I sure am glad I was there."

WHAT DOES A NURSE ANESTHETIST DO?

Nurse anesthetists, also known as *certified registered nurse anesthetists* (*CRNAs*), are registered nurses with advanced training in anesthesiology. Reliable methods of putting a patient to sleep were first developed in the 1840s when the discovery of ether anesthesia revolutionized surgery. Before that time, when surgery offered the only possible chance of saving a person's life (if a gangrenous leg had to be amputated, for example), all that the surgeon could do was to offer alcohol or opium to deaden the pain and then saw off the limb as quickly as possible before the patient went into shock.

Anesthesiologists are physicians who completed a residency in anesthesiology and passed medical board exams in that specialty. Before World War II, only seven anesthesiology physician residency programs were available; in 1942, there were 17 nurse anesthetists for every anesthesiologist. During the first half of the century, medical students and physicians were often trained by nurse anesthetists in anesthesiology techniques.

Approximately 26 million anesthetic procedures are carried out annually in U.S. medical facilities; approximately 65 percent of these are administered by certified registered nurse anesthetists. In two-thirds of rural hospitals, nurse anesthetists are the only anesthesia providers.

Contemporary anesthesiology is far more complicated than in the early days when an ether- or chloroform-soaked cloth or sponge was held up to the patient's face. In advance of surgery, a nurse anesthetist takes the patient's history, evaluates his or her anesthesia needs, and forms a plan for the best possible management of the case (often in consultation with an anesthesiologist). The nurse anesthetist also explains the planned procedures to the patient and answers questions. On the morning of the operation, the nurse anesthetist administers an intravenous (IV) sedative to relax the patient.

Usually a combination of several anesthetic agents is administered by the nurse anesthetist to establish and maintain the patient in a controlled state of unconsciousness, insensibility to pain, and muscular relaxation. Muscular relaxant drugs prevent the transmission of nerve impulses to the muscles to ensure that involuntary movements by the unconscious patient will not interfere with the surgery. Some general anesthetics are administered by inhalation through a mask and tube—the most common are nitrous oxide, halothane, enflurane, and isoflurane. Others are administered intravenously. Because the muscular relaxants prevent patients from breathing on their own, the nurse anesthetist has to provide artificial respiration through a tube inserted into the windpipe.

Throughout the surgery, the nurse anesthetist monitors the patient's vital signs (blood pressure, respiration, heart rate, and temperature) by watching the video and digital displays. The nurse anesthetist is also responsible for maintaining the patient's blood, water, and salt levels and—from moment to moment—readjusting the flow of anesthetics and other medications to ensure optimal results. After surgery, nurse anesthetists monitor their patients' return to consciousness and watch for complications; they may also be involved in postoperative pain management.

General anesthesia is not necessary for all surgical procedures. Nurse anesthetists also work on cases in which they provide various types of local anesthesia—topical, infiltration, nerve block, spinal, and epidural or caudal.

WHAT IS IT LIKE TO BE A NURSE ANESTHETIST?

Juan Quintana has been a certified registered nurse anesthetist (CRNA) since 1997. He is the owner of Sleepy Anesthesia

Associates, an independent nurse anesthesia practice in Texas that works on contract with seven health care facilities. Before becoming a CRNA, Juan worked as a critical care nurse. "After 10 years of working in critical care settings," he explains, "I decided I wanted to function in a more autonomous role. I had the opportunity to observe anesthesia providers who went the extra mile to help their patients, and I was drawn to that possibility. As a CRNA, I could be that person who made patients more comfortable at a time when their trepidation might overwhelm them."

Nurse anesthetists work in urban, suburban, and rural areas. Juan's practice is located in a small rural community. "The provision of services to rural communities comes with both costs and rewards," he says. "My day begins at around 5:30 and 6:00 A.M., depending on how far I need to travel to get to the town in which I will provide anesthesia that morning." Juan covers several rural communities in a 60-mile radius with populations that typically range from 4,000 to 6,000 people. "This means I might travel over 150 miles by the time the day is over," he says.

When Juan arrives at a facility, he changes into scrubs and proceeds to the preoperative holding area to interview his first patient of the day. "After reviewing the information in the patient's chart including lab work, x-rays, EKGs, and history," he says, "I personally interview the patient and validate the information contained in the chart." Then Juan performs a physical examination of the patient and formulates a plan using the information from the chart, patient, and physical examination. "The patient is given choices as available for his or her anesthesia and a discussion of risks, benefits, and potential complications of anesthesia is provided," Juan explains.

Juan then prepares the anesthesia area in checklist fashion to assure that everything is in order and readily available for any circumstance that might be out of the ordinary. "In anesthesia," Juan says, "we say, 'anesthesia is 98 percent of the time absolute beauty and art, 2 percent of the time sheer terror.' The checklist systems assert that when the 2 percent occurs, you're prepared to handle it."

The patient is then brought into the operating room, Juan administers anesthesia, the surgery is performed, and, once completed, the patient is taken to the post-anesthesia care unit. "The beauty of administering anesthesia," Juan explains, "is modifying it to meet the needs of each patient as their physiology, age, health, and emotional state requires. The comfortable/pain-free, slightly sleepy, smiling patient is a testament to your skills in the art of anesthesia."

Juan repeats these duties over and over again during his workday. He says that the environment can get quite hectic as patients are transported in and out of the operating room to start the next surgical procedure. One extra challenge for Juan is that he has to travel between facilities to administer anesthesia to patients. "Many cases involve relatively simple procedures on healthy individuals," he says, "while others involve emergencies on young and old alike who cannot be

To Be a Successful Nurse Anesthetist, You Should . . .

- be able to analyze and solve problems quickly
- have the ability to handle stressful situations
- be able to remain calm in emergencies
- have strong powers of concentration
- have excellent communication skills

advises, "long hours may await you. You may be exposed to blood-borne pathogens, respiratory viruses, and, at times, physical harm from patients. Sometimes no matter how hard you try, how much current information you have, or how well your team works together, you cannot save the patient's life."

Nurse anesthetists also need to be efficient in their time management. "The surgeons have to be kept happy by having the patients moved along quickly without long delays between cases," is how one nurse anesthetist put it. If a nurse anesthetist is slow in finishing one case and setting up for the next, the surgeon may be reluctant to work with that individual again.

moved to a larger facility for one reason or another."

DO I HAVE WHAT IT TAKES TO BE A NURSE ANESTHETIST?

Nurse anesthetists must be able to concentrate intently for lengthy periods. They are responsible for keeping the anesthetized patient alive, which requires careful attention to every detail. They need to be critical thinkers who can analyze problems accurately and swiftly, make decisions, and take appropriate action. All nurses need the ability to remain calm during emergencies; the operating room is one of the most stressful environments around.

"Depending upon the setting in which you choose to practice," Juan Quintana

HOW DO I BECOME A NURSE ANESTHETIST?

After completing his undergraduate degree, Juan Quintana went to work as a surgical ICU nurse primarily working with postoperative open heart, heart transplant, and neurosurgery patients. "I ran the gamut in that area from staff RN to charge RN to head nurse of the area," he says. "As the head nurse, I found I was too distanced from interaction and care with patients." After nearly 10 years as an RN, Juan matriculated into Texas Wesleyan University in Fort Worth, Texas. In 1997, he completed a master's degree in health science and became an advanced-practice nurse. "It is not a short path to follow but contains many rewards along the way," Juan advises. "The curriculum is challenging, and for those who are up to the task, an outstanding practice awaits on the other side of the journey. Set your goals, realize that it takes hard work and perseverance, and you will succeed."

Education

High School

To become a nurse anesthetist, you must first be a registered nurse. Anyone who is interested in a nursing career needs to take a college-preparatory course in high school that gives a good foundation in the laboratory sciences. You need to take biology, chemistry, physics, and mathematics. If your high school offers advanced biology or a human physiology course beyond the introductory biology class, these would be good choices for electives. English classes and other courses that develop communication skills are also important.

High school would be a good time to test your interest in nursing by getting some hands-on experience. There may be opportunities for volunteer work or a part-time job at a hospital, community health center, or nursing home in your community. You might also talk with people in various nursing fields or join the Future Nurses Club or Health Occupation Students of America (http://www.hosa.org).

Postsecondary Training

There are three ways to become a registered nurse—a two-year associate's degree program at a junior or community college, a three-year hospital nursing school program, or a bachelor's degree program (BSN) at a college or university nursing school. Sometimes persons who already have a bachelor's degree in another field enter nursing through a master's-level program (MSN) rather than by earning another bachelor's degree. All programs combine classroom education and actual nursing experience. Part-time or summer jobs in health care offer additional opportunities for exploring the nursing field.

The bachelor's or master's degree route is strongly recommended since a nurse with less than a BSN has few opportunities for advancement. All applicants to nurse anesthetist programs are required to have at least a bachelor's degree. (The other advanced-practice nursing fields—nurse practitioner, clinical nurse specialist, and nurse-midwife—also expect applicants to have a bachelor's degree before beginning specialized training.)

Undergraduate nursing programs include courses in biology, microbiology, human anatomy and physiology, psychology, nutrition, and statistics. Some classes in humanities and social sciences are also required in BSN programs. After com-

Did You Know?

According to the American Association of Nurse Anesthetists, approximately 43 percent of the 30,000 nurse anesthetists in the United States are men—as compared to only 8 percent of nurses in all specialties.

pleting the nursing degree, it is necessary to pass a national licensing exam; only then are you a registered nurse.

Ninety-two nursing anesthesia programs in the United States have been recognized by the Council of Accreditation of Nurse Anesthesia Educational Programs. The American Association of Nurse Anesthetists provides a listing of these programs at its Web site, http://www.aana.com. They last 24 to 36 months and nearly all offer a master's degree. "The master's part of my education was perhaps the most difficult educational experience I had ever encountered," Juan Quintana recalls. "While my bachelor's degree was interesting and involved, the master's course was taxing and excruciating. It required my complete and utmost resolve. I ate, drank, and slept anesthesia. Upon completion of the program, I knew that I had the knowledge to succeed. All that remained was the experience."

There are also a few clinical nursing doctorate programs for nurse anesthetists. Applicants to nurse anesthetist programs must have at least one year of experience as an RN in an intensive care unit; many have considerably more. The admissions process is very competitive.

If you are enrolled in a nurse anesthetist program, expect to take classes in pharmacology (the science of drugs and their uses), anatomy and physiology, pathophysiology (the physiology of disease), biochemistry, chemistry, and physics. You'll also acquire hundreds of hours of anesthesia-related clinical experience in surgery and obstetrics.

Historical Highlights

- The first nurse anesthetist was Sister Mary Bernard, who practiced in Pennsylvania in the 1870s. The first school of nurse anesthetists was founded in 1909 at St. Vincent Hospital in Portland, Oregon. Since then, many schools have been established, including the famous Mayo Clinic Anesthesia Program.

- During World War I, America's nurse anesthetists were the major providers of care to the troops in France. They also trained the French and British nurses and physicians in anesthesia procedures.

- Prior to World War II, anesthesia was considered a nursing specialty. In 1942, there were 17 nurse anesthetists in the United States for every anesthesiologist.

- The nurse anesthesia specialty was formally created on June 17, 1931, when the American Association of Nurse Anesthetists (AANA) held its first meeting.

Certification or Licensing

All registered nurses must be licensed to practice in the United States. For specifics, contact your state's nursing board. (See the National Council of State Boards of Nursing Web site at http://www.ncsbn.org for contact information.)

Nurse anesthetists are required to pass national certification exams given by the Council on Certification of Nurse Anesthetists after completing their educational program. The certification process was initiated by the American Association of Nurse Anesthetists (AANA) in 1945. All states recognize certified registered nurse anesthetist status. Nurse anesthetists are not required to work under the supervision of an anesthesiologist, although some licensing laws do stipulate that they must work with a physician. The American Society of PeriAnesthesia Nurses also offers a certification program.

Internships and Volunteerships

As part of your training, you will be required to complete several nursing internships, or clinical rotations. Usually these rotations are set up through the college or university to be completed at a hospital or other health care facility.

WHO WILL HIRE ME?

Juan Quintana landed his first job at Parkland Hospital in Dallas, Texas, where he functioned as a certified registered nurse anesthetist on staff. "Like all the anesthesia providers at Parkland," he says, "I administered anesthesia to patients for surgery on bone fractures (orthopedics) to major trauma emergencies to providing epidural analgesia for vaginal births."

Many nurse anesthetists are employed by hospitals or outpatient surgery centers (this would include dental and podiatry work as well as same-day surgery). Others are in group or independent practice and provide services to hospitals and other health care centers on a contract basis. Some work for the U.S. Public Health Services. Most rural hospitals rely on nurse anesthetists as their only providers

of anesthesia. Nurse anesthetists are eligible to receive direct Medicare reimbursement (under the 1986 Omnibus Budget Reconciliation Act).

The U.S. military also employs nurse anesthetists. In every 20th-century war, nurse anesthetists were the major providers of anesthesia care, especially in forward-positioned medical facilities. In the Vietnam War, there were three nurse anesthetists for every physician anesthetist. Frank Maziarski, who has been a certified registered nurse anesthetist (CRNA) for more than 45 years, spent many fulfilling years as a CRNA in the Army Nurse Corp, including service in Vietnam. "I decided to become a nurse anesthetist," he explains, "because of the challenge of taking care of very ill persons, in a specialty that was very high tech, using applied physiology, pharmacology, and intensive nursing skills. I wanted to make a difference to some patient every day, to give them hope and freedom from pain." After serving in a variety of clinical and educational positions, Frank retired from the Army as a Lt. Colonel. In 2004 he served as president of the American Association of Nurse Anesthetists.

Because the high-quality, cost-effective anesthesia service provided by nurse anesthetists is widely acknowledged, more and more health care institutions are eager to employ them.

WHERE CAN I GO FROM HERE?

Experienced nurse anesthetists who want new professional challenges beyond direct practice might consider teaching or administrative positions or involvement in research for improved or specialized anesthesia equipment and procedures. Some nurse anesthetists choose to acquire other advanced-practice nursing qualifications so they can be involved in a wider range of nursing activities. Doctoral programs for nurse anesthetists are expected to expand in the near future.

Juan Quintana hopes to continue to expand his business to more facilities and encourage hospitals to use CRNAs to their full extent. He is also the president-elect of the Texas Association of Nurse Anesthetists. "In the future, I hope to continue to represent CRNAs from my state," he says, "and perhaps take a more national role in the future policy making, legislative pursuits, and education of CRNAs everywhere."

WHAT ARE THE SALARY RANGES?

Nurse anesthetists are the highest paid nursing specialists. According to the American Association of Nurse Anesthetists, the average salary for nurse anesthetists is more than $120,000. Salaries may range from the $60,000s for new graduates to more than $150,000 for experienced nurse anesthetists. Earnings vary based on type and size of employer, years of experience, and location, among other factors.

Nurse anesthetists also receive fringe benefits such as paid sick, holiday, and vacation time, medical coverage, 401(k) plans, and other perks offered by the employer.

WHAT IS THE JOB OUTLOOK?

The job outlook for nurse anesthetists is excellent, according to Frank Maziarski.

Related Jobs

- anesthesiologists
- clinical nurse specialists
- community health nurses
- directors of nursing services
- directors of schools of nursing
- nurse-midwives
- nurse practitioners
- office nurses
- perfusionists
- private and general duty nurses
- school nurses

"The U.S. population continues to increase," he explains, "and the number of seniors is growing, requiring more surgeries for diseases of aging. The demand for reconstructive and plastic surgery is also increasing. Advances in technology and pharmacotheraputics are allowing surgery to be performed for pathology never before attempted. And the demand for nurse anesthetists in all branches of the military continues to increase." Frank says that the following subspecialties are especially promising: acute and chronic pain management, obstetrics, cardiovascular and neurosurgery, pediatric surgery, same-day surgery, and office-based practices.

Today, certified registered nurse anesthetists working with anesthesiologists, physicians, and, where authorized, podiatrists, dentists, and other health care providers are the hands-on providers of approximately 65 percent of all anesthetics given each year in the United States. CRNAs work in every setting in which anesthesia is delivered: tertiary-care centers, community hospitals, labor and delivery rooms, ambulatory surgical centers, diagnostic suites, and physicians' offices. CRNAs are the sole anesthesia providers in more than 70 percent of rural hospitals, affording anesthesia and resuscitative services to these medical facilities for surgical, obstetrical, and trauma care. Furthermore, eight nurse anesthetists can be educated for the cost of educating one anesthesiologist. In addition to the much higher annual cost of educating an anesthesiology resident, the total educational process for producing a nurse anesthetist (including undergraduate and graduate work) is on average four years shorter. All of these factors combine to make the likelihood for continued reliance on nurse anesthetists very good.

Nurse Assistants

SUMMARY

Definition
Nurse assistants care for patients in hospitals, nursing homes, and other settings under the supervision of nurses.

Alternative Job Titles
Career nurse (or nursing) assistants (or aides)
Hospital attendants
Nurse or nursing aides
Nursing assistants
Orderlies

Salary Range
$15,000 to $21,000 to $30,000+

Educational Requirements
High school diploma; completion of training program in either a community college or vocational school

Certification or Licensing
Voluntary for hospitals
Required for nursing homes

Employment Outlook
Much faster than the average

High School Subjects
Anatomy and physiology
Biology
English (writing/literature)
Health
Sociology

Personal Interests
Helping people: emotionally
Helping people: physical health/medicine

Helping nursing home residents get showered, dressed, and off to breakfast; taking residents to the bathroom—it had been a hectic morning and now Pam Owens must make a bed. It may not seem like a large task, but the resident is bedridden and fragile and can't be moved about much. Pam will leave the resident in the bed while making it; she'll work slowly and carefully, a contrast from the fast action that's been required of her all morning.

First Pam draws the curtain to protect the resident's privacy. "Are you comfortable, Mrs. Smith?" she asks, adjusting the pillow and raising the bed. When she's certain that the resident is at ease and unexposed, she lowers the side rail and begins to make up half the bed. She then raises the side rail again and helps the resident to the other side of the bed to finish. Before leaving, she checks again with Mrs. Smith to make certain she's comfortable and has everything she needs. Mrs. Smith responds with a smile and she squeezes Pam's hand. Pam leaves the room with the certainty that her tasks are important to the residents and the facility.

Lingo to Learn

acute care Providing emergency services, and general medical and surgical treatment for acute disorders rather than long-term care.

ambulatory care Serving patients who are able to walk.

asepsis Methods of sterilization to ensure the absence of germs.

gerontology A branch of medicine that deals with aging and the problems of the aged.

neonatal Pertaining to newborn children.

pediatrics A branch of medicine concerned with the development, care, and diseases of babies and children.

WHAT DOES A NURSE ASSISTANT DO?

Though the job title suggests someone who assists nurses, *nurse assistants* actually perform many duties independently; in some cases, they become more closely involved with patients or nursing home residents than do registered nurses or licensed practical nurses. Nurse assistants work under the supervision of nurses and perform tasks that allow the nursing staff to perform their primary duties effectively and efficiently.

Nurse assistants perform basic nursing care in hospitals and nursing homes. Male nurse assistants are perhaps better known as *orderlies.* Working independently and alongside nurses and doctors, nurse assis-

tants help move patients, assist in patients' exercise and nutrition, and see to the patients' personal hygiene. They bring the patients their meal trays and help them to eat. They push the patients on stretchers and in wheelchairs to operating and X-ray rooms. They also help to admit and discharge patients. Nurse assistants must keep charts of their work for review by nurses.

About 40 percent of the nurse assistants today work in nursing homes, tending to the daily care of elderly residents. They help residents with baths and showers, meals, and exercise. They help them in and out of their beds and to and from the bathroom. They also record the health of residents by taking body temperatures and checking blood pressures.

Because the residents are living within such close proximity to each other, and because they need help with personal hygiene and health care, a nurse assistant also takes care to protect the privacy of the resident. It is the responsibility of a nurse assistant to make the resident feel as comfortable as possible. Nurse assistants may also work with patients who are not fully functional, teaching them how to care for themselves and educating them in personal hygiene and health care.

The work can be strenuous, requiring the lifting and moving of patients. Nurse assistants must work with partners, or in groups, when performing the more strenuous tasks, so that neither the nurse assistant nor the resident is injured. Some requirements of the job can be as routine as changing sheets and helping a resident with phone calls, while other requirements can be as difficult and unattractive as assisting a resident with elimination and cleaning up a resident who has vomited.

Nurse assistants may be called upon by nurses and physicians to perform the more menial and unappealing tasks, but they also have the opportunity to develop meaningful relationships with residents. Nurse assistants work closely with residents, often gaining their trust and admiration. When residents are having personal problems, or problems with the staff, they may turn to the nurse assistant for help.

Nurse assistants generally work a 40-hour workweek, with some overtime. The hours and weekly schedule may be irregular, however, depending on the needs of the care institution. An assistant may have one day off in the middle of the week, followed by three days of work, then another day off. Nurse assistants are needed around the clock, so beginning assistants may be required to work late at night or very early in the morning.

WHAT IS IT LIKE TO BE A NURSE ASSISTANT?

Pam Owens works in a 120-bed long-term care facility in Winterhaven, Florida. She cares for patients with cancer, Alzheimer's, dementia, and other illnesses and diseases; patients who are recuperating from fractured hips, knee replacements, and car accidents; hospice patients; and those who may simply have no other place to go. She works under the supervision of registered nurses and licensed practical nurses. She

also works with occupational therapists, physical therapists, and dietitians. But mostly she performs her own set of daily responsibilities.

"I start at 7 A.M.," Pam says, "and check all my patients, make sure they are all OK, make sure they all have a washcloth and towel, and take them to the washroom if they need to go. After that, I serve them breakfast, help them get dressed, and take them to therapy."

In addition to caring for patients during the day, Pam must attend to call lights; call lights are the way residents signal the nurse assistants for help. "We are supposed to respond to call lights in a reasonable amount of time—in our facility this is within one to three minutes," she explains. "These go off all day and all night."

At the end of her workday, Pam fills out daily activity sheets for each patient that she cared for. The activity sheets are part of a patient's chart, and doctors and nurses review them to learn more about the status of a patient. "I record," explains Pam, "whether I gave patients a bath or shower, how much I had to help them get dressed, their bowel movements, the percentage of food they ate (the dietitian uses this information to monitor and develop nutritional treatment plans), their vital signs, whether they were continent or incontinent, and other information. I am the eyes and ears for my nurse, and I report anything that I see that is not status quo with the patient." The daily activity sheets are considered legal documents and may be reviewed by state inspectors if any legal questions arise as to the care of a patient. Pam spends about 30 minutes preparing the day's activity sheets.

Pam's day is usually complete at 3:00 P.M., though she occasionally works overtime. "Every now and then, a person might call in sick, and I might stay till 5:00, but that doesn't happen too often."

DO I HAVE WHAT IT TAKES TO BE A NURSE ASSISTANT?

A nurse assistant must care about the work and the patients and must show a general understanding and compassion for the ill, disabled, and the elderly. "You need to have compassion and a love of your job," Pam Owens says. "Otherwise, there is no sense in being a nurse assistant."

Because of the rigorous physical demands placed on a nurse assistant, you should be in good health. Also, the hours and responsibilities of the job won't allow you to take many sick days. Along with this good physical health, you should have good mental health. The job can be emotionally demanding, requiring your patience and stability. You should also be able to take orders and to work as part of a team.

Though the work can often be rewarding, a nurse assistant must also be prepared for the worst. "Dealing with difficult persons, for example, an Alzheimer's or dementia patient, can be very challenging," Pam says. "They may not want to get dressed or eat. They may be verbally abusive, and some of them like to hit. You just have to love them. If you don't love them, you're not going to be able to follow through with your care and get them to do what you want them to do."

To Be a Successful Nurse Assistant, You Should . . .

- be a compassionate person
- be in good health
- be able to perform some heavy lifting
- have a great deal of patience
- take orders well
- be a good team player
- be emotionally stable

Nurse assistants also need to have pride in their work. "You have to be able to look at yourself," explains Pam, "and say 'this is a job that I love to do, and this is my career and I'm proud of it.'"

HOW DO I BECOME A NURSE ASSISTANT?

Education

High School

Communication skills are valuable for a nurse assistant, so take English, speech, and writing courses. Science courses, such as biology and anatomy, will also prepare you for future training. Because a high school diploma is not required of nurse assistants, many high school students are hired by nursing homes and hospitals for part-time work. Job opportunities may also exist in a hospital or nursing home kitchen, introducing you to diet and nutrition, as well as in nursing home activity departments. Also, volunteer work can familiarize you with the work nurses and nurse assistants perform, as well as introduce you to some medical terminology.

Postsecondary Training

Nurse assistants are not required to have a college degree but may have to complete a short training course at a community college or vocational school. These training courses, usually led by a registered nurse, teach basic nursing skills and prepare students for the state certification exam. Nurse assistants typically begin the training courses after getting their first job as an assistant, and the course work is incorporated into their on-the-job training.

Many people work as nurse assistants as they pursue other medical professions; someone interested in becoming a nurse or a paramedic may work as an assistant while taking courses. A high school student or a student in a premedical program may work as a nurse assistant part time before going on to medical school.

Certification or Licensing

Nurse assistants in hospitals are not required to be certified, but those working in nursing homes must pass a state exam. The Omnibus Budget Reconciliation Act (OBRA) passed by Congress in 1987 requires nursing homes to hire only certified nurse assistants. OBRA also requires continuing education for nurse assistants, and periodic evaluations.

Pam Owens became a certified nursing assistant by taking and passing a written test. Today, nurse assistants must take a hands-on test to become certified. "They must demonstrate skills," Pam says, "such as how to give a bath, dress or undress a patient, take blood pressure, transfer people in and out of beds, and other tasks that nurse assistants are expected to perform." Pam feels that certification is a good thing because many aspiring nurse assistants have never been caregivers or taken care of patients and need to learn appropriate skills before they are trusted with the care of a patient. To maintain her certification in Florida, Pam must complete 18 hours of continuing education annually.

WHO WILL HIRE ME?

Forty percent of all nurse assistants work in nursing homes. Other places where they are employed include hospitals, halfway houses, retirement centers, and private homes.

Because of the high demand for nurse assistants, you can apply directly to the health care facilities in your area. Most will probably have a human resources department that advertises positions in the newspaper and interviews applicants.

WHERE CAN I GO FROM HERE?

For the most part, there is not much opportunity for advancement within the job of nurse assistant. To move up in a health care facility requires additional training. Some nurse assistants, after gaining experience and learning medical technology, enroll in nursing programs, or may even decide to pursue medical degrees or opportunities in health care management. Lori Porter worked as a certified nursing assistant for seven years before becoming a nursing home administrator. She also cofounded the National Association of Geriatric Nursing Assistants (NAGNA), the first and only national professional association for nursing assistants in the United States. "I am responsible for the oversight of the association as a whole, membership, operations, education, public policy agenda, and a variety of other tasks," she explains. "I represent the association on a national front through public speaking and negotiating with long-term-care health providers to partner with NAGNA to serve the needs of their CNAs."

A nursing home requires a lot of hard work and dedication, so nurse assistants frequently burn out, or quit before completing their training. Others may choose another aspect of the job, such as working as a home health aide. Helping patients in their homes, these aides see to the client's personal health, hygiene, and home care.

WHAT ARE THE SALARY RANGES?

Although the salaries for most health care professionals vary by region and population, the average hourly wage of nurse assistants is about the same across the country. Midwestern states and less populated areas, where a large staff of nurse assistants may be needed to make up for

Related Jobs

- ambulance attendants
- child care attendants
- emergency medical technicians
- home health aides
- morgue attendants
- occupational therapy aides
- optometric assistants
- perfusionists
- physical therapy aides
- psychiatric aides
- surgical technicians

a smaller staff of nurses and therapists, may pay a little more per hour.

According to the U.S. Department of Labor, nurse assistants earned median hourly wages of $10.31 in 2003. For full-time work at 40 hours per week, this hourly wage translates into a yearly income of approximately $21,440. The lowest-paid 10 percent earned less than $7.49 per hour (approximately $15,580 per year), and the highest-paid 10 percent earned more than $14.51 per hour (approximately $30,190 annually).

Benefits are usually based on the hours worked, length of employment, and the policies of the facility. Some offer paid vacation and holidays, medical or hospital insurance, and retirement plans. Some also provide free meals to their workers.

WHAT IS THE JOB OUTLOOK?

Lori Porter sees a very bright employment future for nursing assistants. "Nurse assisting offers a career freedom rarely found in America," she says. "Once certified, a nurse assistant can go anywhere in the United States and find a position in his or her chosen field within 24 hours. This level of freedom is priceless. The largest growing demographic is geriatrics and, therefore, long-term care offers unlimited opportunities in health care professional growth. Hospital acute care is often depicted as more exciting or prestigious, but those working in long-term care often find their work more challenging and rewarding. I highly recommend the profession in general, but certainly recommend long-term care specifically."

There will continue to be many job opportunities for nurse assistants. Because of the physical and emotional demands of the job, and because of the lack of advancement opportunities, there is a high turnover rate of employees. Also, health care is constantly changing; more opportunities open for nurse assistants as different kinds of health care facilities are developed. Business-based health organizations are limiting the services of health care professionals and looking for cheaper ways to provide care. This may provide opportunities for those looking for work as nurse assistants.

Government and private agencies are also developing more programs to assist dependent people. And as the number of people 65 years of age and older continues to rise, new and larger nursing-care facilities will be needed.

Nurse-Midwives

SUMMARY

Definition
A nurse-midwife is a registered nurse who assists in family planning, pregnancy, and childbirth. Nurse-midwives also provide routine health care for women.

Alternative Job Titles
Certified nurse-midwives

Salary Range
$54,000 to $66,000 to $80,000+

Educational Requirements
Two- to four-year registered nursing program; nine-month to two-year certified nurse-midwife program

Certification or Licensing
Required

Employment Outlook
Much faster than the average

High School Subjects
Anatomy and physiology

Biology
Chemistry
Health
Psychology
Science

Personal Interests
Helping people: emotionally
Helping people: physical health/medicine
Science

The young woman found out last month that she was pregnant. It would be her second child. When she was pregnant the first time, three years ago, she was seeing an obstetrician for her prenatal care. She also had the obstetrician deliver her baby.

But she wanted to do things differently this time. Last time, she felt that she didn't receive the emotional support she needed from her doctor. And with all the pain medication she was given during delivery, she almost felt as if she weren't in the room when her baby was born.

So this time she decided to seek prenatal care from a certified nurse-midwife, who would also deliver her baby. It would be a natural pregnancy and a natural childbirth. And now, after meeting with Heather Bradford, her nurse-midwife, she knew she had made the right decision.

WHAT DOES A NURSE-MIDWIFE DO?
Midwifery, the act of caring for women during childbirth, has been practiced around the world for thousands of years. But in the United States, pregnancy and childbirth are often considered technical medical procedures best left in the hands

of physicians known as obstetricians and gynecologists. Midwifery was historically frowned upon by both the medical community and the public.

Since the 1960s, however, this attitude has changed as more women insist on "natural" methods of giving birth and seek care that is less medically interventive. *Nurse-midwives,* officially known as *certified nurse-midwives (CNMs),* have generally become accepted as respected members of health care teams involved with family planning, pregnancy, and childbirth. A number of studies have even indicated that babies delivered by nurse-midwives are less likely to experience low birth weights and other health complications than babies delivered by physicians.

Most nurse-midwives work at hospitals, family planning clinics, or birthing centers affiliated with hospitals. Some nurse-midwives operate independent practices providing home birth services.

Nurse-midwives examine pregnant women and monitor the growth and development of fetuses. Typically, a nurse-midwife is responsible for all phases of a normal pregnancy, including prenatal care, assisting during labor, delivering the baby, and providing follow-up care. A nurse-midwife always works in consultation with a physician, who can be called upon should complications arise during pregnancy or childbirth. In most states, nurse-midwives are authorized to prescribe and administer medications. Many nurse-midwives provide the full spectrum of women's health care, including gynecological exams.

An important part of nurse-midwifery care is focusing on the education of patients. Nurse-midwives teach their patients about proper nutrition and fitness for healthy pregnancies, and about various positions in labor that help facilitate faster and easier childbirth. Nurse-midwives also counsel their patients in the postpartum period—that is, after birth—about breast-feeding, parenting, and other areas concerning the health of mother and child. Nurse-midwives provide counseling on several other issues, including sexually transmitted diseases, spousal and child abuse, and social support resources. In some cases, counseling extends to patients' family members.

Not all midwives are certified nurse-midwives. Most states recognize other categories of midwives, including *certified* (or *licensed*) *midwives* and *lay* (or *empirical*) *midwives.*

Certified midwives are not required to be nurses in order to practice as midwives. They typically assist in home births or at birthing centers, and are trained through a combination of formal education, apprenticeship, and self-education. Certified midwives are legally recognized in all 50 states. Certified midwives perform most of the services of nurse-midwives, and they generally have professional relationships with physicians, hospitals, and laboratories.

Lay midwives usually obtain their training by apprenticing with established midwives, although some may acquire formal education as well. Lay midwives are midwives who are not certified or licensed, either because they lack the necessary experience and education or because they pursue nontraditional childbirth techniques. Some lay midwives practice only as part of religious communities or specific ethnic groups. Lay midwives typically assist only in home birth situations. Some states have made it illegal for lay midwives to charge for their services. The rest of this article will concern itself only with certified nurse-midwives.

Lingo to Learn

catching babies An informal term used to describe the act of assisting in the delivery of an infant.

cesarean section A surgical procedure to deliver a baby through an incision in the abdomen. The procedure is named after Julius Caesar, who was supposedly born in this way.

episiotomy An incision made between the vagina and anus to provide more clearance for birth.

gynecologist A physician who specializes in the diseases and routine health care of the reproductive systems of women.

natural childbirth A term used to emphasize pregnancy, labor, and childbirth as natural processes. In natural childbirth, pain-reducing and labor-inducing drugs either are not used or are used conservatively.

obstetrician A physician who specializes in childbirth and in prenatal and postpartum care.

Pap smear A procedure in which cells are collected from the cervix; the cells are then examined under a microscope for signs of cancer.

postpartum After childbirth.

prenatal Before childbirth.

WHAT IS IT LIKE TO BE A NURSE-MIDWIFE?

Heather Bradford is a certified nurse-midwife at the Center for Women's Health at Evergreen in Kirkland, Washington. She has been a midwife since 2002. "I've always been interested in women's health and am fascinated with pregnancy and birth as empowering experiences," she says. "Women come to us with so many questions and concerns at the beginning of their pregnancy and after they have a baby they say, 'I think I could climb a mountain!' They are so proud of themselves. It's a powerful thing to watch, especially with women who just had a vaginal birth after a previous cesarean section."

Heather typically works four to six days a week, depending on her schedule. These days consist of call days and regular work at the clinic. "I work in private practice with three other CNMs (and seven obstetricians/gynecologists)," explains Heather. "The midwives share their patients and rotate call between the four of us. Consequently, I am on call approximately one day a week and every fourth weekend."

Nurse-midwives who are on call are responsible for attending patients for labor and birth. Heather begins a typical on-call day (a 24-hour shift) at 6 A.M. by talking on the phone with the previous day's call person to get an update regarding a patient who is in labor. "Typically, our practice delivers 30 to 35 babies a month, so that equates to about a baby a day," she says. "And most babies come at night (your hormones that trigger labor increase at night), so we can pretty much expect to be up every night that we are on call."

If she has no patients in labor, Heather starts her morning at the hospital at 8 A.M. by checking up on any postpartum patients. "After that," she says, "I am responsible for managing all triage calls (such as, 'I think my water broke,' 'I think I have a yeast infection,' 'I ran out of birth control,' 'What can I take for my sinus infection?'), as well as calling patients regarding lab results." Heather also sees about 5 to 10 patients during the day to handle the aforementioned triage work. "Once in a while, we have an induction scheduled, but these are done only if medically necessary."

If it is a clinic day, Heather sees her first patient at about 7:40 A.M. She sees 20 or more patients a day—at least 2 of whom are newly pregnant. "We spend about 30 to 45 minutes with these women," she says, "reviewing their health history as well as providing lots of helpful information about diet and exercise guidelines, normal weight gain, and recommended lab tests. We see our pregnant patients every four weeks until their last month of pregnancy, and then we see them weekly." In addition to prenatal care, Heather provides care after birth, gynecological exams, newborn care, and assistance with family planning decisions,

preconception care, menopausal management, and counseling in health maintenance/disease prevention. "There is lots of variety, and that makes the job exciting and different every day."

Some nurse-midwives, such as Ginger Breedlove, also work as educators. Ginger is the Director and Founder of the Nurse Midwifery Education Program at the University of Kansas School of Nursing. The Program prepares master's-level certified nurse-midwives to provide pregnancy and well-woman care to women in the Greater Kansas City area and the states of Kansas and Missouri (the program was created in collaboration with the University of Missouri-Kansas City School of Nursing). "I consider my career in nursing a lifelong educator role," she says. "Teaching is a significant component of every role in the nursing profession. This includes helping patients and families better understand illness and treatment plans, encouraging health promotion and disease prevention strategies throughout life, and providing knowledge to consumers in order to make better-informed decisions."

Ginger spent 20 years in clinical practice in nursing and nurse-midwifery. "I then decided," she says, "to work at a university school of nursing in order to establish a nurse-midwifery education program in Kansas, and become part of the education team to develop future nursing leaders who work with compassion and caring." In addition to her directorial duties, Ginger teaches advanced-practice nursing and assists in various undergraduate nursing courses. "I believe that expert nurses who

To Be a Successful Nurse-Midwife, You Should . . .

- enjoy working with people
- be independent and able to accept responsibility for your actions and decisions
- have strong observation, listening, and communication skills
- be confident and composed— especially in emergency situations
- be a good listener
- be strong both mentally and physically

have worked in their respective field for a significant number of years provide students with realistic expectations of practice and professional responsibility upon completion of school," she says. "Being able to share a wealth of diverse knowledge, varied experiences in clinical settings across the country and world, and wisdom related to understanding the 'art' of nursing and nurse-midwifery highly influences what graduates embrace and replicate in their own career. I can't imagine following any other pathway through my professional career."

DO I HAVE WHAT IT TAKES TO BE A NURSE-MIDWIFE?

If you are interested in becoming a nurse-midwife, you will need skills that aren't necessarily taught in midwifery programs. Nurse-midwives need to enjoy working with people, learning about their patients' needs, and helping them through a very important life change. They should be sympathetic to the needs of their patients. They need to be independent and able to accept responsibility for their actions and decisions. Strong observation skills are key, as nurse-midwives must be tuned into their patients' needs during pregnancy and labor. Nurse-midwives also need to listen well and respond appropriately. They must communicate effectively with patients, family members, physicians, and other hospital staff, as well as insurance company personnel. Finally, nurse-midwives should be confident and composed, responding well in an emergency and keeping their patients calm.

Nurse-midwives, like many nurses, work long and irregular hours in order to care for their patients. This can be physically and emotionally draining. "Being a part of someone's birth experience is an honor," Heather Bradford says. "It is a true miracle to watch. And who doesn't love being around newborn babies? But staying up all night several nights a week can wear on a person tremendously." Heather considers nurse-midwifery not just a profession, but also a calling. "You have to love it to endure the physical and emotional challenges. But for those who do love it, it is well worth it."

Nurse-midwives share both the joys of childbirth and the tragedies. The birth of babies is a wonderful event, but complications or even death can also occur during childbirth. This is especially difficult for midwives because they become so involved in their patients' lives. "I was once involved with a birth where the baby had a severe cleft lip and the parents did not know ahead of time," Heather recalls. "The family always looks to you for support and guidance, and you have to be 'on'

all the time. So it can also be quite emotionally exhausting."

HOW DO I BECOME A NURSE-MIDWIFE?

Heather Bradford followed a very circuitous route to becoming a nurse-midwife. She started at Boston College and received a Bachelor of Arts in Sociology and was also in the college's premedical training program. "At that point," she says, "I had never heard of a midwife and had never contemplated nursing. I had my sights set on becoming a doctor." After a year of volunteer work, Heather slowly became more interested in nurse-midwifery. "I connected with the philosophy of it more than medicine," she explains. "I liked the idea of seeing the patient in a holistic way." She entered a combined BSN/MSN program at the University of Pennsylvania. "It was sometimes arduous and challenging," she recalls, "mainly because there were times in the BSN portion that I kept thinking to myself, I will never need this information as a CNM. But I really feel that being trained as a nurse makes me a better midwife."

Education

High School

To prepare for a career in midwifery, high school students should focus heavily on science courses. A prospective midwife needs to gain a broad range of education and experience. They are just as much people-focused as they are science-focused—so take courses in English, language, philosophy, psychology, and sociology.

Breast-feeding—Benefits and Bothers

● ● ● ● ●

Midwifery supports the practice of breast-feeding over bottle-feeding. Human milk contains antibodies that protect infants from infections, and breast-feeding strengthens the psychological bond between mother and child.

However, problems sometimes develop with breast-feeding. A breast may become engorged with milk, preventing the infant from sucking properly. In addition, nipples can become sore and cracked, and infections and abscesses can develop in the breasts.

Lactation consultants are health care professionals who help prevent and solve breast-feeding problems. They work in hospitals, public health centers, and private practices. The International Board of Lactation Consultant Examiners certifies lactation consultants.

Among the people certified as lactation consultants are many nurse-midwives, dietitians, physicians, and social workers.

Information about becoming a lactation consultant can be obtained from the International Lactation Consultant Association, 1500 Sunday Drive, Suite 102, Raleigh, N.C. 27607-5151, 919-861-5577, info@ilca.org, http://www.ilca.org.

Try to gain as much work experience as possible. You can volunteer at hospitals (especially at facilities where you can work with adolescents) and become involved in peer-to-peer counseling. These experiences can make a difference in gaining admission into a midwifery program.

Heather Bradford recommends that students try to arrange a job-shadowing experience with a nurse-midwife in their area. She advises students to visit the Find a Midwife section of the American College of Nurse-Midwives Web site, http://www.acnm.org, to contact a nurse-midwife. "Sometimes a patient is even open to having a student be present at her birth," she says. "You will be hooked! Births can be beautiful and often leave you awestruck."

Postsecondary Training

All nurse-midwives begin their careers as registered nurses. In order to become a registered nurse, you must first graduate from either a four-year bachelor's degree program in nursing or a two-year associate's degree program in nursing. (Thirty-nine of the 43 accredited nurse-midwifery schools in the United States require applicants to earn a baccalaureate degree in nursing prior to admission.) After receiving a degree, you will need to apply for admission into an accredited certificate program in nurse-midwifery or an accredited master's degree program in nurse-midwifery. For more information on accredited programs, visit http://www.midwife.org.

Ginger Breedlove recommends that students get experience in maternal child health before entering midwifery school. She says that "students can participate in activities such as working in a hospital labor and delivery unit for one year, teaching or assisting with childbirth education classes, completing continuing education in electronic fetal monitoring surveillance, and reading evidence-based journals about women's health issues."

If you have earned an associate's degree in nursing, you are eligible for acceptance into a certificate program in nurse-midwifery. A certificate program requires 9 to 12 months of study. In order to be accepted into a master's degree program in nurse-midwifery, you will need a bachelor's degree in nursing. A master's program requires 16 to 24 months of study. Some master's programs also require one year of clinical experience in order to earn a degree as a nurse-midwife. Ginger believes that the most successful graduate nurse-midwifery students are those who "have a passion to learn, support from friends/family, a reduced workload/financial responsibilities, and who place academic studies as their top personal priority."

In all of these programs, you will be trained to provide primary care services, gynecological care, preconception and prenatal care, labor delivery and management, and postpartum and infant care. As you train to become a nurse-midwife you will also learn how to perform physical examinations, Pap smears, and episiotomies; repair incisions from cesarean sections; administer anesthesia; and prescribe medications. You will also be trained to provide counseling on such subjects as nutrition, breast-feeding, and infant care, as well as to offer emotional support.

Certification or Licensing

All states and Washington, D.C., require nurses to be licensed. To obtain a license, graduates of approved nursing schools must pass a national examination. Nurses may be licensed by more than one state. In some states, continuing education is a condition for license renewal. Different titles require different education and training levels. For further information, contact your state's nursing board. (See the National Council of State Boards of Nursing Web site at http://www.ncsbn. org for contact information.)

After graduating from a nurse-midwifery program, you will be required to take a national certification examination administered by the American College of Nurse-Midwives. When you pass this examination you will then apply to be licensed to practice nurse-midwifery in the state where you wish to practice. Each state, however, has its own laws and regulations governing the activities and responsibilities of nurse-midwives.

Internships and Volunteerships

Nursing students who pursue a BSN or MSN will be required to complete several nursing internships, or clinical rotations. Usually these rotations are set up through the college or university to be completed at a hospital or other health care facility.

Students in the graduate track at the Nurse Midwifery Education Program at the University of Kansas (the program directed by Ginger Breedlove) are pro-

Midwifery: Past and Present

The practice of midwifery is many thousands of years old. In most cultures around the world, births are usually attended to by midwives rather than physicians. The United States is one of the few countries where births are usually physician-delivered in hospital settings.

Hospitals began to replace homes as the places of birth early in the twentieth century. At the same time, the use of drugs to reduce pain and induce labor became commonplace. In addition, cesarean sections, in which the uterus is cut open for childbirth, increased in frequency.

Though this approach to childbirth undoubtedly decreased infant mortality in the United States, many people began to criticize it during the 1960s. The main criticism was that modern medicine was robbing women of the feelings and sensations associated with childbirth. The natural childbirth movement increased the popularity of midwifery.

Today, midwifery, as practiced by professional nurses who work in consultation with physicians, is generally accepted by the medical establishment.

vided clinical experiences in all courses that involve knowledge and theory related to patient care of women and newborns. Students complete more than 800 hours of clinical practice during this course of study. "In the last 10 weeks of the program, all students are required to complete an 'internship' experience where they move off campus and work in a new health care setting with faculty preceptors," Ginger explains. "This experience allows the students to bring together all their knowledge and previous experiences in master's coursework into one capstone experience. Each student is responsible to work a full-time nurse-midwife schedule (with the preceptor always present) and provide full-scope health care including: prenatal visits, gynecology, preconception counseling, care of women in labor and birth, newborn care in the hospital, family planning, and care of aging women."

see patients and attend deliveries on hospital grounds and use hospital-owned equipment for examinations and other procedures. Additional medical personnel are always available for emergency situations. Other nurse-midwives work in family planning clinics and other health care clinics and privately funded agencies. These nurse-midwives usually have relationships with specific hospitals and physicians in case of an emergency. Finally, some nurse-midwives operate their own clinics and birthing centers, while a small percentage work independently and specialize in home birth deliveries.

WHO WILL HIRE ME?

As a nurse-midwifery student, Heather Bradford became involved in the American College of Nurse-Midwives. Through her work on a legislative committee, she met a midwife in Seattle. "I didn't get involved with networking in mind," she says, "but it really made a difference. As I approached graduation, I asked her if she knew of any job openings, and next thing you know, I secured my first job at the Center for Women's Health at Evergreen."

Hospitals are the primary source of employment for nurse-midwives. Approximately 89 percent of the 7,000 nurse-midwives who are members of the American College of Nurse-Midwives work in clinical practice. More than half work primarily in an office or clinic environment, and physician practices and hospitals are the places where most CNMs are employed. At hospitals, CNMs

WHERE CAN I GO FROM HERE?

With experience, a nurse-midwife can advance into a supervisory role or into an administrative capacity at a hospital, family planning clinic, birthing center, or other facility. Many nurse-midwives choose to continue their education and complete Ph.D. programs. With a doctorate, a nurse-midwife can do research or teaching.

Heather Bradford plans to eventually pursue a doctorate and teach and do research. "While I was a student at Penn," she says, "I had some opportunities to participate in research that looked at factors affecting labor and delivery outcomes, and I really enjoyed it. I would also like to teach midwifery in an academic setting, as well as practice part time so that I can continue to care for women."

WHAT ARE THE SALARY RANGES?

Certified nurse-midwives who work for large hospitals tend to earn more than those working for small hospitals, clinics, and birthing centers. The most experienced nurse-midwives, including those in supervisory, director, and administrative positions, have the highest earnings. Salaries also vary according to the region of the country and whether the employing facility is private or public. Because of their special training, CNMs are among the higher-paying nursing professions. According to the U.S. Department of Labor, the median yearly income for all registered nurses was $54,670 in 2005. This median, however, may actually be closer to the starting salary for a certified nurse-midwife. Nursemidwifejobs.com (http://nursemidwifejobs. com), a division of the company Health Care Job Store that offers job placements to medical professionals, reports that the average salary for a nurse-midwife was approximately $66,615 in 2005. Experienced CNMs in the private sector may earn $80,000 a year or more. Ginger Breedlove reports that new graduates of her Nurse Midwifery Education Program receive average starting salaries of $68,000 a year.

Nurse-midwives generally enjoy a good benefits package, although these too can vary widely. Most nurse-midwives work a 40-hour week. The hours are sometimes irregular, involving working at night and on weekends. This is partly due to the fact that the onset of labor cannot be controlled.

Related Jobs

- community health nurses
- dietitians
- licensed practical nurses
- nurse anesthetists
- nurse practitioners
- nutritionists
- obstetricians/gynecologists
- office nurses
- paramedics
- physician assistants
- private and general duty nurses
- school nurses

WHAT IS THE JOB OUTLOOK?

The number of nurse-midwifery jobs is expected to grow much faster than the average for all occupations through 2014, as nurse-midwives continue to gain a reputation as an integral part of the health care community. Currently, there are more positions than there are nurse-midwives to fill them. This situation is expected to continue for the near future.

Two factors are driving the demand for nurse-midwives. The first factor is the growth of interest in natural childbirth among women. The number of midwife-assisted births has risen dramatically since the 1970s. Some women have been attracted to midwifery because of studies that indicate natural childbirth is healthier for mother and child than doctor-assisted childbirth or those that show greater reliance on drugs and anesthetics in doctor-assisted childbirth. Other women have been attracted to midwifery because it emphasizes the participation of the entire family in prenatal care and labor.

The second factor in the growing demand for nurse-midwives is economic in nature. As society moves toward managed-care programs and the health care community emphasizes cost-effectiveness, midwifery should increase in popularity. This is because the care provided by nurse-midwives costs substantially less than the care provided by obstetricians and gynecologists. If the cost advantage of midwifery continues, more insurers and health maintenance organizations will probably direct patients to nurse-midwives for care.

Despite these rosy predictions, the nationwide market for job *choice* is tight, according to Ginger Breedlove. "Most graduates are entering employment through established relationships within medical groups or hospitals in the communities they reside in," she says. "Regions of the United States with the highest numbers of midwives in practice include the Southwest, West Coast, East Coast, and Deep South." Nurse-midwives may find it more difficult to locate positions in these regions, and may need to adjust their job search to focus on underserved areas.

Nurse Practitioners

SUMMARY

Definition
Nurse practitioners are registered nurses (RNs) who have advanced education in diagnosis and treatment that enables them to carry out many health care responsibilities formerly handled by physicians.

Alternative Job Titles
Acute care nurse practitioners
Family nurse practitioners
Gerontological nurse practitioners

Occupational health nurse practitioners
Pediatric nurse practitioners
Psychiatric nurse practitioners
School nurse practitioners

Salary Range
$54,000 to $69,000 to $100,000+

Educational Requirements
Master's degree

Certification or Licensing
Licensing as an RN is mandatory; certification for nurse practitioners is recommended.

Employment Outlook
Much faster than the average

High School Subjects
Anatomy and physiology
Biology
Chemistry
Health
Mathematics

Personal Interests
Helping people: emotionally
Helping people: physical health/medicine
Science

In working with college students, Harvey Bennett says it is essential to establish a rapport. "You need to be a good listener and make it clear that confidentiality will be respected," he explains.

Harvey, the head nurse practitioner at Vanderbilt University's Student Health Service, spends much of his workday seeing students with a variety of health complaints. An average of 150 students visit the Health Service each day, with problems ranging from colds and sore throats to alcohol-related problems or eating disorders.

Careful assessment of each case is important. Most of the time, it turns out that one of the center's six nurse practitioners can handle the problem without calling in a staff physician.

WHAT DOES A NURSE PRACTITIONER DO?

Nurse practitioners provide health care in a wide range of settings, generally focusing on primary care, health maintenance, and prevention of illness. They carry out many of the medical responsibilities traditionally handled by physicians. They do physical exams, take detailed medical histories, order lab tests and X-rays, and recommend treatment plans.

The nurse practitioner role developed in the 1960s in response to the shortage of physicians and the need for alternative health care providers, especially in remote rural areas. Harvey Bennett was attracted to the profession during its early years because he valued its goal—to keep people out of the hospital by providing good primary and preventive care.

As a result of their advanced training, nurse practitioners are qualified to work more autonomously than staff nurses. In 1986, a study carried out by the U.S. Congress Office of Technology Assessment found that "within their areas of competence, nurse practitioners provide care whose quality is equivalent to that of care provided by physicians." In preventive care and communication with patients, nurse practitioners were found to surpass doctors. There are approximately 115,000 nurse practitioners in the United States, and the number is increasing rapidly.

A nurse practitioner's exact responsibilities depend on the setting in which she or he works and the field of specialization chosen. A nurse practitioner may work in close collaboration with a physician at a hospital, health center, or private practice office or, as in the case of a rural health care provider, may have only weekly telephone contact with a physician. Nurse practitioners may not function entirely independently of a

physician, although the degree of consultation required varies from state to state. As Harvey points out, it is important for nurse practitioners to develop the judgment to recognize when an illness or injury is beyond their level of competence.

Most nurse practitioners have a field of specialization. The most common specialty (and the broadest in its scope) is *family nurse practitioner* (FNP). Family nurse practitioners, who are often based in community health clinics, provide primary care to people of all ages—assessing, diagnosing, and treating common illnesses and injuries. Their interactions with patients have a strong emphasis on teaching and counseling for health maintenance. Nurse practitioners recognize the importance of the social and emotional aspects of health care, in addition to the more obvious physical factors.

Nurse practitioners in other specialties perform similar tasks, though working with different age groups or with people in school, workplace, or institutional settings. *Pediatric nurse practitioners* (PNPs) provide primary health care for children (infants through adolescents). Developmental assessment is an important part of the pediatric nurse practitioner's responsibilities: Is this child within the norms of physical and social growth for his or her age group? *Gerontological nurse practitioners* (GNPs) work with older adults. They are often based in nursing homes.

School nurse practitioners work in school settings and provide primary health care for students in elementary, secondary, or higher education settings. *Occupational health nurse practitioners* focus on employment-related health problems and injuries. They work closely with occupational health physicians, toxicologists, safety specialists, and other occupational health professionals to identify potential dangers and to prevent work-related illness or injury. *Psychiatric nurse practitioners* work with people who have mental or emotional problems. *Cardiac nurse practitioners* work with people who have heart disease or related illnesses.

Women's health care nurse practitioners provide primary care for women from adolescence through old age. In addition to handling overall primary care, they do Pap smears and breast exams, provide information on family planning and birth control, monitor normal pregnancies, and offer treatment and counseling for gynecological problems and sexually transmitted diseases. Some nurse practitioners are also certified in midwifery.

In most states, nurse practitioners are allowed to write prescriptions, but a physician's signature is often required to validate it.

WHAT IS IT LIKE TO BE A NURSE PRACTITIONER?

Harvey Bennett has been a nurse practitioner in Vanderbilt's Student Health Service since 1984. He is certified as a family nurse practitioner. Though he is qualified to provide primary care to per-

> ### Lingo to Learn
>
> **acute** Describes a disease or symptom that begins suddenly and does not last long.
>
> **advanced practice nurses** Nurses with advanced education that enables them to take on many responsibilities formerly carried out by physicians; nurse practitioners, clinical nurse specialists, certified nurse-midwives, and certified registered nurse anesthetists are classed as advanced-practice nurses.
>
> **chronic** Describes a disease or condition that develops gradually and often remains for the rest of the person's life, such as glaucoma.
>
> **clinical** Pertaining to direct, hands-on medical care; from the Greek word for "bed."
>
> **licensed practical nurse** An individual trained in basic nursing who usually works under the supervision of a registered nurse.
>
> **Pap smear** A test that examines cells (taken during a pelvic exam) to detect cancers of the cervix.
>
> **protocol** A written plan (prepared in advance) that details the procedures to be followed in providing care for a particular medical condition.
>
> **wellness** A dynamic state of health in which a person moves toward higher levels of functioning—a term often used by NPs.

sons of all ages, in his present position his practice is confined to the Vanderbilt student population—undergraduates who are generally 18 to 22 and graduate and professional students who may be in their 20s, 30s, and 40s.

After completing the nurse practitioner program at Vanderbilt, Harvey spent six years working as a family nurse practitioner based in rural health clinics in Alabama and Georgia. Each clinic was staffed by a nurse practitioner; there was a physician "somewhere in the county." During his Georgia years, the nearest hospital was 35 miles away. The shortage of doctors and hospitals meant that the nurse practitioners formed long-term relationships with the people they served and had the satisfaction of knowing that they were making a difference in people's lives. It also meant that they were likely to have people knocking on the door in the middle of the night with a medical emergency. In both Alabama and Georgia, Harvey found a high level of acceptance from patients, but in Alabama there was considerable hostility to nurse practitioners from the medical establishment. During the Reagan administration, federal funding for clinics was cut, so Harvey returned to Nashville.

At Student Health, Harvey spends most of his time seeing students with health problems. He takes a history from each patient, does a physical, and orders lab tests (if indicated). Treatment is based on a protocol developed by the nurse practitioners and doctors; as long as the complaint can be handled within the protocol, the nurse practitioner works without consulting the doctor.

In assessing each case, it is essential to find out whether the reported symptoms may actually reflect a more serious under-

To Be a Successful Nurse Practitioner, You Should . . .

- be strongly committed to making a positive difference in people's lives

- have patience and the ability to remain calm in an emergency

- find teaching and counseling as satisfying as dramatic medical interventions

- be committed to life-long learning

- be able to identify those medical situations where it is necessary to call in a physician

lying problem. For example, in many cases, students suffering from depression come to the center complaining of headaches, stomach pains, or fatigue.

Teaching and counseling are important parts of the job. College students are at a formative age, and Harvey tries to make a positive impact on their daily health habits. Health topics he discusses with them include alcohol and tobacco use, diet, seat belt use, and the need for bicycle safety helmets. Students often need assistance in making the connection between the symptoms they are experiencing and their behavior (such as smoking or excessive consumption of alcohol). In addition to seeing patients, Harvey, as head nurse practitioner, is also responsible for scheduling and quality control.

DO I HAVE WHAT IT TAKES TO BE A NURSE PRACTITIONER?

A nurse practitioner needs to enjoy working with people and to be strongly committed to making a positive difference in people's lives. Nurse practitioners must develop excellent communication skills. Being a good listener is essential, as is the ability to encourage people to answer questions about personal matters that they may find difficult to talk about. Anyone going into the health care field needs to have patience and flexibility and the ability to remain calm in an emergency.

Since nurse practitioners work more independently than nurses traditionally do, it is important for them to develop the capacity to take active responsibility in health care situations. At the same time, they must have the judgment to identify those situations that are beyond their competence and to call in a physician or other specialist.

Because the nurse practitioner role is strongly focused on health maintenance and prevention, a person considering becoming a nurse practitioner should find teaching and counseling at least as satisfying as dramatic medical interventions.

A nurse practitioner has to be prepared for the possibility of friction with professional colleagues. The nurse practitioner profession is still new, and some physicians are uncomfortable with it; some display hostility to the idea of nurses functioning in autonomous roles. The nurse practitioner seems to be perceived as a threat by some physicians.

Relations with staff nurses can also be a problem for nurse practitioners at times because some staff nurses resent taking orders from anyone except a doctor. Some patients who have never encountered a nurse practitioner before may be concerned about "just seeing the nurse instead of the doctor." All these situations need to be handled in a mature and professional way.

The problems involved in dealing with insurance companies are also a major source of stress for many nurse practitioners. Although the nurse practitioner is widely recognized as a cost-effective provider of health care, insurance regulations make it difficult for them to receive direct reimbursement.

Harvey Bennett believes that NPs must "be committed to lifelong learning due to the rapid pace of change required to adapt your practice to new information regarding health and disease and therapeutic approaches. I also believe that with the increasing globalization of economies and the influx of economic and political refugees, NPs must have an awareness of and sensitivity to the particular cultural and religious practices as they impact on the patient's health beliefs and behaviors."

HOW DO I BECOME A NURSE PRACTITIONER?
Education
High School

Future nurse practitioners should take a well-balanced college preparatory course in high school, with a good foundation in the sciences. Obviously, biology and chemistry are important courses. If your high school offers anatomy and physiology as a follow-up to the basic biology course, that would be a good elective. You also need to take courses in the humanities and social sciences. Classes that improve communication skills are especially helpful for anyone going into a people-oriented field like nursing.

The high school years are also a good time to start getting some hands-on experience in health care. Try doing volunteer work at a local hospital, community health center, or nursing home. There are probably nurse practitioners in your community who would be glad to discuss their work with you and let you follow them around for a few days to observe.

Debbie Bishop, a cardiac nurse practitioner at St. Francis Hospital in Evanston, Illinois, recommends that students volunteer in a health care organization such as a hospital, nursing home, or clinic to learn more about the field. "This will give you a wealth of information and knowledge," she says, "and give you a sense of whether or not you feel comfortable working in health care. From that end, you could go a variety of different ways— you could look at nursing school, medical school, PA school, or perhaps a career in a medical laboratory."

Postsecondary Training

You need to be a registered nurse (RN) before you may become a nurse practitioner. There are three ways to become an RN: an associate's degree program at a junior or community college, a diploma program at a hospital school of nursing, or a bachelor's degree program at a college or university. All programs combine classroom study and clinical experience in hospitals and other health care settings.

A bachelor's degree is generally necessary for anyone who wants to go on for the additional training (usually a master's degree) required to become a nurse practitioner. A student who begins nursing study in an associate's degree or diploma program may transfer into a bachelor's degree program later. Students with an undergraduate major other than nursing may also enter nursing degree programs, although they may need to fulfill some additional prerequisites.

In nursing school, students study the theory and practice of nursing, taking such courses as human anatomy and physiology, psychology, microbiology, nutrition, and statistics. Students in bachelor's degree programs also study English, humanities, and social sciences. After finishing their educational program, students must pass a national examination in order to be licensed to practice nursing in

FYI

The nurse practitioner role developed in the 1960s in response to the shortage of physicians and the need for alternative health care providers.

their state and to use the initials "RN" after their name.

A master's degree is usually required to become a nurse practitioner. Programs last one to two years and provide advanced study in diagnostic skills, health assessment, pharmacology, clinical management, and research skills. Classroom work is combined with hands-on clinical practice. Usually the student begins with generalist work and later focuses on preparation for a specific nurse practitioner specialty. Admission to good nurse practitioner programs is very competitive.

Certification or Licensing

Not all states require nurse practitioners to be nationally certified; however, certification is strongly recommended by those in the profession. Certification in a variety of specialties is offered by such organizations as the American Nurses Association, the American Academy of Nurse Practitioners, the Pediatric Nursing Certification Board, and the Society of Urologic Nurses and Associates. Certification typically involves passing a written exam, and requirements for recertification usually include completing a certain amount of continuing education. Exact requirements vary according to the certifying group.

All states and Washington, D.C., require a license to practice nursing. To obtain a license, graduates of approved nursing schools must pass a national examination. Nurses may be licensed by more than one state. In some states, continuing education is a condition for license renewal.

State requirements for licensing and registration of nurse practitioners vary. All states except Georgia license them to prescribe medications independently, although some states have restrictions regarding the prescription of controlled substances. For specifics, contact your state's nursing board. (See the National Council of State Boards of Nursing Web site at http://www.ncsbn.org for contact information.)

Internships and Volunteerships

Nurse practitioner students are required to complete several internships, or clinical rotations. Usually these rotations are set up through the college or university to be completed at a hospital or other health care facility. As an NP student, Debbie Bishop received clinical experience where she spent one day a week in a physician's office working with a physician or a nurse practitioner. "I would see patients and would do all the tasks that I currently do now," she says, "but I was supervised by a preceptor. In nursing school, you do clinical rotations with a whole group of nursing students, but in NP school you have more independence as a nurse practitioner student. Since I was studying family medicine, I did rotations in pediatrics, women's health, and internal medicine, and then I did two rotations in acute care. I saw the whole gamut from newborn to acute care to pregnancy to chronic illnesses, which was exactly what I wanted to do because I wanted that diversity and responsibility before I found the job that I am in now."

WHO WILL HIRE ME?

Debbie Bishop landed her first and current job as a result of a school project. "One of my tasks as a student was to do a lot of teaching," she explains. "I had a teaching project with one of my classes that had to do with research my current employer was conducting on cardiac markers (which basically are blood tests to determine if a patient has had a heart attack). I got involved with him [my current employer] via the research, and he helped me out with my project. He was looking for a physician assistant, but I convinced him it would be much more beneficial to hire a nurse practitioner. And lo and behold, that's how I ended up where I am."

Nurse practitioners are employed in hospitals, clinics, physicians' offices, community health centers, rural health clinics, nursing homes, mental health centers, educational institutions, student health centers, nursing schools, home health agencies, hospices, prisons, industrial organizations, the military, and other health care settings. In the states that allow nurse practitioners to practice independently, self-employment is an option.

The particular specialty you pursue is obviously a major factor in determining your employment setting. Another important factor is the degree of autonomy you desire. Nurse practitioners in remote rural areas have the most autonomy, but they must be willing to spend a lot of time on the road visiting patients who are unable to get to the clinic, to be on call at all hours, and to make do with less than optimal facilities and equipment.

The career services office of your nursing school is a good place to begin the employment search. Contacts you have made in clinical settings during your nurse practitioner program are also useful sources of information on job opportunities. Nursing registries, nurse employment services, and your state employment office have information about available jobs. Nursing journals and newspapers list openings. If you are interested in working for the federal government, contact the Office of Personnel Management for your region. Applying directly to hospitals, nursing homes, and other health care agencies is also an option for nurse practitioners.

WHERE CAN I GO FROM HERE?

Nurse practitioners have many avenues for advancement. After gaining experience, they may move into positions that offer more responsibility and higher salaries. Some choose to move into administrative or supervisory positions in health care organizations or nursing schools. They may become faculty members at nursing schools or directors of nursing at a hospital, clinic, or other health agency.

Some advance by doing additional academic and clinical study that gives them certification in specialized fields. Those with an interest in research, teaching, consulting, or policy-making in the nursing field would do well to consider earning a Ph.D. in nursing.

In the next five years or so, Harvey Bennett plans to reduce his workload, "but I plan to continue to work as an NP," he says, "with a focus on the local Hispanic population."

Debbie Bishop plans to continue as a nurse practitioner and pursue expanded roles in teaching, education, and maybe open her own practice. "I love the patient interaction nurse practitioners have, and being able to see the improvement in a person's health means the most to me," she says.

WHAT ARE THE SALARY RANGES?

Geographic location, experience, and specialty area of practice are all factors that influence salary levels for nurse practitioners. The U.S. Department of Labor reports the median annual income for registered nurses as $54,670 in 2005. NPs, however, tend to earn more than this amount. According to NP Central, an on-line information provider, nurse practitioners (including all specialties) working full time averaged an annual income of $73,235 in 2004. According to the 2005 National Salary Survey done by *Advance for Nurse Practitioners,* a news magazine for NPs, the average salary for nurse practitioners (all specialties) was $74,812. Details of the survey show that average salaries vary by specialties and settings. For example, NPs working in their own private practice earned on average $90,574, and those specializing in emergency department medicine earned $84,835 annually. At the other end of the pay scale, however, were NPs working in family practice, who averaged

Related Jobs

- community health nurses
- directors of nursing services
- directors of schools of nursing
- nurse anesthetists
- nurse-midwives
- office nurses
- physician assistants
- private and general duty nurses
- school nurses

$72,048, and those in college health service settings, who averaged $61,400 annually. The survey also found that NPs working in California had the highest average earnings by state, making $80,674. Some practitioners earned even more than this amount, with salaries exceeding $100,000.

Full-time nurse practitioners' benefits vary. Those in their own practices must provide their own retirement plans. NPs employed by hospitals, clinics, and schools generally receive health insurance, paid vacation and sick days, and retirement plans. Some employers also pay for continuing education.

WHAT IS THE JOB OUTLOOK?

The job outlook for nurse practitioners is excellent, since the nurse practitioner is being increasingly recognized as a provider of the high-quality yet cost-effective medical care that the nation's health care system needs. More and more, people are recognizing the importance of preventive health care, which, of course, is one of the nurse practitioner's greatest strengths. All nurse practitioner specialties are expected to continue growing. Harvey Bennett feels that the employment outlook for NPs is strong, especially in underserved areas such as rural and inner-city settings. "A fast-growing specialty," he says, "is the acute care NP who generally works in hospital critical care or subspecialty practices."

There should also be an especially strong demand for gerontological nurse practitioners, as the percentage of the U.S. population in the over-65 age group increases. The Midwest and the South are expected to be the areas of greatest growth in demand for nurse practitioners.

Nurse practitioner organizations are working to promote legislation that will increase the degree of autonomy available to nurse practitioners and make it easier for them to receive insurance company reimbursement. This should make the profession an even more attractive route of advancement for RNs.

At the same time, it is important for those entering the profession to have realistic expectations. Some nurse practitioners report increasing frustration with recent cutbacks in the health care industry that make it difficult to persuade insurance companies to approve for reimbursement the treatment plans considered necessary by health care professionals. Problems with insurance companies and current restrictions on autonomy lead to burnout and disillusionment for some nurse practitioners, who emerged from their master's degree programs with idealistic goals for their profession.

Nursing Instructors

SUMMARY

Definition
Nursing instructors teach patient care to nursing students in classroom and clinical settings. They demonstrate nursing skills to students and monitor their hands-on learning during patient care. Some instructors specialize in teaching specific areas of nursing such as pediatrics or oncological nursing.

Alternative Job Titles
Nursing educators

Nursing professors
Nursing teachers

Salary Range
$32,000 to $53,000 to $86,000+

Educational Requirements
Master's degree

Certification or Licensing
Licensing as an RN is required

Employment Outlook
Much faster than the average

High School Subjects
Anatomy and physiology

Biology
Chemistry
Health
Mathematics

Personal Interests
Helping people: emotionally
Helping people: physical health/medicine
Science
Teaching

Students learn in different ways. "Some learn by listening," nursing instructor Gail DeLuca explains, "some by touching, some by seeing, and some by conceptualizing. As a teacher, it's a challenge to present lessons in a variety of ways so that each student will be able to learn in his or her style. Most of all, it's important to develop a trusting relationship with the student to facilitate the teaching process."

WHAT DOES A NURSING INSTRUCTOR DO?

Nursing instructors teach in colleges and universities or nursing schools, both in classroom and clinical settings. Their duties depend on the facility, the nursing program, and the instructor's education level. Some nursing instructors specialize in specific subjects such as chemistry or anatomy, or in a type of nursing activity such as pediatric nursing.

Many health care facilities partner with area nursing programs, so the students can actually practice what they are learning under the supervision of nursing staff and instructors. For example, the students may spend time in a hospital environment learning pediatrics and surgical care and additional time in a nursing home setting learning the health care needs of the elderly and handicapped. Classroom instruction and clinical training depend on the nursing program and the degree conferred.

Teaching load and research requirements vary by institution and program. Full professors usually spend more of their time conducting research and publishing than assistant professors, instructors, and lecturers. Often nursing instructors actively work in the nursing field in addition to teaching.

Nursing instructors must spend a lot of preparation time outside the classroom and clinical setting. For example, the instructor must work with head nurses or charge nurses to determine the students' patient assignments. They must review patients' charts and be well informed about their current conditions prior to the student nurses appearing for their clinical instruction. Plus, there are the usual teaching responsibilities such as course planning, paper grading, and test preparation. Involvement often extends beyond the classroom.

Nursing instructors at colleges and universities are often expected to be involved with the community. They may be required to speak to community groups or consult with businesses, and they are encouraged to be active in professional associations and on academic committees. In addition, many larger institutions expect professors to do research and be published in nursing or medical journals.

Nursing instructors work in colleges, universities, or nursing schools. Their clinical instruction can take place in any number of health care facilities including doctors' offices, medical clinics, hospitals, institutions, and nursing homes. Most health care environments are clean and well lighted. Inner-city facilities may be in less than desirable locations, and safety may be an issue.

All health-related careers have some health and disease risks; however, adherence to health and safety guidelines greatly minimizes the chance of contracting infectious diseases such as hepatitis and AIDS. Medical knowledge and good safety measures are also needed to limit exposure to toxic chemicals, radiation, and other hazards.

WHAT IS IT LIKE TO BE A NURSING INSTRUCTOR?

Gail DeLuca is a nursing instructor at the Marcella Niehoff School of Nursing at Loyola University in Chicago, Illinois. She has been a nurse for more than 20 years and an educator since 1997. "Even though I really enjoyed my patient contact," she says, "I always had an interest in education. One of my friends, a distinguished educator, encouraged me to apply for a teaching position at Loyola. It was a good fit, and I really love what I do. Nursing is

Q. What's New in Learning?
A. Preceptorships

A preceptorship is really a new and improved version of shadowing. You know shadowing, like when you go to work with your parent and follow him or her around to see what he or she does on the job. Preceptorships take shadowing a huge step forward and are really something to look into. A preceptorship is an arrangement where a student (that would be you) is assigned on a one-to-one basis to a clinical nurse expert in a certain area. What's innovative about this method is that you are not only learning what someone else does as a nurse, but you are also learning how you will react and respond to nursing. That's a whole new ball game! Basically, this year-long adventure in nursing is the best hands-on class you can have, with your very own expert to make sure you know what you're doing. Look into this type of opportunity when you're starting an entry-level job or looking for supplementary learning.

Medical Surgical Nursing Clinical for the senior undergraduate students, which takes place on a cardiac telemetry floor at Loyola Medical Center, and Intro to Nursing to incoming freshmen.

"In Advanced Health Assessment, students are taught to complete a health history and physical examination and to understand the information they've obtained in terms of patient health or illness. Additionally, they learn to identify and recommend screenings and health behaviors necessary to keep people at their healthiest.

"The Physical Assessment in Clinical Nursing is similar, but it is taught at the undergraduate level and not specific to diagnosis and management as it is in the graduate program.

"In the Nurse Practitioner Clinical, I supervise 7 to 10 nurse practitioner students who are learning their specialty out in the field. My role in this clinical is to follow these students individually out in the field. These students are using the most current research and clinical guidelines to help them make health decisions for their patients. Students are required to submit clinical papers and create presentations as part of the class. I grade them and provide feedback. It is Loyola's goal that when the NP student graduates he or she will be a beginning researcher, writer, and clinician.

"Clinical instruction at the senior undergrad level incorporates all the coursework students have taken and applies it to a patient in a clinical setting. I work with students on a post-open-heart/cardiac telemetry floor at Loyola Medical Center.

such a broad a field that you can never get bored. It pays well, and nurses are well-respected by the community."

Gail teaches both undergraduate and graduate nursing students. "Currently, I teach Advanced Health Assessment for the nurse practitioner/clinical nurse specialist graduate students, Physical Assessment for the undergrad seniors, and a Nurse Practitioner Clinical. Other classes that I frequently teach are Advanced

This clinical strives to integrate all the sciences and to view the patient as an entire person, and part of a family and a community. It is a very holistic approach to patient care.

"The freshman course is more of an introduction to nursing and self exploration. At this level, freshmen have many ideas about what is a nurse. The course seeks to have the freshmen understand just what is nursing, and also challenges them to explore themselves and their own ideas and how this relates to their futures as nurses."

Gail spends a great deal of time preparing for these classes, as well as grading papers and answering student e-mails. "I don't think that students understand how much behind-the-scenes work is involved even before you begin creating and giving a lecture, as well as test creation and all the followup," she says. "To prepare for my classes, I reexamine all the required content, reread the chapters, go over the lecture, go over the PowerPoint, and make sure that I've answered all of the questions in my mind that students may want to ask," she says. "At the graduate level, my students come from many different professional backgrounds. They're already nurses, some might be from critical care, some might be from other areas in the hospital, while others work in the community. The challenge, then, is how to make the class applicable to everyone as well as interesting."

Like many nursing instructors, Gail strives to be current in her field and combines her teaching duties with part-time work as a nurse practitioner. "I practice

To Be a Successful Nursing Instructor, You Should . . .

- enjoy teaching, nursing, and interacting with students
- have excellent organizational and leadership skills
- be able to demonstrate skilled nursing techniques to students
- stay abreast of new information in the medical field through continuing education and other methods

part time as a family nurse practitioner at Poronsky Family Practice in Palos Heights, Illinois," she says. "I also volunteer once a month as a NP at Community Health Clinic in Chicago where I see patients who have no health insurance and no ability to pay for a regular office visit. The care is excellent and free to the patient."

DO I HAVE WHAT IT TAKES TO BE A NURSING INSTRUCTOR?

In order to succeed as a nursing instructor, you must enjoy teaching, nursing, and interacting with students. "The students think I'm giving to them, but they're actually giving to me all the time," Gail says. "The students keep me on my toes. They're very energizing, they really ask a lot of critical questions, and even if you're teaching the same content, every student group is a whole new experience. I love being able to help them along and teach them, develop relationships with them, and actually watch them grow and become the kind of professional nurses that nursing was meant to be."

Successful nursing instructors should also have excellent organizational and leadership skills. You should be able to demonstrate skilled nursing techniques. Since you will be responsible for all the care your students administer to patients, you must have good supervisory skills, be calm under pressure, and be patient and respectful of each individual. "My intent is not only to teach the basic content that specialty students need to learn," Gail says, "but as the student becomes advanced, my role is to mentor the thinking of the student on how to ask the right questions in each situation to gain the correct information." In addition, you should be able to teach your students the human side of nursing that is so important in patient and nurse relationships. New medical technologies, patient treatments, and medications are constantly being developed, so nursing instructors must stay abreast of new information in the medical field. To stay up to date, Gail reads monthly professional journals, such as *Consultant*, *American Journal for Nurse Practitioners*, *Advance for Nursing Practitioners*, *American Family Physician*, and *MedWatch*. "As high tech as nursing becomes, and as much information as we gain," Gail asserts, "it's the nurse-patient relationship that really creates the healing."

HOW DO I BECOME A NURSING INSTRUCTOR?

Education

High School

If you are interested in becoming a nursing instructor, take classes in health and the sciences to prepare you for a medical career. Since nursing instructors begin as nurses themselves, you need to take classes that will prepare you for nursing programs. Talk to your guidance counselor about course requirements for specific programs, but plan on taking biology, chemistry, mathematics, and English courses to help build the strong foundation necessary for nursing school.

Postsecondary Training

Most nursing instructors first work as registered nurses and, therefore, have completed either a two-year associate's degree program, a three-year diploma program, or a four-year bachelor's degree program in nursing. Which of the three training programs to choose depends on your career goals. As a nurse, you should also have considerable clinical nursing experience before considering teaching.

Most universities and colleges require that their full-time professors have doctoral degrees, but many hire master's degree holders for clinical teaching and part-time and temporary teaching positions. Two-year colleges may hire full-time teachers who have master's degrees. "To be an educator you need to have a minimum of a master's degree," Gail advises. "If students want to make teaching or nursing research their career, I recommend they get their Ph.D. To get a Ph.D. when you're young is a huge, huge value. It allows you to get your research started, your grant writing started, and allows you to become one of the nursing greats."

Certification and Licensing

In order to practice as a registered nurse, you first must become licensed in the state in which you plan to work. Licensed RNs must graduate from an accredited school of nursing and pass a national examination. In order to renew their license, RNs must show proof of continued education and pass renewal exams. Most states honor licenses granted in other states, as long as scores are acceptable. For further information, contact your state's nursing board. (See the National Council of State Boards of Nursing Web site at http://www.ncsbn.org for contact information.)

Membership in professional nursing associations is an excellent way for nurses and nursing educators to stay up to date regarding certification, licensing, and continuing education requirements, as well as to network with colleagues. Gail is a member of Sigma Theta Tau (an honor society for nurses), the American Academy of Nurse Practitioners, and the Illinois Society for Advanced Practice Nursing.

Internships and Volunteerships

Hospital-based nursing programs usually have a clinical learning program set up on-site. Other non-hospital-based nursing programs may set up a partnership with local hospitals or other health care facilities. The Marcella Niehoff School of Nursing at Loyola offers both—a university education with an affiliated medical center. Loyola University, where Gail works, offers an undergraduate capstone course called Clinical Role Transition. "Students understand the enormity of their responsibility as a nurse and need to transition from student to a professional role," says Gail. "What this course does is essentially provide each individual student with a one-on-one internship with a nurse. The student works the nurse's schedule and progresses from taking one patient to doing about 70 percent of the nurse's assignment and responsibilities. The student learns to think critically, to analyze, and to problem solve. It is a 168-hour internship and readies the student to be a graduate nurse."

WHO WILL HIRE ME?

It is necessary to complete the required education and obtain a license before you can practice as a nurse. But newly licensed nurses continue to learn in their first position. As a new nurse, Gail targeted a charge nurse whom she admired. "She was well respected, very bright, and a good mentor," Gail says, "and I asked her if I could work on her floor. It never occurred to me until later in my career the importance of that first position. I was so fortunate and am so grateful for her input."

After graduating from an approved nursing program and passing licensure examinations, you can apply directly to hospitals, nursing homes, companies, and

Nursing Instructors: Top Employers and Mean Earnings

Colleges and universities	18,080	$59,580
Junior colleges	12,780	$52,810
General medical and surgical hospitals	3,170	$65,240
Technical and trade schools	1,530	$46,840
Management of companies and enterprises	390	$42,100

Source: U.S. Department of Labor, 2005

government agencies for employment. Jobs can also be obtained through school career services offices, employment agencies specializing in placement of nursing personnel, or through states' employment offices. Other sources of jobs include nurses' associations, professional journals, and newspaper want ads.

Approximately 35,000 nursing instructors are employed in the United States. They work in hospitals, clinics, colleges, and universities that offer nursing education programs. Instructors' jobs can vary greatly, depending on the employer. Many nursing instructors associated with hospitals or medical clinics work in the nursing field in addition to teaching. Those employed by large universities and colleges are more focused on academia, conducting medical research and writing medical reports of their findings.

WHERE CAN I GO FROM HERE?

In hospitals and clinics, nursing instructors generally begin in staff education and advance by moving up in staff ranks and education. Positions with higher levels of authority, and higher pay, include clinical nurse specialists, advanced practice nurses, nurse supervisors or managers, or medical administrators.

Those who work in nursing schools, colleges, or universities may advance through the academic ranks from a part-time adjunct to a full-time instructor to assistant professor to associate professor, and finally to full professor. From there, those interested in administration may become deans or directors of nursing programs. As professors advance in their careers, they frequently spend less time in the classroom and more time conducting research, public speaking, and writing.

Gail is happy as an instructor and sees herself continuing to evolve in her role through the supportive mentorship of all the Loyola faculty. "To say they are outstanding is an understatement," she says.

As a nurse practitioner, Gail sees herself educating the public about preventative care. "By the time I see people as a nurse practitioner," she says, "they're overweight, have pre-diabetes, or have other preventable illnesses. There are so many little health behaviors people can do to create positive changes in their life, but they may have no idea how to do it."

WHAT ARE THE SALARY RANGES?

Educational background, experience, responsibilities, geographic location, and the hiring institution are factors influencing the earnings of nursing instructors. According to the U.S. Department of Labor, nursing instructors and teachers had median annual earnings of $53,160 in 2005. Ten percent earned less than $32,850 annually, and 10 percent earned more than $86,570 annually.

Full-time faculty typically receive such benefits as health insurance, retirement plans, paid sick leave, and, in some cases, funds for work-related expenses such as educational conferences.

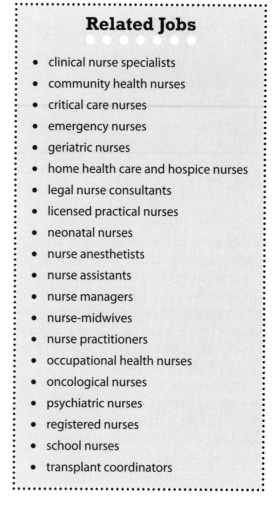

Related Jobs

- clinical nurse specialists
- community health nurses
- critical care nurses
- emergency nurses
- geriatric nurses
- home health care and hospice nurses
- legal nurse consultants
- licensed practical nurses
- neonatal nurses
- nurse anesthetists
- nurse assistants
- nurse managers
- nurse-midwives
- nurse practitioners
- occupational health nurses
- oncological nurses
- psychiatric nurses
- registered nurses
- school nurses
- transplant coordinators

WHAT IS THE JOB OUTLOOK?

Several developments will create good employment opportunities for nursing instructors. The U.S. Department of Labor projects that employment for registered nurses will grow much faster than the average through 2014. Those practicing nursing specialties will also be in great demand. Because of this, there will be a corresponding demand for nursing instructors. The AACN reports that 41,683 qualified applicants to baccalaureate nursing programs were not accepted in 2005; nearly 75 percent of responding schools said that an insufficient number of faculty members was a factor for not accepting all applicants. As more students apply to nursing school, more nursing instructors will be

Interview: Suzanne Letellier, Health Educator

Suzanne Letellier is the program coordinator for the Milwaukee Area Health Education Center (http://www.milahec.org) in Milwaukee, Wisconsin. The center seeks to "improve access to health care in Southeastern Wisconsin's underserved communities, through the development of community-based, client-oriented, culturally relevant, collaborative health professions education programs." The center is just 1 of 51 AHEC programs in 46 states that are administered by the National Area Health Education Center Organization. For more information on these programs, visit http://www.nationalahec.org.

Suzanne was kind enough to speak with the editors of *What Can I Do Now?: Nursing* about her career as a health educator (a relatively new career that is growing in popularity) and programs offered by her organization.

Q. Can you describe a day in your life as a program coordinator?

A. Each day is completely different. It usually involves a lot of communication: e-mails, phone calls, and meetings. I give presentations on health careers to high school students and cultural competency trainings for health care professionals. I've also worked with area hospitals and clinics to coordinate/plan such trainings. I serve on some local health committees that work to improve the health of our community.

We are a very small nonprofit organization. There are four full-time staff people and a part-time staff person. I have my own office and spend about half of my time in it. I do a lot of work in the community, so I am out and about meeting with people. I also travel to other parts of the state for various meetings and conferences. Occasionally, I will go out of the state for a national conference.

Q. What is involved when you give presentations on health careers to high school students?

A. The main objective of these presentations is to show students the enormous variety of health careers that are out there; they often only think of doctor, nurse, and dentist. There are literally hundreds of different jobs in health care, and we want to open their eyes to this.

Q. What other programs are you involved in?

A. One of my AHEC colleagues developed a curriculum that we will be promoting to the high schools and middle schools in our region. One lesson in the curriculum will be about general health careers (kind of like what I am already doing), and the other lessons will each focus on a specific health career and will include hands-on activities. We, the AHEC staff, will offer to come into the classrooms to teach the curriculum.

Q. What do you like most about your job?

A. I like the variety of activities that I can be involved in and being able to network in the community. It is a pleasure to work for a nonprofit that has an honorable mission. I enjoy presenting and teaching.

needed to teach students and make up for staffing shortages. Additionally, nursing faculty age continues to rise. This means that through the first decade of the twenty-first century a large percentage of nursing school faculty will retire. Their replacements, naturally, are drawn from the teaching faculty, and this should also add to a shortage of and demand for nursing teachers.

Registered Nurses

SUMMARY

Definition

Registered nurses (RNs) administer medical care to sick or injured individuals and help people achieve health and prevent disease.

Alternative Job Titles

Staff nurses

Salary Range

$38,000 to $54,000 to $79,000+

Educational Requirements

Associate's degree through an accredited junior college; diploma from a nursing school; or bachelor's degree

Certification or Licensing

Required for certain specialties (certification)
Required (licensing)

Employment Outlook

Much faster than the average

High School Subjects

Anatomy and physiology
Biology
Chemistry
Health
Mathematics

Personal Interests

Helping people: emotionally
Helping people: physical health/medicine
Science

It's three in the morning in the intensive care unit. Nurses on the night shift are making their rounds, listening to the instruments that monitor their patients, changing IV bags, or giving medicine. In the emergency room several cases come in all at once; even though they are seven hours into their shift, the trauma nurses immediately snap to in a flurry of activity. Their ability to react quickly and make decisions under pressure can make the difference between life and death.

Meanwhile, at a retirement community not far away, a live-in nurse assists her client to the bathroom, walking slowly to help her safely navigate the long hallway from her bedroom. Although it is in the middle of the night, the nurse shows no hint of irritation or fatigue. It is her job to help her patient in any way she can.

WHAT DOES A REGISTERED NURSE DO?

Just as the title "doctor" encompasses numerous specialties and branches of study, the title *registered nurse* is an umbrella term, covering many different aspects of nursing. Although nurses work in various health care facilities, they have three basic goals: to assist the ill, elderly, or people with disabilities in the recovery or maintenance of life functions; to prevent illness and relapse of illness; and to promote health in the community. Most nurses come into contact with patients more frequently than other members of the health care community. Doctors are busy with diagnosis and the creation of treatment plans, and often do not have time to carry out the plans themselves. Because of this, nurses often provide the human element in a patient's treatment. They observe a patient's symptoms and evaluate progress or lack of progress. Nurses are also responsible for educating their patients and families on how to cope with a long-term illness or disability.

The field of nursing is broken down by the setting in which a nurse works. A registered nurse typically works under the guidance of a physician, who develops a care plan for a patient that the nurse helps to administer. But the specific work of each nurse can take many forms. *General duty nurses* offer bedside nursing care and observe the progress of the patients. They may also supervise licensed practical nurses and aides. *Surgical nurses* are part of a logistical team in the operating room that supports the surgeon. They sterilize instruments, prepare patients for surgery, and coordinate the transfer of patients to and from the operating room. A *maternity nurse*, or *neonatal nurse*, looks after newborn infants, assists in the delivery room, and educates new mothers and fathers on basic child care. A *head nurse* directs and coordinates the activities of the nursing staff. Other hospital staff nurses are trained to work in intensive care units, the emergency room, and the pediatric ward.

Lingo to Learn

case manager A nurse or administrator who coordinates the medical care of a patient.

crash cart The cart that carries medicines, equipment, and machines that may be needed in an emergency situation in an intensive care unit or emergency room.

extubate To remove a breathing tube from a patient.

intubate To insert breathing apparatus into the throat of a patient who is unable to breathe satisfactorily.

nursing home A long-term care facility that provides the elderly and chronically ill with health care and assistance with daily activities, such as bathing, eating, and dressing.

skilled nursing facility A facility that provides round-the-clock medical care by registered nurses and other licensed health care professionals.

vital signs The temperature, pulse rate, breathing rate, blood pressure, and level of pain of a patient.

Registered nurses work in varied settings. *Home health nurses* provide nursing care, prescribed by a physician, to patients at home. They assist a wide range of patients, such as those recovering from illnesses and accidents, and must be able to work independently. *Private duty nurses* may work in hospitals or in a patient's home. They are employed by the patient they are caring for or by the patient's family. Their duties are carried out in cooperation with the patient's physician.

Office nurses work in clinics or at the private practice of a physician. Their duties may combine nursing skills—taking blood pressure, assisting with outpatient procedures, educating patients—with administrative or office duties such as scheduling appointments, keeping files, and answering phones. Nurses in this field may work for a health maintenance organization (HMO) or an insurance company.

Nursing home nurses direct the care of residents in long-term-care facilities. The work is similar to that done in hospitals; however, a nursing home nurse cares for patients with conditions ranging from a hip fracture to Parkinson's disease. *Public health nurses*, or *community health nurses*, work with government and private agencies to educate the public about health care issues. Their work might include creating a community blood pressure testing site, speaking about nutrition and disease, and providing immunizations and disease screenings for members of their community. Many schoolchildren are screened by *public health nurses*, or *school nurses*, for such conditions as poor vision and scoliosis.

Occupational health nurses, or *industrial nurses*, provide nursing care in a clinic at a work site. They provide emergency care, work on accident prevention programs, and offer health counseling.

WHAT IS IT LIKE TO BE A REGISTERED NURSE?

Erin Moran is a registered nurse who works in the emergency department (ED) of a university hospital that has a Level I trauma center. She has been a registered nurse for five years. Erin typically works from 7:30 P.M. to 8:00 A.M. three days a week and works day shifts about once every six weeks. Because she has experience as an oncology nurse, she also fills in as needed in her hospital's oncology department.

Patients with a variety of illnesses and injuries come to Erin's emergency department for treatment. "Broken bones, flu-like symptoms, stab wounds, gunshot victims, women in labor, people having asthma attacks, heart attacks, motor vehicle accident victims...basically we get them all," she says. Erin's emergency department has 28 beds, and she takes care of anywhere from two to nine patients during her shift. "In overflow situations, we've had as many as 60 patients in beds in the hallways," she says.

ED registered nurses at Erin's hospital work in one of the following capacities: *triage nurse, fast-track nurse, team leader, charge nurse*; or they are responsible for a block of ED rooms. (Note: these positions may have different names at other hospitals.)

"Triage," Erin explains, "is a place where you gather information on the patient, such as name, age, date of birth, vital signs, chief complaint (such as abdominal pain, nausea, dizziness, etc.), medical history, medications they are taking, and allergies. This information helps us create a general picture of the patient and his or her health." Once the triage nurse has this information, he or she assigns a color-coded care level that the patient fits under. "As a triage RN," Erin says, "you must quickly decide the severity of the patient's status and color code them accordingly. The more serious the condition, the faster the patient will receive a bed in the ED and be treated by a physician."

Fast-track nurses treat patients who don't need extensive medical workups or treatment. "For example," Erin explains, "a fast-track patient may be someone who cut his finger on glass and needs stitches and a tetanus shot. Or somebody who fell, has knee pain, and needs an X-ray." Patients in these settings are treated in anywhere from 20 minutes to 2 hours, depending on the level of activity in the emergency department.

Team leaders oversee the RN assignments in the emergency department. "In our ER," Erin says, "there are three teams, and for each team there is one registered nurse who works as a team leader. Team leaders facilitate the movement of patients and are on hand to help out in emergency situations or cover for other nurses who are helping out in emergency situations."

Charge nurses are sort of like the dispatcher of the emergency department. "They monitor the pulse of the ED," Erin explains, "making sure that the triage RNs, team leaders, and physicians are all communicating so the patients are seen in an efficient manner." They also are responsible for coordinating with an administrator (known by a variety of titles, depending on the hospital) who is responsible for the overall operation of the hospital and coordination with the fire department, police department, and private ambulance companies.

FYI

The first U.S. school of nursing was established in 1872 at the New England Hospital for Women and Children in Boston.

Emergency department nurses who are assigned to a certain block of rooms are responsible for the care of patients (including taking vital signs, administering medication, etc.). Once a patient has been treated, these nurses are responsible for sending the patient home, to an inpatient room, or to another facility. They might also help with trauma cases and communicate with emergency services technicians in the field caring for patients who are in transit to the hospital.

At the end of her shift, Erin gives a verbal report to the new covering RN about her patients. "For example," she says, "I tell him or her about a patient's chief complaint, past medical history, medications administered, response to these medications, and current condition. Of course, my replacement can also refer to the patient's written chart that I've maintained during my shift, to any lab tests that have come back, and to physician orders."

Erin works overtime if she is in the midst of a situation that has occurred on her shift. "You don't just go home when the shift is over," Erin says. "If there is a life-threatening change in the patient's status, I stay and help the oncoming RN until the situation is resolved or a team leader can replace me."

DO I HAVE WHAT IT TAKES TO BE A REGISTERED NURSE?

You should enjoy working with people and be able to handle patients who may experience fear or anger because of an illness. Patience, compassion, and calmness are qualities needed by anyone working in this career. In addition, you must be able to give directions as well as follow instructions and work as part of a health care team. Anyone interested in becoming a registered nurse should also have a strong desire to continue learning because new tests, procedures, and technologies are constantly being developed for the medical world. Erin is currently taking a course to meet new standards established for triage by her hospital.

More than anything else, nurses must be genuinely concerned for their patients. "You have to be an advocate for your patient," Erin says. "You have to ensure that people are getting the best and safest care in the most efficient manner."

Nursing can be an emotionally demanding and stressful occupation. "Our ER is undergoing restructuring and, because of this," Erin explains, "the number of patients we see each day has increased—despite the fact that we are working under a budget that allows for fewer nurses." Asked what makes nursing worth the emotional stress and responsibility, Erin replies, "there is grat-

To Be a Successful Registered Nurse, You Should . . .

- have keen observational skills
- be able to work under pressure
- follow orders precisely
- be well organized
- be caring and sympathetic
- handle emergencies calmly

ification when you can save a patient's life or provide resources to a patient . . . such as providing outpatient care contact information to people with psychiatric problems."

HOW DO I BECOME A REGISTERED NURSE?
Education
High School

"Be sure to take advantage of all the science classes that are offered at your high school," Erin advises, "and really focus on chemistry, biology, and anatomy and physiology. Psychology, sociology, and statistics will also be useful. These are some of the core classes you will have to take as an undergrad, so it is really helpful to take these subjects while you are in high school." Communication skills are vital to successful nurses, so English and speech courses will also be useful.

It is possible to volunteer in many of the places nurses work, in order to decide if nursing is the career you want. Hospitals will take on high school volunteers as candy stripers or assistants, delivering mail and flowers, visiting with patients, and doing routine office work. While volunteerships at this level are not really concerned with patient treatment, they enable the prospective nurse to understand the way the hospital works and who is responsible for what duty.

While volunteering, you may be given more opportunity as a technician or as an aide to contribute to patient care. In many cases, if hospitals know you are seriously considering a career in nursing, they will give you better opportunities for hands-on involvement and experiences. Hospitals have a vested interest in training people to be nurses, especially if it means they will be able to hire somebody who is already familiar with the workings of their administration and setup.

Postsecondary Training

There are three training programs for registered nurses: associate's degree programs, diploma programs, and bachelor's degree programs. All three programs combine classroom education with actual nursing experience. Associate's degrees in nursing usually involve a two-year program at a junior or community college that is affiliated with a hospital. Many associate's degree nurses seek further schooling in bachelor's programs after they have found employment, in order to take advantage of tuition reimbursement programs.

The diploma program is conducted through independent nursing schools and teaching hospitals and usually lasts three years.

A bachelor's degree is recommended for nurses who must compete in an era of cutbacks and small staffs. Additionally, bachelor's degree programs are recommended for those who may want to go into administration or supervision. It is also required for jobs in public health agencies and for admission to graduate school.

Certification or Licensing

Those who pass an accredited nursing program are known as nurse graduates, but must still pass the licensing exam to become a registered nurse. Licensing is required in all 50 states, and license renewal or continuing education credits are also required periodically. In some cases, licensing in one state will automatically grant licensing in reciprocal states. For further information, contact your state's nursing board. (See the National Council of State Boards of Nursing Web site at http://www.ncsbn.org for contact information.)

You will need additional training if you wish to advance into specialized practices, administration, and teaching. This may include further clinical training within the hospital in an area such as pediatrics or gerontology, or entering a master's degree program. A variety of certifications are offered in these and other nursing specialties.

Internships and Volunteerships

Nursing students are required to complete several nursing internships, or clinical rotations, as part of their postsecondary training. Depending on your educational program, your school may offer these opportunities on-site or have agreements with nearby hospitals and medical centers. Rotations focus on specific practice areas such as oncology, geriatrics, surgery, or pediatrics.

WHO WILL HIRE ME?

The most obvious place to look for a nursing job is in a hospital. Nurses also are needed in retirement communities, government facilities, schools, and private practices. In fact, nursing in hospitals is not expected to grow as fast as other aspects of nursing, due to rising costs and a general trend away from inpatient care. The reductions caused by fewer available hospital jobs will be taken up by increased opportunities in newer fields. Insurance companies now hire registered nurses to assist in case management and to ensure that insured patients are getting the correct kind of care from their health care providers. One of the fastest-growing fields in nursing is home health care. Nurses who care for people on a part-time basis in their homes are in great demand for a variety of reasons. Technology has enabled many people to live free of health care institutions, but these people may still require assistance with some of their treatments.

Many surgical centers and emergency medical centers are taking the place of hospital emergency rooms. This will provide work for nurses who require a flexible schedule but who do not wish to work in a hospital. The number of older people with functional disabilities is growing, and jobs will be available in long-term care facilities for specialized conditions such as Alzheimer's disease.

Registered nurses should look in local newspapers and on the Internet for positions, in addition to contacting preferred employers to ask what they may have available. Many professional nursing associations offer job listings at their Web sites or in their professional journals and newsletters. Knowing where you would like to work, achieving educational credits in that field, and making sure those in charge of hiring know you are available are the key steps to finding a desirable nursing position.

WHERE CAN I GO FROM HERE?

Experienced registered nurses can advance in many ways. Those who want challenges beyond direct patient care may become teachers or administrators. Others continue their education and become clinical nurse specialists, nurse practitioners, certified nurse-midwives, or nurse anesthetists. Master's degrees and doctorates are required for many of these positions.

In five years as a registered nurse, Erin has tried out several specialties. "So far," she says, "I've worked in a community hospital, on an orthopedic unit, at a university hospital on a hematology/oncology floor, and now as an emergency room nurse. There are so many opportunities available: nurse practitioners, research, sales, management, informatics, teaching, school nurses, or working in a clinic or office setting. Right now, though, I enjoy hands-on patient care, and that's where I plan to stay."

WHAT ARE THE SALARY RANGES?

According to the U.S. Department of Labor, registered nurses had median annual earnings of $54,670 in 2005. Salaries ranged from less than $38,660 to more than $79,460. Earnings of RNs vary according to employer. Registered nurses who worked for employment services earned $64,720, those who worked at hospitals earned $57,820, and RNs who worked at nursing and personal-care facilities earned $51,510.

Most health care employers provide a good benefits plan for their workers, as well as flexible work schedules, child care, and bonuses. Educational incentives take the form of in-house training and tuition reimbursement, which can enable nurses to increase their skills and potential for advancement at no or little cost to themselves.

Related Jobs

- clinical nurse specialists
- community health nurses
- critical care nurses
- emergency nurses
- geriatric nurses
- home health care and hospice nurses
- legal nurse consultants
- licensed practical nurses
- nurse anesthetists
- nurse assistants
- nurse managers
- nurse-midwives
- nurse practitioners
- nursing instructors
- occupational health nurses
- oncological nurses
- paramedics
- physician assistants
- psychiatric nurses
- school nurses
- transplant coordinators

WHAT IS THE JOB OUTLOOK?

As with most health care fields, nursing is expected to grow much faster than average in the next decade. As the cost for medical specialists skyrockets, more general health care practitioners will be in demand for the services that they can provide at less cost. Technological advances in patient care and the health care needs of an aging population have created a demand for skilled nurses in many areas. Ambulatory, home health, and outpatient care are expected to provide the most employment opportunities, while need for nurses in hospitals will grow less rapidly. Registered nurses will be in high demand in nursing homes and in facilities that care for critically and terminally ill patients.

There are also many part-time job openings for nurses who do not want a full-time position.

Staying aware of trends in health care will give prospective nurses a good idea of the job market for their skills. Trade journals, association membership materials, and health care laws all discuss the course that health care is taking today, and are a valuable source of information for predicting where the future demand in nursing will be.

Surgical Nurses

SUMMARY

Definition
Surgical nurses care for patients before, during, and after surgical procedures. From preoperative assessment to assisting the surgical team to postoperative evaluation, the surgical nurse uses specific medical knowledge and technical skills to provide patient care.

Alternative Job Titles
Circulating nurses
Day surgery preop nurses
Floor nurses
Intra-op nurses

Medical surgical nurses
Operating room nurses
Perioperative nurses
Post-anesthesia care unit nurses
Postop nurses
Preop nurses
Recovery room nurses
RN first assistants
Scrub nurses

Salary Range
$38,000 to $63,000 to $79,000+

Educational Requirements
Nursing degree; completion of on-the-job training

Certification or Licensing
Voluntary (certification)
Required (licensing)

Employment Outlook
Much faster than the average

High School Subjects
Anatomy and physiology
Biology
Chemistry
Health
Mathematics

Personal Interests
Helping people: emotionally
Helping people: physical health/medicine
Science

The little girl's eyes are wide with fright as she clutches her mother's hand as if a large wave is going to wash her away.

Plastic surgical nurse Marcy Dienno knows just what to do. She takes the little girl's hand and calmly begins to explain what will happen next in surgery.

"Once I take you into the operating room," she explains, "I will move you over to another bed. I will put a seat belt across your legs, similar to the one you wear in a car. Sticky pads that do not hurt will be put on your shoulders and left side. I will then put on a blood pressure cuff, like the one they put on you when you came for your pre-visit, and another sticky pad on your finger. Once all these are on, the sleep doctor will give you a mask and let you breathe some special air that will make you sleepy. None of this hurts. The mask might smell a little funny, kind of like plastic, but we add a special flavor to make it smell better. Once you are asleep, we will put a small plastic tube in your hand called an IV (this is how we give you your breakfast) and some other lines that will let us watch you and give you medicine during the surgery. Once we get you all ready, Dr. Jones will fix your face and when the surgery is finished, we will wrap your head with a special turban dressing. We will then wake you up and send you to the unit for recovery. Do you have any questions?"

The young girl looks at her parents and Marcy, smiles, and shakes her head no.

Everything is going to be just fine, Marcy thinks to herself.

WHAT DOES A SURGICAL NURSE DO?

When most people think of nurses, the image of a *surgical nurse* handing an instrument to a surgeon is probably what comes to mind. Surgical nurses assist surgeons during operations ranging from a tonsillectomy to open-heart surgery. The duties of the surgical nurse can be divided into three areas, although all of the areas overlap: preoperative (before the operation), intra-operative (during the operation), and postoperative (after the operation). For an overview of surgical nursing specialties, see the sidebar "Surgical Nursing Specialties."

The duties of a surgical nurse begin long before the patient is wheeled into the operating room and continue long after the operation is over. Through all aspects of the job, the surgical nurse has to remain observant and continually assess the patient. High-stress situations call for the surgical nurse to be calm and cool while meeting the needs of both the surgical team and the patient.

Before surgery, the surgical nurse must prepare a patient physically, emotionally, and mentally for the upcoming surgical procedure. First, the surgical nurse assesses the patient's current state. Is the patient showing signs of stress? Is he or she in any physical pain? Does the patient have enough information about the procedure to help with any anxiety or fear? After assessing the patient, the surgical nurse may explain the upcoming surgery in more detail, take steps to alleviate stress, and measure the patient's vital signs (heart rate, blood pressure, etc.). Many times, the patient may not be ready for surgery, and the operation is postponed. The surgical nurse must make this judgment call and alert the

---

Lingo to Learn

allograft A specific surgery in which diseased tissue or organs are replaced with healthy tissue or bones from a living donor or a cadaver.

ambulatory care Surgical care for patients in outpatient settings with short recovery times.

arthroscopic surgery Outpatient surgery using small instruments and incisions. This generally involves a joint or knee and utilizes a camera and telescope.

clinical surgical nurse specialist A nurse who has a graduate degree and is an expert in a surgical specialty.

surgeon, who then decides if the patient is strong enough to go through with the procedure.

Another major responsibility is communicating to the family of the patient as much information as possible about the nature of the surgery, its expected length, predicted results, and usual outcomes. Although the surgeon usually describes her primary goal for the surgery and the method she'll be using to the patient's family, surgical nurses are often able to give more detailed information about the patient's well-being.

Another surgical nurse is responsible for preparing the operating room for the surgery, including choosing and sterilizing the correct instruments and tools, setting up medical machinery, and keeping accurate count of the tools that will be used in the procedure. During surgery, the surgical nurse's primary duty is to act as the patient's advocate—the patient's voice while he or she is sleeping and unable to speak for him or herself. The surgical nurse also assists the surgeons in the operating room. The nurse must anticipate the needs of the surgical team and react to any changes in the patient's physical state. Since all surgery has a certain amount of risk, operations must be performed as quickly as possible. Because of this, surgical nurses must be familiar with many different procedures and the instruments and tools that are used to perform them. During the operation, the surgical nurse must be prepared to act on the surgeon's instructions.

After the operation, the surgical nurses in the recovery room or post-anesthesia care unit (PACU) continue to evaluate the patient, but at this stage the questions are a little different. How is the patient responding to the surgery? Is the medication relieving any postoperative pain the patient may have? Is the patient recovering as expected? Any and all variations are reported to the attending physician or surgeon. Also, the surgical nurse relays the pertinent information concerning the surgery and its results to the patient's family.

Once discharged from the PACU, the patient is either sent to the day surgery discharge area to begin getting ready to go home, or to the surgical floor to begin

To Be a Successful Surgical Nurse, You Should . . .

- have compassion and be willing to put your patient's needs first
- be flexible to work odd hours and be on call
- be alert and constantly aware of the patients under your care
- be able to cope with the physical and mental demands of emergency situations
- follow instructions completely and pay attention to detail
- relate well to people and have strong communication skills

the healing process. In the latter case, a surgical floor nurse is assigned to the patient and monitors his or her progress and administers any medications prescribed by the surgeon or physician.

WHAT IS IT LIKE TO BE A SURGICAL NURSE?

Marcy Dienno has been a plastic surgical nurse for 26 years. But, surprisingly, she never thought she would work in this career. "It just happened," she explains. "My original plan was to work in the operating room for a year, and then move into oncology nursing. I also had no intention of working with children for an extended period of time. However, after working with children and seeing just how fascinating the operating room was, within months, I was hooked on both—children and surgery."

It's no wonder that Marcy finds great satisfaction as a part of the surgical medical team. Surgical nursing is an exciting, fast-paced career that constantly challenges a nurse's ability to cope under pressure. But the rewards of helping to save a person's life far outweigh even the most frightening situations.

Surgical nurses usually work an extended day to evening shift since most surgeries are scheduled during that time. Common shifts include 7:00 A.M. to 3:30 P.M., 3:00 P.M. to 11:30 P.M., 11:00 P.M. to 7:30 A.M. Most surgical nurses are also on call, so if an emergency situation arises or the staff is short on a given day, a surgical nurse can be called in to work. Most nurses dislike that aspect of the job and

say it is the most difficult part of being a surgical nurse.

Long hours are often the norm for surgical nurses as well. Regular shifts plus emergency surgeries can add up to a lot of high-stress work and very little sleep. "Patients need heath care professionals 24 hours a day, seven days a week," Marcy says. "Therefore nurses' hours are not always the best, and one must expect to work difficult shifts and some holidays. Overtime is a must in the operating room. Trauma cases come in at all hours, and each patient requires a minimum of two nurses (not to mention the numerous other members of the surgical team)."

Some surgical nurses get to travel to conferences or even to other countries to work with other health care professionals. Marcy had the opportunity to travel with one of her colleagues to assist in the development of a plastic surgery/craniofacial clinic. "For me, this experience has been one of the highlights of my plastic surgical nursing career," she says. "How humbling it was to visit foreign lands, where everything is valued and not simply thrown away. Where even the simplest gesture is appreciated and nothing is taken for granted. You can not help returning home forever changed by such experiences."

Some surgical nurses, such as Cecelia Grindel, also work as educators. She has been a medical-surgical nurse who has had a particular interest in oncology nursing for 35 years. She is currently the associate director for Graduate Programs at the Byrdine F. Lewis School of Nursing at Georgia State University. As

Surgical Nursing Specialties

Surgical nurses are nurses who care for surgical patients; this includes *floor nurses* (who work on surgical units) and *perioperative nurses*. Floor nurses get "inpatients" ready for surgery and send these patients to the operating holding area when the operating room nurses are ready for the patient.

- *Perioperative nurses* include *day surgery preop nurses*, who check patients in and get them ready for the day's surgery. Problems arising with the patient are generally picked up by these nursing professionals. If a problem is discovered, the day surgery preop nurse notifies anesthesia and surgery and the patient is reassessed at this time.

- *Intra-op nurses* include the *scrub nurse* and *circulating nurse*. Scrub nurses select and organize supplies and medical instruments that will be used during the surgery. The circulating nurse is a non-sterile member of the surgical staff. From the operating room, the circulating nurse acts as a liaison between the surgical team and the rest of the hospital during and after an operation. These nurses are also known as *operating room nurses*.

- *Post-anesthesia care unit nurses,* who take over from the operating room nurses once the surgery is completed. They assess the patient for pain, bleeding, breathing, general vital signs, etc. They are also known as *postop nurses* and *recovery room nurses*.

- The position of *RN first assistant* is a relatively new career in surgical nursing. RN first assistants are registered nurses who have gone through a formal postsecondary training program that involves both classroom and supervised clinical education. RN first assistants work directly with surgeons in the operating room and in office settings seeing preop and postop patients. They may also check on preop and postop patients, but they are not floor nurses. For more information on this specialty, visit http://www.aorn.org/patient/rnfafact.htm.

associate director, Cecelia teaches, conducts research, and oversees the implementation of the master's and doctoral programs at the School of Nursing. "I enjoy teaching nursing students about the fascinating world of nursing practice," she says, "and have been able to teach students at the undergraduate, master's, and doctoral levels. I particularly enjoy teaching about health conditions and illnesses of adults. Of course, oncology nursing practice is my favorite topic, but I also find care of patients with cardiac disease, respiratory disease, and renal disease particularly intriguing." Cecelia also serves as the president of the Academy of Medical-Surgical Nurses. "We are the only specialty organization devoted to medical-surgical nurses and the care of adults," she says. "We have developed a scope and standards of practice and have published many position statements on important issues in nursing. We are proud of what we have accomplished and are very excited about our future."

DO I HAVE WHAT IT TAKES TO BE A SURGICAL NURSE?

Most nurses describe the odd hours as the most demanding part of their job. Never knowing when they will have to drop what they are doing and go into a high-stress situation, surgical nurses are called upon to be very flexible. To be a surgical nurse, you have to be willing to put your life on hold sometimes.

Surgical nurses deal with situations ranging from minor surgery to life-and-death surgical procedures. "High levels of stress are a definite part of work as a surgical nurse," Marcy Dienno says, "and this stress can take its toll on the most seasoned nurse. Life-and-death situations can occur at any time and, as the surgical nurse involved with the patient, you find yourself in the middle of these situations. As part of a surgical team, you must be able to deal with the pressure that comes with holding a person's life in your hands. You must be able to react quickly to emergencies by drawing on your technical knowledge and experience." Marcy feels that a person who is best suited for surgical nursing "should possess the ability to assess a situation and react to it at a moment's notice. In my experience, I have found the surgical nurse to be the glue that holds the team together."

Marcy also believes that the ability to work as a member of a team is key. "In the operating room, you have to have excellent communication skills and a close working relationship with other team members," she says. "This type of nursing is not a one-person job but a team effort, and every member of the team must be valued for his or her respective expertise." Strong communication skills are important when dealing with family members as well. Marcy says that parents are often fearful of handing their child over to strangers. "As I take the child from the parents," she says, "I turn to them, look them in the eye, and say 'I will treat Mary Jane as though she were my own.' I say this to each and every one of my parents because I can think of no better commitment to them. What better care can I give than the care I would give my own children?"

Surgical nurses also must be willing to continue to learn throughout their careers. "With the ever-changing technology and advances in medicine in today's health care field, learning new things is essential to remain current in the practice," says Diane Teresczenko, a surgical nurse and Operative Services Manager at West Suburban Medical Center in Oak Park, Illinois. "It is important to read professional journals specific to surgical nursing. . . . Other methods of staying up to date include formal seminars and professional meetings. In-services provided by the hospital and the nursing unit are mandatory for each new piece of equipment or procedure introduced to the environment." Diane says that every surgical nurse at her hospital is required to attend a formal presentation and complete a successful return demonstration, to assure that he or she has a clear understanding of the equipment or procedure. "There cannot be any compromises in maintaining a safe environment for the surgical patient," she says.

If you get woozy at the sight of blood, this is probably not the best career choice for you. But, if you are fascinated by the workings of the human body or intrigued by how modern medical procedures can prolong life, this may be your best bet. This isn't a profession for people who want a nine-to-five job that they can leave behind when they get home. Surgical nursing is a field for people who want to make a difference for other people and are willing to give a large portion of their own lives to do so.

Excerpt from the Nurses' Code of Ethics

1. To conserve life, alleviate suffering, and promote health.

2. To give nursing care that is not influenced or altered by the personality of the patient, race, social status, religion, or any other external factor.

3. To maintain high standards of ethics in personal life and to practice good citizenship.

4. To keep up-to-date with current nursing practice to be adequately prepared to give the best possible care to the patient.

5. To carry out orders with the greatest skill possible.

Source: The American Nurses Association Code of Ethics

HOW DO I BECOME A SURGICAL NURSE?
Education
High School

In all states you must graduate from a nursing program and then be licensed. To enter a nursing program, you must have a high school diploma. As a high school student, you should take as many science, biology, health, and mathematics classes as you can. And, because communication skills are so important in the nursing field as a whole and surgical nursing in particular, you should also take speech and English classes.

You should also take first aid courses that are provided by your school or other agencies. Some high schools have future nurses clubs that help students explore careers in nursing.

On the practical side, you can gain a lot of hands-on experience through volunteering or getting a part-time job in a hospital.

Postsecondary Training

To become a surgical nurse, you must first complete a four-year baccalaureate program, a three-year hospital diploma program, or a two-year associate's degree program and pass a licensing exam. In nursing school, you'll take classes in nursing theory, humanities, sciences, and human growth and development. You'll also take part in clinical experience programs at hospitals and other health care facilities in the last two years of your degree program.

After earning a nursing degree, you must also enroll in a formal, postgraduate operating room course or participate in a hospital in-service program that focuses on the development of the necessary skills and techniques of surgical nursing. After Marcy Dienno earned her BSN, she gained on-the-job experience in the operating room in her employer's orientation program. "The training was intense and stressful due to the highly critical area in which I was working," Marcy says, "however, the support I received from more experienced nurses helped tremendously."

Diane Teresczenko received her training for this profession through a variety of methods. "When I began my surgical nursing career," she explains, "I received 'on-the-job' training. This included knowledge from experienced OR nurses that was passed on to me through shadowing, precepting, classroom practice, along with many hours that I spent independently studying the names and function of all the many instruments and equipment required. Within six months of starting in the OR, I was fully oriented to each of the specialties (General, Gynecological, Ophthalmology, Ear/Nose/Throat, Orthopedics, Plastics, Urology, Neuro, and Peripheral/Vascular surgeries), and I began taking on call responsibilities for emergency case coverage." Diane says that many hospitals and colleges today offer perioperative courses that are specially designed for teaching an RN interested in pursuing a surgical nursing career.

Certification or Licensing

All states and the District of Columbia require nurses to obtain a license to practice. To obtain a license, graduates of approved nursing schools must pass a national examination. Nurses may be licensed by more than one state. In some states, continuing education is a condition for license renewal. For further information, contact your state's nursing board. (See the National Council of State Boards of Nursing Web site at http://www.ncsbn.org for contact information.)

Several voluntary certifications are available to surgical nurses. The Perioperative Nursing Certification Board offers the Certified Nurse: Operating Room (CNOR) designation to applicants who have earned a BSN, spent two years gaining work experience in surgical nursing, completed 2,400 hours of perioperative practice, and passed an examination. The board also offers certification to RN first assistants.

Applicants who have earned a BSN; spent two years (of the last five) working as an RN in an adult medical-surgical clinical setting; completed 3,000 hours of clinical practice as a staff nurse, clinical nurse specialist, clinical educator, faculty member, manager, or supervisor; and passed an examination can earn the designation of certified medical-surgical registered nurse. This certification is offered by the Academy of Medical-Surgical Nurses and the Medical-Surgical Nursing Certification Board.

The American Society of Plastic Surgical Nurses (ASPSN) strongly recommends that all nurses working in the field of plastic surgery become certified. This voluntary certification requires that plastic surgical nurses have a minimum of two years experience in the field and pass an examination. "Certification is a great way to show your skill level, competency, knowledge of specific plastic surgical procedures, and level of dedication to the field," says Marcy Dienno. "The exam is similar to the state nursing boards and requires periodic recertification, usually by continuing education units (CEUs)." Plastic surgical nurses who meet these requirements are known as certified plastic surgical nurses.

Marcy finds that the best way to stay up to date about her field is through membership in professional associations. "I read the journals, attend conferences, collect CEUs, and network with peers," she explains. "Being part of a professional organization makes remaining current easy. I am also certified, so I must maintain a certain number of CEUs to hold my certifications. Certification is a great way to keep current because recertification requirements encourage nurses to remain current on relevant issues by requiring a certain number of continuing education credits."

Internships and Volunteerships

As part of your nursing degree, you will be required to complete several internships, or clinical rotations. Usually these clinicals are set up through the college or university to be completed at a hospital or other health care facility. Clinical rotations expose you to various areas of nursing care, such as pediatrics, community health, or geriatric care.

Volunteering is an excellent way to gain experience and build up your résumé. Contact hospitals, nursing homes, and other health care facilities to find out about volunteering (or maybe even part-time employment) as a nurse's aide or office helper. Not only will you learn while doing, you may also make valuable contacts that can be helpful in getting a job later in your career.

WHO WILL HIRE ME?

Marcy Dienno landed her first job as a staff nurse in the operating room at Children's Hospital of Philadelphia. "I rotated through all services," she says. "I did everything from minor ear surgery to open-heart surgery. As I learned more about the various surgical specialties, I developed a love for neurosurgery and specialized in that area. I then moved into the cardiac arena and worked with that specialty. Leaving that, I became the educator for the operating room complex and was in charge of orienting new nurses as well as developing a continuing education program for staff nurses." Marcy gradually found herself working more and more with the plastic surgeons. When a specialty position opened up in plastics, Marcy knew she had to take it. She did and has been involved with plastic surgery ever since. "The children are incredible," she says, "the parents grateful, and the surgeons technically superior, supportive, and encouraging to my professional development within the specialty of plastic surgery."

Nursing graduates often seek employment in the same hospital or health care facility in which they completed their clinical work. It's important to select a college or university that has a strong

What Are the Benefits of Association Membership?

Who better to ask than Marcy Dienno, past president of the American Society of Plastic Surgical Nurses (ASPSN), one of the leading professional associations representing surgical nurses. While Marcy's answers reflect the opportunities available through the ASPSN, future nurses will find that many associations offer similar benefits to their membership. According to Marcy (and in her own words), the top benefits of membership (in no particular order) in the ASPSN include:

1. *Plastic Surgical Nursing Journal.* In this journal, members receive opportunities to earn CEUs specific to the field of plastic surgery, updates on current techniques, exposure to the newest products coming on the market, and the opportunity to become published themselves.

2. *Newsletter.* Members receive clinical updates, news of upcoming chapter and regional events, educational opportunities, government relations updates, scholarship and grant information, and possible employment opportunities.

3. *Web site.* Our Web site includes a member directory, a discussion area (where nurses can post pertinent questions to nurses around the country and Canada), and information on the latest industry changes. It also offers members the ability to register online for upcoming events and review ASPSN's approved standards of care.

4. *Conference.* Members have the ability to attend conferences (including two national conferences) at a reduced registration rate. Conference attendees gain personal development, professional education pertinent to their specific practice, peer-to-peer networking/problem solving, and access to numerous vendors showing the newest state-of-the-art products available.

5. *Member directory.* This is an invaluable tool to our members as it allows for easy access to members from all over the country and Canada. Members utilize this tool for help with patient referrals, planning future meetings, and peer-to-peer networking. This tool is consistently a favorite among members.

6. *Continuing education validity of specialty.* Although the certification exam is open to members and nonmembers alike, association members have the opportunity to network with peers prior to sitting for the certification exam. Review courses are offered at various locations, and history shows that those taking the review course have a high pass rate.

clinical program. The best programs will be affiliated with a hospital or outpatient facility so that nursing students can work during their schooling to fulfill experience requirements.

The two major employment areas for surgical nurses are hospitals and ambulatory surgery centers (outpatient surgery centers). Hospitals in the larger cities usually employ many surgical nurses to meet the needs of the high number of patients and surgeries that are necessary. Outpatient surgery is on the rise due to hospitals trying to cut costs by releasing patients earlier and moving many surgical procedures that were once inpatient to outpatient status. Although hospitals employ the most nurses overall, nursing jobs in outpatient facilities are growing every year.

The first place a new graduate should visit when looking for a nursing position is the career services office at the college or university he or she has attended. The staff should be able to provide leads and contact information, and sometimes they will set up interviews immediately with certain health care facilities. Often the places a nursing student worked during clinical experience programs for college are the best starting points for employment. Job seekers can also go the traditional route by checking the employment advertising in the newspaper. Nursing magazines such as *American Nurse, Nursing,* and *RN* can usually be found in the larger libraries and often contain advertisements for open positions.

The following associations publish materials that contain job listings or hospital listings: Academy of Medical-Surgical Nurses, American Hospital Association, American Medical Association, American Nurses Association, American Society of Plastic Surgical Nurses, Association of Perioperative Registered Nurses, and the National Student Nurses Association. You'll find contact information for these associations at the end of this book.

Advancement Possibilities

- *Clinical surgical nurse specialists* supervise and guide surgical nurses through daily routines. Clinical nurse specialists also conduct research and develop nursing techniques.

- *Nurse managers for operating rooms* coordinate and oversee nursing areas of the surgical unit. Nurse managers assist head nurses and their staff with difficult surgical situations.

- *Nurse practitioners* perform many tasks without supervision that are usually reserved for physicians, such as treating common ailments, administering medications, and examining patients.

- *Nursing instructors* provide classroom and clinical instruction to nursing students.

The Internet also provides a wealth of employment listings that are updated daily. Job seekers should search the Internet with keywords such as "nursing and employment," "nursing and jobs," and "nursing and career." Check out the "Surf the Web" chapter at the end of this book, too.

WHERE CAN I GO FROM HERE?

"One of the great things about working as a surgical nurse is the opportunity to advance your career," Diane Teresczenko says. She began her career in the operating room as a staff nurse, and as she gained experience, advanced to the positions of surgical resource nurse and operating room clinical educator. In Diane's current position as Operative Services Manager, her responsibilities include 24-hour accountability for the operating room, post-anesthesia care unit, same-day services unit, and the pre-admission testing unit. "Surgical nursing has so many opportunities for advancement within the specialty," says Diane. "It is a field that has proven to be exciting and highly rewarding for me. If I had to choose a career today, knowing what I know about surgical nursing, there is not a doubt in my mind that I would once again make the same career choice that I made so many years ago."

It's important to continue to educate yourself if you want to advance to higher-skilled, more responsible positions. A master's degree and then a doctorate are both steps that may need to be completed for certain positions. You may want to become a clinical nurse specialist in the medical-surgical area or perhaps you'll shift laterally to become a clinical nurse specialist in a slightly different area. Whatever your goal, more education and ongoing experience is the key. You may even decide to become your own boss as a nurse practitioner.

There is also a great deal of advancement opportunity on the business side of nursing. You can use your experience and knowledge to manage an ambulatory care center. You may even advance to high-level management jobs within a hospital or health organization. The opportunities are really wide open.

Marcy Dienno is content with her career for now. "But once my children are through college . . . I would like to return to school to obtain my master's in pediatric plastic surgical nursing. I hope to join an organization that periodically travels to Third World countries offering care to children suffering from craniofacial anomalies such as cleft lips and palates."

WHAT ARE THE SALARY RANGES?

Salary ranges for surgical nurses often depend on what region of the country they are working in and the level of education and experience attained. According to the Association of Perioperative Registered Nurses, staff perioperative nurses working in smaller facilities earned average salaries of $57,700 in 2006. Staff perioperative nurses who were employed in larger facilities earned an average of $63,800. According to the U.S. Department of Labor, registered nurses (including surgical nurses) earned salaries that ranged from less than $38,660 to $79,460 or more in 2005.

Hospitals usually have very attractive benefits packages to go along with salary. Often this includes tuition reimbursement to help you further your education while you work. If you work for a government hospital, you will get state employee benefits, which are usually very comprehensive.

WHAT IS THE JOB OUTLOOK?

The job outlook for surgical nursing, and nursing in general for that matter, is

Related Jobs

- clinical nurse specialists
- critical care nurses
- emergency room nurses
- nurse anesthetists
- nurse-midwives
- nurse practitioners
- operating room technicians
- transplant nurses

excellent and shows no sign of changing in the near future. Nursing is expected to grow much faster than the average for all occupations in the United States through 2014. While the outlook for general nurses is excellent, its employment focus is shifting from hospitals to outpatient care. This is not necessarily true for surgical nurses. Although hospitals are trying to cut costs by moving patients out of the hospital more quickly and by making more operations outpatient, this does not diminish the need for surgical nurses. Whether in the hospital setting or in an ambulatory care setting, surgical nurses continue to be in high demand.

Another factor that is affecting nursing is the growth of the segment of the American population that is 65 and over. As this elderly population grows and as people live longer, there is more of a chance that body organs and systems will wear out, creating a need for surgical care. Surgical nurses will continue to be in high demand as the population ages.

The increasing need for surgical care will also increase the number of surgeries performed in ambulatory care settings. Surgical nurses with specific skills and techniques will be in high demand to meet the ambulatory care needs.

Hospitals may try to offset costs by using more part-time nurses. Currently, one-fifth of all nurses work on a part-time schedule. This may be less of a factor for surgical nurses because of their education and experience levels. Marcy Dienno has the best of both worlds; she has worked part time since her children were born. "This has not stopped my advancement or travel," she says, "all of which happened after moving from a full-time to a part-time status. I've been lucky to be able to have my cake and eat it too. I have a wonderfully fulfilling career and the ability to spend time at home with my children. Some days it's a juggling act, but it's worth it."

SECTION 3

Do It Yourself

Now that you've read about different careers in nursing, what do you think is the most important characteristic a prospective nurse should have? If you think it's the desire to help others, then you're developing a good understanding of this profession. The fact is that nursing, above all else, is about caring for other people, so nurses must put their patients first. It's certainly true that nurses find their work intellectually stimulating, challenging, exciting, and personally fulfilling—but they find their ultimate reward in the care and comfort they give to others.

After this desire to help, what do you suppose is the next most important characteristic of a prospective nurse? Is it academic ability? Practical nursing skills? Bedside manner? Personal maturity? Dedication to the work even under difficult circumstances? You probably know by now that all of these things are equally important. If you're not quite convinced of that, consider a nursing student who gets straight As in her classes but can't calm down a nervous patient to give him his medication. Or consider a nursing student who gets along beautifully with all of the patients he works with but is never on time to feed or bathe them. They both may have the desire to serve and other skills besides, but their behavior may prove harmful to their patients—and it certainly won't endear them to prospective employers.

We can conclude that nurses must be strong in three general areas, broadly defined as academic ability, practical skills, and personal qualities. This may seem a bit overwhelming, but you can easily start to evaluate and improve your proficiency in these areas right now, while you are still in high school. This section will introduce you to some of the many ways in which you can test your aptitude for nursing and begin to prepare for a nursing career.

❑ ACADEMIC ABILITY

Academic ability is undoubtedly the area you're most familiar with, since you spend at least nine months out of the year working on it! If you want to be a nurse, you simply must be confident of your abilities in biology, chemistry, composition, mathematics, and the other subjects that are essential to the profession. That's not to say that you must enjoy all these subjects and earn top grades in them, but you must be comfortable with each one. If you need to improve in one or more of these subjects—and most people have plenty of room for improvement—start now by really applying yourself and asking your teachers for advice and assistance. Good performances in high school classes will not only aid your nursing school applications, but they'll also make your college classes much more manageable.

❑ PRACTICAL SKILLS

Practical skills are those that are specific to nursing: giving a patient an injection, assisting a physician, comforting an accident victim. Naturally, you will learn and practice these skills in college, but you can start working on some of them while you're still in high school. Doing so will give you a real advantage and added confidence in nursing school, and will also give you the chance to explore the profession before making a commitment to it. You may be able to learn enough right now to start thinking about pursuing a nursing specialty such as pediatrics or midwifery. Then, too, you may learn that you are not as well suited to the profession as you thought. If you feel faint at the sight of blood or constantly lose your patience with those who are ill and not in good humor, don't you want to know this before you invest time and money in training to become a nurse?

❏ PERSONAL QUALITIES

The personal character traits needed for nursing are not as easy to quantify as the other skills and abilities. Nurses are, of course, unique individuals with different likes, dislikes, backgrounds, aspirations, and qualities. But they do share a profound sense of dedication, responsibility, and maturity. While these characteristics are important to virtually every profession, they are absolutely vital to nursing, where the health and well-being of others is on the line. Again, you don't have to wait until you're a full-time nursing student to put your character to the test. You can take advantage of many opportunities right now to examine and improve upon your sense of responsibility and maturity. In fact, you'll probably find that almost all of the opportunities mentioned below require a bit more dedication and mature behavior than most of the situations you've been in before.

❏ PREPARING FOR NURSING: ACADEMIC ABILITY

As we've said, preparing academically for a nursing career is something you're already doing five days a week for the better part of the year. So why would you want to work on biology or chemistry over the summer as well? There are a number of reasons. If you need to improve on certain subjects, summer gives you the extra time you need to do so. If you're already doing well in school, use and expand your knowledge during the summertime instead of slowly forgetting what you've learned—or try a subject, perhaps anatomy or nutrition, that your school doesn't offer. And since many summer study opportunities are offered by colleges and universities around the country, they give you the chance to experience college-level classes and campus life before you're even out of high school.

Check out "Get Involved" in Section 4, What Can I Do Right Now, for a sampling of the academic camps and study programs that are available. Remember that we don't endorse any of these programs, but we do want you to check them out for yourself. And be sure to check around your own area or at your preferred colleges to see what's available there.

❏ PREPARING FOR NURSING: PRACTICAL SKILLS

You probably already know of a few ways to get hands-on nursing experience right now: volunteering in a hospital, taking a first aid course, or joining a Future Nurses club, if your school has one. These are all great options that will be discussed further on, but you have a wider range of options than this. You're almost certain to find one that's right for you.

In Your School

Future Nurses Club

You may be able to get your first experience of the nursing profession while gaining practical skills right in your own high school. Past students with an interest in nursing may have teamed up with a teacher or counselor to form a Future Nurses club. If so, you may find the club—similar to Future Farmers or Future Teachers clubs—very helpful in terms of hands-on learning and motivation. After all, it's easier to take on volunteer projects and push yourself to study harder when you have the support of others who share your goals. Together, you and the other future nurses will probably visit facilities such as hospitals and nursing schools, do some volunteer work to practice practical skills, and enjoy guest speakers with careers in the field of nursing.

But what if your school doesn't have a Future Nurses club? If you're really sold on the idea—and if you can sell it to a few other classmates—why not start your own club? That may sound daunting, but all you really need to start a Future Nurses club is some prospective members, a teacher or counselor to act as adviser, a place to hold regular meetings, and your principal's permission. With students and faculty working together, you can plan creative activities for the club and publicity to attract more members.

Health Occupations Students of America/SkillsUSA

If you are taking health occupations classes in high school, you are probably already familiar with Health Occupations Students of America or Vocational Industrial Clubs of America. These are national organizations specifically for vocational students—and if your school is affiliated with either or both, they can be a real boost to your future in nursing.

Health Occupations Students of America (HOSA) has been working since 1976 "to promote career opportunities in the health care industry and to enhance the delivery of quality health care to all people." HOSA is an integral part of the health occupations curriculum in its member schools. One of its most visible activities is the annual Competitive Events Program, held at the state and national levels. Qualifying HOSA participants compete in many skill, leadership, and related events, including CPR/First Aid, Medical Terminology, and Practical Nursing. HOSA also sponsors an annual National Conference. Remember, to participate in HOSA events, you must work with your school, so speak to a teacher or counselor about your interest in the organization.

SkillsUSA

SkillsUSA works with trade and technical students as well as those in health occupations, but like HOSA, it works through schools and in their curricula. Also like HOSA, SkillsUSA has a highly visible annual competition, called the

SkillsUSA Championships. It's a large event with local, state, and national levels of competition in such categories as Basic Health Care Skills, First Aid/CPR, Health Knowledge Bowl, Health Occupations Professional Portfolio, Nurse Assisting, and Practical Nursing. Work with your school officials to determine if SkillsUSA is an option for you. Their Web site can be found at http://www.skillsusa.org/.

Blood Drive

Whether or not your school already has formal clubs for prospective nurses, there is one experience of practical nursing that is possible at almost every school: a blood drive. Usually managed by the Red Cross, blood drives are often sponsored by Key Clubs, student councils, and even individual students with great organizational abilities. By getting involved in the sponsorship of a blood drive, you'll get to work with medical professionals, witness the functions they carry out, and perform a real service for people in need of blood transfusions.

In Your Community

Volunteering

Hospitals. Outside of school programs, the most familiar way to gain practical nursing experience is probably volunteering at a hospital, also called "candy-striping." This is so popular because it's available in most communities and so intimately connected to the work of professional nurses. Naturally, the specifics of volunteering vary among hospitals, but there is a lot of common ground. First of all, you can expect to undergo some kind

of training—a couple of hours or a couple of days—to work on the skills needed in your particular duties. You will probably have to wear some kind of uniform and a name badge to make your identity and position clear to both patients and staff. And you will have to commit yourself to a schedule, so that the hospital can depend on you. Beyond this, the actual days and hours you work and the specific duties you perform are between you and the hospital's volunteer coordinator.

Your options will depend upon the size of the hospital you choose and whether it is a general, children's, or veterans hospital. One rather exceptional example of a hospital for Denver-area residents to consider is The Children's Hospital of Denver, which has nearly 1,900 people in its Association of Volunteers. The Junior Volunteers program is for those ages 13 to 18, who work in departments throughout the hospital and in fund-raising campaigns. Those working directly with patients may help feed them, make their beds, take their temperatures, or assist their nurses by running errands, fetching supplies, and doing some paperwork. These are some of the most basic duties in nursing, and if you enjoy performing them, it's a good indication that you're on the right career path. If you are in the Denver area, you may contact The Children's Hospital of Denver via the Association of Volunteers at 303-861-6887 or via its Web site at http://www.thechildrenshospital.org/public/helpkids/volunteer.

Incidentally, volunteering at a children's hospital or in the children's ward of a general hospital could be your stepping-stone to a career as a pediatric nurse. It's obviously a great way to get experience in that specialty, and it will also rid you of any misconceptions you might have about caring for sick children. Some people considering pediatric nursing think it's mainly about seeing cute kids and healing a few bumps and bruises. But even as a volunteer, you will find that children are demanding patients and that many of their illnesses and injuries are as serious and distressing as those that afflict adults.

Hospices. Hospices and similar institutions generally care for the terminally ill and those with specific diseases such as cancer or AIDS. They sometimes accept teen volunteers, too, so if you are familiar with one in your area, get in touch to see if you can be of service. You would gain basic nursing skills and also see if that is the kind of work environment you might like to work in professionally.

Nursing Homes. If previous experiences in your life have taught you that you get along with the elderly especially well, consider volunteering at a nursing home or other facility for the aged. In terms of nursing duties, you can usually be of as much use in these institutions as in hospitals or hospices. You can also offer your own companionship to the elderly, who may rarely get to socialize with younger people or who may be far away from their own children and grandchildren. You can also work with older people by participating in such programs as Visiting Pets and Meals on Wheels. These may be community-run services or you might access them through a local church. If these experiences confirm that you have a particular talent for working with the elderly, you might consider specializing as a geriatric nurse.

CPR and First Aid

Finally, you should seriously consider taking a class in CPR or First Aid—or both. Your local Red Cross, YMCA, or hospital most likely offers this kind of training for a reasonable fee. CPR and First Aid skills are obviously of great importance to every nurse, in every specialty, in every employment situation, and you can get a head start. But before you actually become a nurse—and even if you eventually decide not to go into nursing at all—CPR and First Aid courses will allow you to react promptly and effectively to medical emergencies around you. How should you react if a teacher faints in class? What should you do if a classmate cuts herself badly in industrial arts? If you've taken the proper courses, you'll know.

Besides CPR and First Aid, the Red Cross offers a number of courses and programs that are worth exploring. They can provide you with the training needed to educate your peers and your community about HIV/AIDS, general health issues, swimming and water safety, and disaster response. Each local Red Cross office has different programs available, so call the one nearest you to see what it has to offer teens. You might also want to check out the Red Cross's extensive Web site —which will help you locate the office in your area—at http://www.redcross.org.

❑ PREPARING FOR NURSING: PERSONAL QUALITIES

You've probably come to the conclusion that most of the activities listed in this section have required the important personal qualities of a nurse we discussed earlier: dedication, responsibility, and maturity. If so, you're absolutely right! All of the volunteer activities involve other people depending on you, and you'll need all of these qualities to measure up to your duties. Volunteering probably won't be easy at first, but persevering and learning how to make the situation better can help you become more dedicated, responsible, and mature.

The camps and study programs listed in "Get Involved: A Directory of Camps, Programs, Competitions, and Other Opportunities" can do the same. Taking college-level courses, working on science projects with people you've just met, and living away from home—possibly in another state—are very different from volunteer work, but these sorts of experiences demand the same qualities of you. And they can bring those qualities out of you.

A final personal quality that has been implied throughout this section—and is central to the field of nursing—is, of course, generosity. The giving of yourself to ensure the well-being of others is a quality you can practice anywhere and everywhere. If you would like to make an especially generous effort in connection with nursing, you might consider doing charity work. It need not take much time: Helping out with the March of Dimes once a year will help combat birth defects. Distributing red ribbons to raise AIDS awareness may take a few hours on a single Saturday. But doing such things genuinely helps others and puts your own good intentions to work right now. The March of Dimes, various AIDS-prevention groups, and many more charitable organizations are as accessible as your phone book.

If one or more of the suggestions in this chapter and other chapters sound interesting to you, put pen to paper or pick up the phone and make a call. These suggestions are just the tools that you must put to use. It's your career, your future—and only you can plan it and start working toward it. Contact some of the organizations listed in this book or similar ones in your area and speak to the person who coordinates the program that interests you. Often, he or she will take some time to speak with you about your career goals, your personal situation, and how you might fit into the program he or she runs. If that program doesn't seem right for you, ask for suggestions about other opportunities and organizations. Take the initiative and find the best way to explore your future in nursing right now.

SECTION 4

What Can I Do Right Now?

Get Involved

Now that you've read about some of the different careers available in nursing, you may be anxious to experience this line of work for yourself, to find out what it's really like. Or perhaps you already feel certain that this is the career path for you and want to get started on it right away. Whichever is the case, this section is for you! There are plenty of things you can do right now to learn about nursing careers while gaining valuable experience. Just as important, you'll get to meet new friends and see new places, too.

In the following pages you will find programs designed to pique your interest in nursing and start preparing you for a career. You already know that this field is complex, and that to work in it you need a solid education. Since the first step toward a nursing career will be gaining that education, we've found more than 35 programs that will start you on your way. Some are special introductory sessions, others are actual college courses—one of them may be right for you. Take time to read over the listings and see how each compares to your situation: how committed you are to nursing, how much of your money and free time you're willing to devote to it, and how the program will help you after high school. These listings are divided into categories, with a description of the program given following its name or the name of the sponsoring organization.

❏ THE CATEGORIES

Camps

When you see an activity that is classified as a camp, don't automatically start packing your tent and mosquito repellent. Where academic study is involved, the term "camp" often simply means a residential program including both educational and recreational activities. It's sometimes hard to differentiate between such camps and other study programs, but if the sponsoring organization calls it a camp, so do we! For an extended list of camps, visit http://www.kidscamps.com.

College Courses/Summer Study

These terms are linked because most college courses offered to students your age must take place in the summer, when you are out of school. At the same time, many summer study programs are sponsored by colleges and universities that want to attract future students and give them a head start in higher education. Summer study of almost any type is a good idea because it keeps your mind and your study skills sharp over the long vacation. Summer study at a college offers any number of additional benefits, including giving you the tools to make a well-informed decision about your future academic career. Study options, including some impressive college and university programs, account for most of the listings in this section—primarily because higher education is so crucial to every nursing career.

Competitions

Competitions are fairly self-explanatory, but you should know that there are only a few in this book because many science (including nursing-related) competitions are sponsored at the local and regional levels and are impractical to list here. What this means, however, is that if you are interested in entering a competition, you shouldn't have much trouble finding one yourself. Your guidance counselor or science, health, or math teachers can help you start searching in your area.

Employment and Internship Opportunities

As you may already know from experience, employment opportunities for teenagers can be very limited. This is particularly true in nursing, which requires workers with bachelor's and even graduate degrees. Even internships are most often reserved for college students who have completed at least one or two years of study in the field. Still, if you're very determined to find an internship or paid position in nursing, there may be ways to find one. See Section 3: Do It Yourself in this book for some suggestions.

Field Experience

This is something of a catchall category for activities that don't exactly fit the other descriptions. But anything called a field experience in this book is always a good opportunity to get out and explore the work of nursing professionals.

Membership

When an organization is in this category, it simply means that you are welcome to pay your dues and become a card-carrying member. Formally joining any organization brings the benefits of meeting others who share your interests, finding opportunities to get involved, and keeping up with current events. Depending on how active you are, the contacts you make and the experiences you gain may help when the time comes to apply to colleges or look for a job.

In some organizations, you pay a special student rate and receive benefits similar to regular members. Many organizations, however, are now starting student branches with their own benefits and publications. As in any field, make sure you understand exactly what the benefits of membership are before you join.

Finally, don't let membership dues discourage you from making contact with these organizations. Some charge dues as little as $25 because they know that students are perpetually short of funds. When the annual dues are higher, think of the money as an investment in your future and then consider if it is too much to pay.

PROGRAM DESCRIPTIONS

Once you've started to look at the individual listings themselves, you'll find that they contain a lot of information. Naturally, there is a general description of each program, but wherever possible we also have included the following details.

Application Information

Each listing notes how far in advance you'll need to apply for the program or position, but the simple rule is to apply as far in advance as possible. This ensures that you won't miss out on a great opportunity simply because other people got there ahead of you. It also means that you will get a timely decision on your application, so if you are not accepted, you'll still have some time to apply elsewhere. As for the things that make up your application—essays, recommendations, etc.—we've tried to tell you what's involved, but be sure to contact the program about specific requirements before you submit anything.

Background Information

This includes such information as the date the program was established, the name of the organization that is sponsoring it financially, and the faculty and staff who will be there for you. This can help you—and your family—gauge the quality and reliability of the program.

Classes and Activities

Classes and activities change from year to year, depending on popularity, availability of instructors, and many other factors. Nevertheless, colleges and universities quite consistently offer the same or similar classes, even in their summer sessions. Courses like Introduction to Nursing and Biology 101, for example, are simply indispensable. So you can look through the listings and see which programs offer foundational courses like these and which offer courses on more variable topics. As for activities, we note when you have access to recreational facilities on campus, and it's usually a given that special social and cultural activities will be arranged for these programs.

Contact Information

Wherever possible, we have given the title of the person whom you should contact instead of the name because people change jobs so frequently. If no title is given and you are telephoning an organization, simply tell the person who answers the phone the name of the program that interests you and he or she will forward your call. If you are writing, include the line "Attention: Summer Study Program" (or whatever is appropriate after "Attention") somewhere on the envelope. This will help to ensure that your letter goes to the person in charge of that program.

Credit

Where academic programs are concerned, we sometimes note that high school or college credit is available to those who have completed them. This means that the program can count toward your high school diploma or a future college degree just like a regular course. Obviously, this can be very useful, but it's important to note that rules about accepting such credit vary from school to school. Before you commit to a program offering high school credit, check with your guidance counselor to see if it would be accepted at your school. As for programs offering college credit, check with your chosen college (if you have one) to see if they will accept it.

Eligibility and Qualifications

The main eligibility requirement to be concerned about is age or grade in school. A term frequently used in relation to grade level is "rising," as in "rising senior": someone who will be a senior when the next school year begins. This is especially important where summer programs are concerned. A number of university-based programs make admissions decisions partly in consideration of GPA, class rank, and standardized test scores. This is mentioned in the listings, but you must contact the program for specific numbers. If you are worried that your GPA or your ACT scores, for example, aren't good enough, don't let them stop you from applying to programs that consider such things in the admissions process. Often, a fine essay or even a personal account of your dedication and eagerness can compensate for statistical weaknesses.

Facilities

We tell you where you'll be living, studying, eating, and having fun during these programs, but there isn't enough room to go into all the details. Some of this information can be important: what is and isn't accessible for people with disabilities, whether the site of a summer program has air-conditioning, and how modern the laboratory and computer equipment are. You can expect most program brochures and application materials to address these concerns, but if you still have questions about the facilities, just call the program's administration and ask.

Financial Details

While a few of the programs listed here are fully underwritten by collegiate and corporate sponsors, most of them rely on you for at least some of their funding. 2005 prices and fees are given here, but you should bear in mind that costs rise slightly almost every year. You and your parents must take costs into consideration when choosing a program. We always try to note where financial aid is available, but really, most programs will do their best to ensure that a shortage of funds does not prevent you from taking part.

Residential versus Commuter Options

Simply put, some programs prefer that participating students live with other participants and staff members, others do not, and still others leave the decision entirely to the students themselves. As a rule, residential programs are suitable for young people who live out of town or even out of state, as well as for local residents. They generally provide a better overview of college life than programs in which you're only on campus for a few hours a day, and they're a way to test how well you cope with living away from home. Commuter programs may be viable only if you live near the program site or if you can stay with relatives who do. Bear in mind that for residential programs especially, the travel between your home and the location of the activity is almost always your responsibility and can significantly increase the cost of participation.

❏ FINALLY . . .

Ultimately, there are three important things to bear in mind concerning all of the programs listed in this volume. The first is that things change. Staff members come and go, funding is added or withdrawn, supply and demand determine which programs continue and which terminate. Dates, times, and costs vary widely because of a number of factors. Because of this, the information we give you, as current and detailed as it is, is just not enough on which to base your final decision. If you are interested in a program, you simply must write, call, fax, or e-mail the organization concerned to get the latest and most complete information available. This has the added benefit of putting you in touch with someone who can deal with your individual questions and problems.

Another important point to keep in mind when considering these programs is that the people who run them provided the information printed here. The editors of this book haven't attended the programs and don't endorse them: we simply give you the information with which to begin your own research. And after all, we can't pass judgment because you're the only one who can decide which programs are right for you.

The final thing to bear in mind is that the programs listed here are just the tip of the iceberg. No book can possibly cover all of the opportunities that are available to you—partly because they are so numerous and are constantly coming and going, but partly because some are waiting to be discovered. For instance, you may be very interested in taking a college course but don't see the college that interests you in the listings. Call the institution's Admissions Office! Even if they don't have a special program for high school students, they might be able to make some kind of arrangements for you to visit or sit in on a class. Use the ideas behind these listings and take the initiative to turn them into opportunities!

❏ THE PROGRAMS
Academic Study Associates (ASA)
College Courses/Summer Study

Academic Study Associates has been offering residential and commuter pre-college summer programs for young people for more than 20 years. It offers college credit classes and enrichment opportunities in a variety of academic fields, including natural sciences (which includes chemistry, mathematics, psychology, and science—important classes for future nurses), at the University of Massachusetts–Amherst, the University of California–Berkeley, Emory University, and Oxford University. In addition to classroom work, students participate in field trips, mini-clinics, and extracurricular activities. Programs are usually three to four weeks in length. Fees and deadlines vary for these programs—visit the ASA Web site for further details. Options are also available for middle school students.

Academic Study Associates (ASA)

ASA Programs
10 New King Street
White Plains, NY 10604-1205
800-752-2250
summer@asaprograms.com
http://www.asaprograms.com/home/asa_home.asp

American Assembly for Men in Nursing

Membership

The assembly is a support organization for male nurses. Members of the general public who have an interest in nursing can apply to become associate members. Contact the assembly for more information.

American Assembly for Men in Nursing Foundation

PO Box 130220
Birmingham, AL 35213
205-802-7551
aamn@aamn.org
http://www.aamn.org

American Association of Critical-Care Nurses (AACN)

Membership

This is a professional association for critical-care nurses. Members of the public who are interested in the field of critical-care nursing can apply for affiliate membership. Members receive access to literature databases at the AACN Web site; subscriptions to *Critical Care Nurse, American Journal of Critical Care, AACN News*, and AACN's e-newsletter *Critical Care Newsline;* and are eligible for schol-

arships, grants, and awards. Contact the association for more information.

American Association of Critical-Care Nurses

101 Columbia
Aliso Viejo, CA 92656-4109
800-899-2226
info@aacn.org
http://www.aacn.org

American Collegiate Adventures (ACA)

College Courses/Summer Study

American Collegiate Adventures offers high school students the chance to experience and prepare for college during summer vacation. Adventures are based at the University of Wisconsin in Madison; they vary in length from three to six weeks. Participants attend college-level courses taught by university faculty during the week (for college credit or enrichment) and visit regional colleges and recreation sites over the weekend. All students live in comfortable en suite accommodations, just down the hall from an ACA resident staff member. Courses vary but usually include such basics as Introduction to Biology and Introduction to Chemistry—perfect for those planning to pursue a degree in nursing. Programs in Italy and Spain are also available. Contact American Collegiate Adventures for the current course listings, prices, and application procedures.

American Collegiate Adventures

1811 West North Avenue, Suite 201
Chicago, IL 60622-1598
800-509-7867

info@acasummer.com
http://www.zfc-consulting.com/
    webprojects/americanadventures

American Council for International Studies' Summer Fast Track and Summer Adventure Programs

College Courses/Summer Study

The American Council for International Studies (ACIS) offers two study-abroad programs for high school students who are interested in science and other subjects. Students in its Summer Fast Track Program can take science-related college courses for credit at the University of California–Berkeley (and nonscience courses for credit at colleges in England, France, Italy, Spain, and Russia). Recent classes at the University of California–Berkeley's program included General Psychology and Drugs and the Brain. Fees, the number of college credits available, and courses vary by program; visit the ACIS Web site for further details. The Council also offers less structured educational programs in Costa Rica, Italy, Australia, and New Zealand via its Summer Adventure Program. Programs last anywhere from 17 to 30 days. Students are immersed in the artistic and cultural history of their host countries, stay in three- to four-star hotels, and are provided with breakfast and dinner daily. Contact the Council for more information. Scholarships are available for both programs.

American Council for International Studies
c/o American Institute for Foreign Study

Summer Programs
River Plaza
9 West Broad Street
Stamford, CT 06902-3788
877-795-0813
accounts@acis.com
http://www.summeradvantage.com

Association of Women's Health, Obstetric and Neonatal Nurses (AWHONN)

Membership

This organization represents nurses who specialize in the care of women and newborns. Its members include neonatal nurses, OB/GYN and labor and delivery nurses, women's health nurses, nurse scientists, nurse executives and managers, childbirth educators, and nurse practitioners. It offers associate membership status for non-nurses who are "involved or interested in women's health, obstetric, or neonatal specialty." Membership benefits include access to AWHONN online forums, subscriptions to *The Journal of Obstetric, Gynecologic and Neonatal Nursing, Every Woman,* and *AWHONN Lifelines,* and the opportunity to participate in the organization's annual conference. Contact the association for more information.

Association of Women's Health, Obstetric and Neonatal Nurses (AWHONN)
2000 L Street NW, Suite 740
Washington, DC 20036-4912
800-673-8499
http://www.awhonn.org

Boston University High School Honors Program/Summer Challenge Program

College Courses/Summer Study

Two summer educational opportunities are available for high school students interested in science and other majors. Rising high school seniors can participate in the High School Honors Program, which offers six-week, for-credit undergraduate study at Boston University. Students take two for-credit classes (up to eight credits) alongside regular Boston University students, live in dorms on campus, and participate in extracurricular activities and tours of local attractions. Classes can be taken in such subject areas as biochemistry, biology, biomedical-clinical, chemistry, mathematics, physical science, and psychology. The program typically begins in early July. Students who demonstrate financial need may be eligible for financial aid. Tuition for the program is approximately $3,550, plus registration/program fees ($350) and room and board options ($1,598 to $1,718). Rising high school sophomores, juniors, and seniors in the University's Summer Challenge Program learn about college life and take college classes in a noncredit setting. The program lasts two weeks and is offered in three sessions. Students get to choose two seminars (which feature lectures, group and individual work, project-based assignments, and field trips) from a total of eight available programs. Seminar choices include Science, Psychology, Visual Arts, Business, Law, International Politics, Creative Writing, and Persuasive Writing. Students live in dorms on campus and participate in extracurricular activities and tours of local attractions. The cost of the program is approximately $2,550 (which includes tuition, housing, meals, and sponsored activities). Visit the University's Summer Programs Web site for more information.

Boston University Summer Programs

755 Commonwealth Avenue
Boston, MA 02215-1401
617-353-5124
summer@bu.edu
http://www.bu.edu/summer/highschool

The Center for Excellence in Education

Field Experience

The goal of the Center for Excellence in Education (CEE) is to nurture future leaders in science, technology, and business. And it won't cost you a dime: all of CEE's programs are absolutely free. Since 1984, the CEE has sponsored the Research Science Institute, a six-week residential summer program held at Massachusetts Institute of Technology. Seventy-five high school students with scientific and technological promise are chosen from a field of more than 700 applicants to participate in the program, conducting projects with scientists and researchers. You can read more about specific research projects online.

The Center for Excellence in Education
8201 Greensboro Drive, Suite 215
McLean, VA 22102-3813
703-448-9062
cee@cee.org
http://www.cee.org

College and Careers Program
College Course/Summer Study

The Rochester Institute of Technology (RIT) offers its College and Careers Program for rising seniors who want to experience college life and explore career options in science, computing, liberal arts, and other subject areas. The program, founded in 1990, allows you to spend a Friday and Saturday on campus, living in the dorms and attending four sessions on the career areas of your choice. Past science-related sections included Computers in a Science or Pre-Med Track; Medical Ultrasound: Seeing Through Sound; Medical Sciences: Medical Detective—You Make the Call!, Biotechnology/Genetic Engineering: How to Clone a Dinosaur; Bioinformatics: The Human Genome Project; Premedical Studies: So, You Want to Be a Doctor?; and Chemistry: The Wonders of Chemistry. In each session, participants work with RIT students and faculty to gain hands-on experience in the subject area. This residential program is held twice each summer, usually once in mid-July and again in early August. The registration deadline is one week before the start of the program, but space is limited and students are accepted on a first-come, first-served basis. For further information about the program and specific sessions on offer, contact the RIT admissions office.

College and Careers Program
Rochester Institute of Technology
Office of Admissions
60 Lomb Memorial Drive
Rochester, NY 14623-5604
585-475-6631
https://ambassador.rit.edu/careers2006/

Cornell University Summer College
College Courses/Summer Study

As part of its Summer College for High School Students, Cornell University offers two Medicine and Health Professions seminars for high school students who have completed their junior or senior years: Body, Mind, and Health: Perspectives for Future Medical Professionals; and Biological Research and Health Professions. The Summer College session runs for six weeks from late June until early August. It is largely a residential program designed to acquaint you with all aspects of college life. The Medicine and Health Professions seminars are just two of several such seminars offered by Cornell to allow students to survey various disciplines within the field and interact with working professionals. The seminar meets several times per week and includes lectures and field trips to research laboratories, clinicians' offices, and surgery suites. In addition, Summer College participants take college-level courses of their own choosing. You must bear in mind that these are regular undergraduate courses condensed into a very short time span, so they are especially challenging and demanding. Besides the course material, you will learn time management and study skills to prepare you for a program of undergraduate study. The university awards letter grades and full undergraduate credit for the courses you complete. Residents live and eat on campus, and enjoy access to the university's recreational facilities and special activities. Academic fees total around $3,400, while housing, food, and recreation fees amount to an additional $1,600. Books, travel, and an application fee are extra. A very limited amount of financial aid is available. Applications are due in early May, although Cornell advises that you submit them well in advance of the deadline; those applying for financial aid must submit their applications by early April. Further information and details of the application procedure are available from the Summer College office.

Cornell University Summer College for High School Students
Summer College
B20 Day Hall
Ithaca, NY 14853-2801
607-255-6203
http://www.sce.cornell.edu/sc/
explorations/medicine.php

Early Experience Program
College Courses/Summer Study
The University of Denver invites academically gifted high school students interested in science and other subjects to apply for its Early Experience Program, which involves participating in university-level classes during the school year and especially during the summer. This is a commuter-only program. Interested students must submit a completed application (with essay), official high school transcript, standardized test results (PACT/ACT/PSAT/SAT), a letter of recommendation from a counselor or teacher, and have a minimum GPA of 3.0. Contact the Early Experience Program Coordinator for more information, including application forms, available classes, and current fees.

University of Denver
Office of Academic Youth Programs
Early Experience Program
Attn: Pam Campbell, Coordinator
1981 South University Boulevard
Denver, CO 80208
303-871-2663
pcampbe1@du.edu
http://www.du.edu/education/ces/
ee.html

Exploration Summer Programs (ESP)
College Courses/Summer Study
Exploration Summer Programs has been offering academic summer enrichment programs to students for nearly 30 years. Rising high school sophomores, juniors, and seniors can participate in ESP's Senior Program at Yale University. Two three-week residential and day sessions are available and are typically held in June and July. Participants can choose from more than 80 courses in science (such

as anatomy and physiology, biomedical ethics, chemistry, and microbiology) and other areas of study. Students entering the eleventh or twelfth grades can take college seminars, which provide course work that is similar to that of first-year college study. All courses and seminars are ungraded and noncredit. In addition to academics, students participate in extracurricular activities such as tours, sports, concerts, weekend recreational trips, college trips, and discussions of current events and other issues. Tuition for the Residential Senior Program is approximately $4,100 for one session and $7,400 for two sessions. Day-session tuition ranges from approximately $2,100 for one session to $3,795 for two sessions. A limited number of need-based partial and full scholarships are available. Programs are also available for students in grades four through nine. Contact ESP for more information.

Exploration Summer Programs
470 Washington Street
PO Box 368
Norwood, MA 02062-0368
781-762-7400
http://www.explo.org

Frontiers at Worcester Polytechnic Institute

College Courses/Summer Study

Frontiers is an on-campus research and learning experience for high school students who are interested in science, mathematics, and engineering. Areas of study include biology and biotechnology, mathematics, aerospace engineering,

computer science, electrical and computer engineering, mechanical engineering, physics, and robotics. Participants attend classes and do lab work Monday through Friday. Participants also have the opportunity to try out one of five communication modules: creative writing, elements of writing, music, speech, and theatre. In addition to the academic program, you will attend evening workshops, live performances, field trips, movies, and tournaments. Applications are typically available in January and due in March. Tuition is about $2,000; this covers tuition, room, board, linens, transportation, and entrance fees to group activities. A $500 nonrefundable deposit is required. For more information, contact the Program Director.

Worcester Polytechnic Institute
Frontiers Program
100 Institute Road
Worcester, MA 01609-2280
508-831-5286
frontiers@wpi.edu
http://www.admissions.wpi.edu/
    Frontiers

Health Occupations Students of America (HOSA)

Competition, Conference, Membership

HOSA has been working since 1976 "to promote career opportunities in the health care industry and to enhance the delivery of quality health care to all people." It is an integral part of the health occupations curriculum in its member schools. The organization offers a variety of competitions at the state and national levels. Qualifying HOSA participants compete in a variety of skill, leadership, and related events, including CPR/First Aid, Medical Spelling, Medical Math, Medical Terminology, First Aid/Rescue Breathing, Personal Care, Practical Nursing, Nursing Assisting, Speaking Skills, Job Seeking Skills, and Interviewing Skills. HOSA also sponsors an annual National Conference and teams up with a variety of organizations to offer scholarships. To participate in HOSA events, you must work with your school, so speak to a counselor or teacher about your interest in the organization.

Health Occupations Students of America

6021 Morriss Road, Suite 111
Flower Mound, TX 75028-3764
800-321-HOSA
http://www.hosa.org

Intel Science Talent Search
Competition

Since 1942, Science Service has held a nationwide competition for talented high school seniors who plan to pursue careers in medicine, science, engineering, and math. Those who win find themselves in illustrious company: former winners have gone on to win Nobel Prizes, National Medals of Science, and MacArthur Foundation fellowships. High school students in the United States and its territories, as well as American students abroad, are eligible to compete for more than $1 million in scholarships and prizes awarded to participants, including the top one for $100,000. If you'd like to enter next year's competition, contact the Talent Search for more information.

Intel Science Talent Search

1719 N Street NW
Washington, DC 20036-2801
202-785-2255
http://www.sciserv.org/sts

Intern Exchange International Ltd.
Employment and Internship Opportunities

High school students ages 16 to 18 (including graduating seniors) who are interested in gaining real-life experience in medicine can participate in a month-long summer internship in London, England. Participants will work as interns with hospital and clinic staff at St. Thomas' Hospital, St. Bartholomew's Hospital, or Hammersmith Hospital. There is also a veterinary medicine and community services/social services program. The cost of the program is approximately $6,200 plus airfare; this fee includes tuition, housing (students live in residence halls at the University of London), breakfast and dinner daily, housekeeping service, linens and towels, special dinner events, weekend trips and excursions, group activities including scheduled theater, and a Tube Pass. Contact Intern Exchange International for more information.

Intern Exchange International Ltd.

2606 Bridgewood Circle
Boca Raton, FL 33434-4118
561-477-2434

info@internexchange.com
http://www.internexchange.com

Junior Scholars Program at Miami University–Oxford College
Courses/Summer Study

Academically talented high school seniors can earn six to eight semester hours of college credit and learn about university life by participating in the Junior Scholars Program at Miami University–Oxford. Students may choose from more than 40 courses, including Microorganisms and Human Disease, Principles of Human Physiology, and Aging in American Society. In addition to academics, scholars participate in social events, recreational activities, and cocurricular seminars. Program participants live in an air-conditioned residence hall. Fees range from approximately $1,750 to $2,865, depending on the number of credit hours taken and applicant's place of residence (Ohio residents receive a program discount). There is an additional fee of approximately $150 for books. The application deadline is typically in mid-May. Visit the program's Web site for additional eligibility requirements and further details.

Junior Scholars Program at Miami University–Oxford
Robert S. Smith
202 Bachelor Hall
Oxford, OH 45056-3414
513-529-5825
juniorscholars@muohio.edu
http://www.units.muohio.edu/
    jrscholars

Junior Science and Humanities Symposium (JSHS)
Conference

The Junior Science and Humanities Symposium encourages high school students (grades 9 through 12) who are gifted in the sciences, engineering, and mathematics to develop their analytical and creative skills. There are nearly 50 symposia held at locations all around the United States—including Georgetown University, the University of Toledo, and Seattle Pacific University—so that each year some 10,000 students are able to participate. Funded by the U.S. Army Research Office since its inception in 1958 (and by the U.S. Army, Navy, and Air Force since 1995), the JSHS has little to do with the military and everything to do with research. At each individual symposium, researchers and educators from various universities and laboratories meet with the high school students (and some of their teachers) to study new scientific findings, pursue their own interests in the lab, and discuss and debate relevant issues. Participants learn how scientific research can be used to benefit humanity, and they are strongly encouraged to pursue such research in college and as a career. To provide further encouragement, one attendee at each symposium will win a scholarship of about $3,000 and the chance to present his or her own research at the national Junior Science and Humanities Symposium. Finalists from each regional JSHS win all-expense-paid trips to the national symposium, where the top research students can win additional scholarships worth up to $16,000 and trips to the prestigious London International

Youth Sciences Forum. For information about the symposium in your region and for eligibility requirements, contact the national Junior Science and Humanities Symposium.

Junior Science and Humanities Symposium (JSHS)
Academy of Applied Science
24 Warren Street
Concord, NH 03301-4048
603-228-4520
phampton@aas-world.org
http://www.jshs.org

Medcamp
Camps
Arizona high school students in their junior and senior years have the opportunity to attend Medcamp during their summer vacation. The University of Arizona Health Sciences Center (AHSC) has sponsored this free, three-day career camp every July since 1992. High schools around the state nominate one boy and one girl for the program; the nominees may then submit an application and essay, by which the final participants are selected. If you are chosen to attend Medcamp, you will then explore medical careers while living on the University of Arizona campus under the supervision of medical students. During the day, there are classes, laboratory experiences, hospital tours, and opportunities to speak with and watch health care professionals at work. You leave with a better overall understanding of the health care industry and information on specific careers such as nursing, physical and occupational therapy, and pharmacy. If you are interested in attending Medcamp, discuss it with your science teacher, who should receive nomination forms from the AHSC.

Medcamp
University of Arizona Health
  Sciences Center
Office of Public Affairs
1501 North Campbell Avenue,
  PO Box 245095
Tucson, AZ 85724-5095
520-626-7301
riley@u.arizona.edu
http://www.ahsc.arizona.edu/opa/
  medcamp

National Federation of Licensed Practical Nurses (NFLPN)
Membership
The NFLPN is a professional association for licensed practical nurses. Supporters of the federation can apply for membership, which entitles them to subscriptions to organization publications and the opportunity to attend its annual conference, among other benefits. Contact the NFLPN for more information.

National Federation of Licensed Practical Nurses (NFLPN)
605 Poole Drive
Garner, NC 27529-5203
919-779-0046
http://www.nflpn.com

Nursing Camp at Briar Cliff University
Camps
High school juniors and seniors who are considering a career in nursing can learn

more about the field by attending Briar Cliff University's summer nursing camp. Attendees participate in clinical experiences, learn first aid and CPR, job shadow actual nurses, and work closely with Briar Cliff nursing faculty and graduates. Specialty areas of study include emergency room, hospital (medical-surgical), intensive care, labor and delivery, nursery, operating room, pediatrics, and public health. Students who successfully complete the camp earn one hour of college credit. Nursing Camp is held for five days in late June and/or early July. Participants live in a residence hall. Tuition is approximately $265 and covers four nights of lodging, all meals from Monday lunch through Friday lunch, and transportation to clinical experiences and recreational activities. Visit the program's Web site for more information.

Nursing Camp at Briar Cliff University

Dr. Ruth Dankanich Daumer
Chairperson, Department of Nursing
3303 Rebecca Street
Sioux City, IA 51104-2324
800-662-3303, ext. 5458
ruth.daumer@briarcliff.edu
http://www.briarcliff.edu/
    departments/nursing/camp.asp

Nursing Camp at Seattle Pacific University

Camps

High school students who are interested in nursing can attend the Nursing Camp at Seattle Pacific University, a weeklong camp where young people can explore

nursing careers and make new friends in the process. Participants can watch nurses in action, become certified in CPR, learn to take blood pressure and a pulse, and talk with nursing faculty and recent graduates about the field. Specialty areas include emergency room, home health, intensive care, labor and delivery, nursery, pediatrics, and operating room. Students live in residence halls while attending the camp, which is held in late June. Tuition is approximately $595, and includes lodging, all meals from Sunday dinner through Saturday lunch, and transportation to hospital clinicals and recreation activities. Some financial aid is available. The application deadline is typically in late April. Visit the Web site listed below for more information.

Nursing Camp at Seattle Pacific University

School of Health Sciences
3307 Third Avenue West, Suite 106
Seattle, WA 98119-1922
206-281-2233
http://www.spu.edu/nursing/
    nursingcamp

Pre-College Program at Johns Hopkins

College Courses/Summer Study

Johns Hopkins University welcomes academically talented high school students to its summertime Pre-College Program. Participants in this program live on Hopkins' Homewood campus for five weeks beginning in early July. They pursue one of 27 programs leading to college credit; those interested in nursing should strongly consider enrolling in the Biology or the History of Science and Technology Program. Recent courses included Introduction to Biological Molecules, which surveys the important structures and functions of macromolecules involved in biological processes, and Modern Medicine: A Historical Introduction, a scientific and historical look at medicine from the Renaissance to today. Course work is supplemented with presentations by research scientists, laboratory tours, and visits to the famous Johns Hopkins Hospital and Medical School. All participants in the Pre-College Program also attend workshops on college admissions, time management, and diversity. Students who live in the Greater Baltimore area have the option of commuting. Contact the Office of Summer Programs for financial aid information, costs, and deadlines. As of July 1, applicants must be at least 15, have completed their sophomore, junior, or senior year, and have a minimum GPA of 3.0. All applicants must submit an application form, essay, transcript, two recommendations, and a nonrefundable application fee (rates vary by date of submission). For more information, including an application form, contact the Office of Summer Programs.

Pre-College Program

Johns Hopkins University
Wyman Park Building, Suite G4
3400 North Charles Street
Baltimore, MD 21218-2685
800-548-0548
summer@jhu.edu
http://www.jhu.edu/~sumprog/
    pre-college

Science Is Fun! Camp
Camp

The Center for Chemical Education at Miami University of Ohio sponsors a series of Terrific Science Camps each summer. Local third through seventh graders are welcome to attend the Science Is Fun! Camp. It lasts three hours every day for one week during the month of July. As a participant, you explore the fascinating world of science. The cost for this commuter camp is approximately $100, and free tuition is available to students truly in need of financial aid. Admission is made on a first-come, first-served basis, so you should apply well before the deadline in late April. For an application form and more information on this year's camp, contact Terrific Science Programs.

Terrific Science Programs

Kitty Blattner
200 Levey Hall
Miami University Middletown
Middletown, OH 45052-3497
513-727-3318
http://www.units.muohio.edu/
    continuingeducation/summer/
    youth_programs/youth.htmlx

Science Olympiad
Competition

The Science Olympiad is a national competition based in schools. School teams feed into regional and state tournaments, and the winners at the state level go on to the national competition. Some schools have many teams, all of which compete in their state Science Olympiad. Only one team per school, however, is allowed to represent its state at the national contest, and each state gets a slot. There are four divisions of Science Olympiad: Division A1 and A2 for younger students, Division B for grades 6 through 9, and Division C for grades 9 through 12. There is no national competition for Division A.

A school team membership fee must be submitted with a completed membership form 30 days before your regional or state tournament. The fee entitles your school to a copy of the Science Olympiad Coaches and Rules Manual plus the eligibility to have up to 15 students at the first level of your state or regional contest. Fees vary from state to state. The National Science Olympiad is held in a different site every year, and your school team is fully responsible for transportation, lodging, and food.

Specific rules have been developed for each event and must be read carefully. There are numerous different events in each division. You and your teammates can choose the events you want to enter and prepare yourselves accordingly. Winners receive medals, trophies, and some scholarships.

For a list of all Science Olympiad state directors and a membership form, go to the Science Olympiad Web site. You can also write or call the national office for information.

Science Olympiad
National Office
5955 Little Pine Lane
Rochester, MI 48306-2109
248-651-4013
http://www.soinc.org

Secondary Student Training Program (SSTP) Research Participation
College Courses/Summer Study

The University of Iowa invites those who have completed grade 10 or 11 to apply to its Secondary Student Training Program (SSTP). The program allows students to explore a particular area of science or health care—such as microbiology, internal medicine, pathology, pediatrics, or surgery—while experiencing the career field of scientific research. Participants work with university faculty in one of the many laboratories on campus, studying and conducting research projects for approximately 40 hours per week. At the end of the program, which usually runs from late June to early August, you present your project to a formal gathering of faculty, staff, and fellow SSTP participants. Throughout the program you also take part in various seminars on career choices and the scientific profession, and a variety of recreational activities designed especially for SSTP participants. Students live in University of Iowa dormitories and use many of the facilities on campus. The admissions process is highly competitive and is based on an essay, transcript, and recommendations. Those who complete the program have the option of receiving college credit from the University of Iowa. Applications are due by mid-March, and applicants will be notified of the decisions by mid-May. Tuition fees, room, and board generally total around $2,000; spending money and transportation to and from the university are not included. Financial aid is available. For an application form, financial aid information, and to discuss possible research projects, contact the Secondary Student Training Program.

Summer Programs
Opportunity at Iowa
University of Iowa
224 Jessup Hall
Iowa City, IA 52242-1316
800-553-4692, ext. 5-3876
william-swain@uiowa.edu
http://www.uiowa.edu/~provost/oi/sstp

SkillsUSA
Competitions
SkillsUSA offers "local, state and national competitions in which students demonstrate occupational and leadership skills." Students who participate in its SkillsUSA Championships can compete in categories such as Basic Health Care Skills, First Aid/CPR, Health Knowledge Bowl, Health Occupations Professional Portfolio, Nurse Assisting, and Practical Nursing. SkillsUSA works directly with high schools and colleges, so ask your guidance counselor or teacher if it is an option for you. Visit the SkillsUSA Web site for more information.

SkillsUSA
PO Box 3000
Leesburg, VA 20177-0300
703-777-8810
http://www.skillsusa.org/

Smith Summer Science and Engineering Program at Smith College
College Courses/Summer Study
Female high school students who are interested in careers in medicine, science, or engineering can participate in Smith College's Science and Engineering Program. Students in this month-long residential program take either two two-week-long research courses or one four-week-long research course. Recent courses included Biology, Chemistry, Women's Health, Astronomy, Engineering, the Mathematics of Cryptography, and Writing. Participants give two oral presentations about their work, one at the midpoint of the program and one at the conclusion of the program. In their free time, students participate in a variety of extracurricular activities, such as sports, nature walks, movie nights, museum tours, and cultural activities. For more information on the program, contact the Director of Educational Outreach.

Smith Summer Science and Engineering Program
Smith College
Director of Educational Outreach
Clark Hall
Northampton, MA 01060-6301
413-585-3060
gscordil@smith.edu
http://www.smith.edu/
   summerprograms/ssep

Summer at Delphi
College Courses/Summer Study
Whether you're trying to catch up or get ahead on a course, Summer at Delphi may offer the opportunity you need. The Delphian School is a private, nonsectarian day and residential school for students ages 5 to 17, but its summer session is open to students (boarding school ages 8 to 18; day

school ages 5 to 18) from other schools around the country. Delphi adheres to the educational philosophy of L. Ron Hubbard, who created innovative study methods and emphasized the responsibility of the individual for his or her own academic success. Many of the courses offered for high school students during Summer at Delphi are perfectly suited for those considering a nursing career; recent classes included Anatomy and Physiology, Basic First Aid, Cell Biology, Chemistry, the Circulatory System, Dissecting, and Nutrition & Exercise. You can also work on such fundamentals as algebra and composition. Each course curriculum is personally tailored to your needs, so you are not held back or left behind by other students. All students, however, participate in computer training, service projects, and various trips and activities. You may enroll as a day or resident student.

Contact The Delphian School for program costs and dates, to discuss its educational philosophy, and to determine if it is right for you.

Summer at Delphi

The Delphian School
20950 SW Rock Creek Road
Sheridan, OR 97378-9740
800-626-6610
summer@delphian.org
http://www.summeratdelphi.org

Summer College for High School Students at Syracuse University
College Courses/Summer Study

The Syracuse University Summer College for High School Students features a Liberal Arts/Arts & Sciences Program for those who have just completed their sophomore, junior, or senior year. The Summer College lasts six weeks and offers a residential option so participants can experience campus life while still in high school. The program has several aims: to introduce you to the many possible majors and study areas within this general area; to help you match your aptitudes with possible careers; and to prepare you for college, both academically and socially. Students attend classes, listen to lectures, and take field trips to destinations that are related to their specific area of interest. All students are required to take two courses during the program and receive college credit if they successfully complete the courses. Admission is competitive and is based on recommendations, test scores, and transcripts. The total cost of the residential program is about $5,300; the commuter option costs about $3,800. Some scholarships are available. The application deadline is in mid-May, or mid-April for those seeking financial aid. For further information, contact the Summer College.

Syracuse University Summer College for High School Students

111 Waverly Avenue, Suite 240
Syracuse, NY 13244-2320
315-443-5297
sumcoll@syr.edu
http://summercollege.syr.edu

Summer Program for Secondary School Program at Harvard University
College Courses/Summer Study

High school students who have completed their sophomore, junior, or senior year may apply to Harvard's Summer Program for Secondary School Program. Students who live on campus take either two four-unit courses or one eight-unit course for college credit. Commuting students may take only one four-unit course for college credit. Recent science-related courses included Introductory Biology, Principles of Genetics, Introduction to Immunology, General Chemistry, and Organic Chemistry. In addition to academics, students can participate in extracurricular activities such as intramural sports, a trivia bowl, a talent show, and dances. Tuition for the program ranges from $2,125 (per four-unit course) to $4,250 (per eight-unit course). A nonrefundable registration fee ($50), health insurance ($110), and room and board ($3,725) are extra. The application deadline for this program is mid-June. Contact the program for more information.

Harvard University

Summer Program for Secondary
　School Program
51 Brattle Street
Cambridge, MA 02138-3701
617-495-4024
http://www.summer.harvard.
　edu/2005/programs/ssp.jsp

Summer Scholars Program at Birmingham-Southern College
College Courses/Summer Study

Rising high school seniors in Birmingham-Southern College's Summer Scholars Program can take two courses in science, humanities, social sciences, art, mathematics, philosophy, or religion for college credit. In addition to the classes, students take field trips to the Civil Rights Institute and other cultural and natural destinations. Accepted students receive a full tuition scholarship to participate in the program; textbooks, room, meals, and an activity fee (totaling approximately $1,325) are extra. At the conclusion of the nearly three-week program, three Summer Scholars will be awarded scholarships worth as much as $8,000 over four years at Birmingham-Southern College. The scholarships will be awarded based on the participant's grades in the two classes and their participation in extracurricular activities. To apply, students must submit an application, an official high school transcript, a recommendation from their guidance counselor, and PLAN, PSAT, ACT, or SAT scores. For more information, visit the Summer Scholars Web site.

Summer Scholars Program

c/o Program Coordinator
Birmingham-Southern College
900 Arkadelphia Road
Birmingham, AL 35254-0002
800-523-5793
dmdriski@panther.bsc.edu
http://www.bsc.edu/admission/
　summer/summerscholar.htm

Summer Scholars Program at Wright State University (WSU)
College Courses/Summer Study

If you are a rising junior or senior who is considering a nursing career, you can participate in WSU's Summer Scholars Program, where you can take up to eight credit hours of college-level course work. Past courses included Biology, Chemistry, Communications, Computer Science,

Economics, English, French, Geology, German, History, and Mathematics. Students are required to pay half of the total tuition; the Summer Scholars Program pays for the other half. Two one-month sessions and one two-month session are available. The application deadline is typically in April. Contact the WSU Office of Pre-College Programs for more information.

Wright State University
Office of Pre-College Programs
120 Millett Hall
3640 Colonel Glenn Highway
Dayton, OH 45435-0001
937-775-3135
precollege@wright.edu
http://www.wright.edu/academics/
  precollege

Summer Study at Penn State
College Courses/Summer Study

High school students who are interested in science and other fields can apply to participate in Penn State's Summer Study programs. The six-and-a-half-week College Credit Program begins in late June and recently offered the following science-related classes: Introduction To Biobehavioral Health, Human Body: Form And Function, Genetics, Ecology & Evolution, Structure and Functions of Organisms, Introduction to Health Services Organization, Intro to Human Development and Family Studies, Infant and Child Development, Adolescent Development, and Introductory Principles of Nutrition. Students typically choose one college credit course (for three or four credits) and

either an enrichment class/workshop or the Kaplan SAT prep class. Students who have completed the 10th, 11th, and 12th grades are eligible to apply. The three-and-a-half-week Non-Credit Enrichment Program is held in early July and recently featured science-related classes such as Paging Dr. (Your Name Here): Careers & Trends in Healthcare and Beauty and the Beast: Health and Wellness. Students who have completed the 9th, 10th, and 11th grades are eligible for the program. Tuition for the College Credit Program is approximately $6,000, while tuition for the Non-Credit Enrichment Program is approximately $4,000. Limited financial aid is available. Contact the program for more information.

Penn State University
Summer Study Program
900 Walt Whitman Road
Melville, NY 11747
800-666-2556
info@summerstudy.com
http://www.summerstudy.com/
  pennstate

Summer Youth Programs
College Courses/Summer Study

Michigan Technological University offers the Summer Youth Program for students in grades 6 through 11. Participants attend one of four weeklong sessions usually held during the months of July or August, choosing either to commute or to live on campus. Students undertake an "exploration" in one of many career fields—including science—through field trips and discussions with MTU faculty and other professionals. Science classes recently offered included Chemistry, Clinical Laboratory Sciences, Genetic Engineering, Medical Physiology, and Microbiology. The cost of the Summer Youth Program is approximately $510 for the residential option, $300 for commuters. Applications are accepted up to one week before the program begins.

Summer Youth Program
Michigan Technological University
Youth Programs Office, Alumni
  House
1400 Townsend Drive
Houghton, MI 49931-1295
906-487-2219
http://youthprograms.mtu.edu

Women in the Sciences and Engineering (WISE) Week
Camp

The Pennsylvania State University (Penn State) offers a Women in the Sciences and Engineering (WISE) Week program in June for female rising juniors and seniors. Participants are academically talented with strong math and science skills, headed for college, and considering career paths in health, science, and engineering. Students apply to one WISE option, either Sciences or Engineering. Competition is considerable as only 36 young women are accepted into each option. Accommodation is in a campus residence hall with collegiate women as your supervisors. The cost of the program is about $350, which covers everything except transportation to and from Penn State's University Park Campus; a limited number

of need-based scholarships are available. A completed application form, one letter of recommendation, an essay, any recent standardized test scores, and a current high school transcript must be submitted by the beginning of April. Members of minority groups and students with physical disabilities are strongly encouraged to apply. For further information about WISE Week and the application process, contact the program.

**Women in the Sciences and
Engineering (WISE) Week**
Women in the Sciences
  &Engineering (WISE) Institute
319 Boucke Building
University Park, PA 16802
814-865-3342
nap2@psu.edu
http://www.equity.psu.edu/wise/
  wisecamp.asp

Young Scholars Program: Biology
College Courses/Summer Study

The Young Scholars Program is sponsored by the University of Maryland for motivated juniors and seniors. Participants in the three-week program spend July exploring the field of biology and taking a college-level course. College credit is awarded to students who satisfactorily complete the course. Participants live in the residence halls at the University of Maryland and take their meals on campus or in selected College Park restaurants. To apply, you must submit an application form, an essay, two letters of recommendation, a current transcript, and an application fee of $50 by mid-May. Admissions decisions are based primarily on the recommendations, a GPA of 3.0 or better, and overall academic ability. For further details (including information on cost of tuition) and an application form, visit the Web site below or contact the Summer Sessions and Special Programs staff.

Summer Sessions and Special Programs

Mitchell Building, 1st Floor
University of Maryland
College Park, MD 20742
877-989-7762
http://www.summer.umd.edu/
   youngscholars

Read A Book

When it comes to finding out about nursing, don't overlook books. (You're reading one now, after all.) What follows is a short, annotated list of books and periodicals related to nursing. The books range from fiction to personal accounts of what it's like to be a nurse, to professional volumes on specific topics, such as death and dying and dealing with doctors. Don't be afraid to check out the professional nursing journals, either. The technical stuff may be way above your head right now, but if you take the time to become familiar with one or two, you're bound to pick up some of what is important to nurses, not to mention begin to feel like a part of their world, which is what you're interested in, right?

We've tried to include recent materials as well as old favorites. Always check for the most recent editions, and, if you find an author you like, ask your librarian to help you find more. Keep reading good books!

❏ BOOKS

Anderson, Peggy. *Nurse.* New York: Berkley Books, 1990. A major best-selling account of the life of Mary Benjamin, RN. A remarkable and entertaining book about the life of a nurse—her thoughts and feelings, daily duties, and life-and-death experiences.

Barnum, Barbara Stevens. *Spirituality in Nursing: From Traditional to New Age.* New York: Springer, 2003. Gives a thorough and accessible overview of spirituality, cast as a component of nursing theory and practice. Addresses such major nursing issues as healing, religion, ethics, disease, and death.

Belkin, Lisa. *First, Do No Harm.* New York: Fawcett Books, 1994. An absorbing novel by a former *New York Times* correspondent about the inner workings of Hermann Hospital in Houston, Texas. Examines many profound and complicated questions about life and death.

Billings, Diane McGovern, and Judith A. Halstead. *Teaching in Nursing: A Guide for Faculty.* 2nd ed. Philadelphia: W. B. Saunders, 2004. Winner of the AJN Book of the Year award, this is a great resource for nurses interested in a teaching career. Covers important teaching tools necessary to be a nurse educator.

Boyer, Mary Jo, and Elaine Dreisbaugh. *Math for Nurses: A Pocket Guide to Dosage Calculation and Drug Preparation.* 5th ed. Philadelphia: Lippincott Williams & Wilkins, 2002. Step-by-step math guide for calculating drug dosages. Includes a handy card that features basic equivalents and conversions.

Burkhardt, Margaret A., and Alvita K. Nathaniel. *Ethics And Issues In Contemporary Nursing.* 2nd ed. Stamford, Conn.: Thomson Delmar Learning, 2001. This book covers ethical issues in the nursing professions, and gives models on how to make these important decisions.

Canfield, Jack, Mark Victor Hansen, Mary Mitchell-Autio, and LeAnn Thieman. *Chicken Soup for the Nurse's Soul: 101 Stories to Celebrate, Honor and Inspire the Nursing Profession.* Deerfield Beach, Fla.: HCI, 2001. An inspiring and entertaining collection of short stories celebrating nurses and their heroic work.

Cardillo, Donna. *Your First Year as a Nurse: Making the Transition from Total Novice to Successful Professional.* Three Rivers, Minn.: Three Rivers Press, 2001. Survival tips on how to succeed as a nurse. Much of this author's research is based on actual interviews with both new and seasoned nurses in the United States and Canada.

Catalano, Joseph T. *Nursing Now: Today's Issues, Tomorrow's Trends.* 3rd ed. Philadelphia: F. A. Davis, 2002. Discusses models of nursing, ethical dilemmas, cultural diversity, leadership, as well as other issues important to the field of nursing.

Cox, Helen C., Mittie D. Hinz, Mary Ann Lubno, and Susan Newfield (eds.). *Clinical Applications of Nursing Diagnosis: Adult, Child, Women's, Psychiatric, Gerontic, and Home Health Considerations.* 4th ed. Philadelphia: F.A. Davis, 2002. A standard text for nursing patient-assessment, which discusses a wide range of health patterns and complications and examines the role of the nurse in each case.

Craven, Ruth F., and Constance J. Hirnle. *Fundamentals of Nursing: Human Health and Function.* 2nd ed. Philadelphia: Lippincott Williams & Wilkins, 2004. The consummate textbook for the first nursing course. Provides colorful, well-written, and thorough coverage of all basic nursing concepts, theory, and skills.

Croft, Jennifer. *Careers in Midwifery.* New York: Rosen, 1995. An overview of the history of midwifery, the categories of certification and training, birth settings, and career planning. Addresses midwives versus traditional heath care debate.

Davis, Anne J., Mila A. Arosker, and Joan Liaschensko. *Ethical Dilemmas and Nursing Practice.* Upper Saddle River, N.J.: Prentice Hall, 1997. A broad discussion of health care ethics and an outline of selected ethical approaches of nursing practice. A useful account of the moral dilemmas nurses typically face, from abortion to mental illness.

Dossey, Barbara Montgomery, Lynn Keegan, and Cathie E. Guzzetta. *Holistic Nursing: A Handbook for Practice.* 4th ed. Sudbury, Mass.: Jones and Bartlett, 2005. Describes the many ways in which nurses can complement traditional medical techniques with such alternative healing procedures as therapeutic touch, massage, guided imagery, and music.

Douglas, Ellen, and Elizabeth Spencer. *Apostles of Light: A Novel.* Jackson, Miss.: Banner Books, 1994. A novel about nursing home patients in the Southern United States and the nurses who care for them.

Eliopoulos, Charlotte. *Gerontological Nursing.* 5th ed. Philadelphia: Lippincott Williams & Wilkins, 2000. An accessible and comprehensive basic gerontology text, focusing on health promotion and self-care. Clear, concise, and practically oriented, this text is the perfect guide to understanding and meeting the challenges of providing services to elderly patients in a variety of settings.

Ellis, Rosemary. *Selected Writings of Rosemary Ellis: In Search of the Meaning of Nursing Science.* New York: Springer, 1996. A wonderful collection of writings by one of nursing's most penetrating thinkers and treasured scholars. Written with clarity, grace, and wit, this is an invaluable resource to nurse researchers, theorists, educators, and students.

Felice-Farese, Susan J., ed. *Poetic Expressions in Nursing . . . Sharing the Caring.* Long Branch, N.J.: Vista, 1994. A unique collection of poetry relating to the nursing profession.

Frederickson, Keville. *Opportunities in Nursing Careers.* 2nd ed. New York: McGraw-Hill, 2003. Offers good vocational guidance for a variety of nursing careers, exploring the financial benefits of each.

Friedman, Marilyn M. *Family Nursing: Research, Theory, and Practice.* 4th ed. Upper Saddle River, N.J.: Prentice Hall, 2002. A thorough survey of the educational requirements, procedures, and vicissitudes of family nursing.

Galanti, Geri-Ann. *Caring for Patients from Different Cultures: Case Studies from American Hospitals.* 3rd ed. Philadelphia: University of Pennsylvania Press, 2003. Collection of case studies that illustrate how to avoid cross-cultural misunderstandings in the nursing workplace.

Hegner, Barbara, Barbara Acello, and Esther Caldwell. *Nursing Assistant: A Nursing Process Approach.* 9th ed. Stamford, Conn.: Thomson Delmar Learning, 2003. Covers important knowledge and skills needed by nursing assistants. Also includes a step-by-step guide to more than 160 common procedures.

Iyer, Patricia W. *Legal Nurse Consulting: Principles and Practices.* 2nd ed. Boca Raton, Fla.: CRC Press, 2002. An important reference to the growing field of legal nurse consulting. Gives practical information for the many practice opportunities for legal nurse consultants.

Katz, Janet R., Carol J. Carter, Joyce Bishop, and Sarah Lyman Kravits. *Keys to Nursing Success.* 2nd ed. Upper Saddle River, N.J.: Prentice Hall, 2003. Gives students insight and advice for a career as a nurse.

Kuhse, Helga. *Caring: Nurses, Women, and Ethics.* Boston: Blackwell, 1997. Discusses the often troubled relations between nurses and physicians, nursing ethics, and the nursing environment.

Leonard, Peggy C. *Building a Medical Vocabulary.* 5th ed. St. Louis: Mosby, 2003. Excellent guide to the language of health care. Teaches the fundamental word parts that are used as the "building blocks" of more complicated terminology.

McKinney, Anne. *Real-Resumes for Nursing Jobs: Including Real Resumes Used to Change Careers and Resumes Used to Gain Federal Employment.* Fayetteville, N.C.: Prep, 2003. This book gives tips on how to create a winning résumé— perfect for new grads or those interested in crossing over to other health care fields. Also includes examples of actual résumés and helpful information on obtaining federal government jobs.

Novotny, Jeanne M., Doris T. Lippman, Nicole K. Sanders, and Joyce J. Fitzpatrick, eds. *101 Careers in Nursing.* New York: Springer, 2003. This book gives a quick overview of 101 different nursing careers, as well as their education requirements and compensation ranges. Also includes a chapter on career searches and certification.

Perry, Anne Griffin, and Patricia A. Potter. *Clinical Nursing Skills and Techniques.* St. Louis: Mosby, 2003. An introductory text outlining the fundamental skills and knowledge of nursing, from bathing patients to recognizing vital signs.

Peterson, Veronica. *Just the Facts: A Pocket Guide to Nursing.* St. Louis: Mosby, 2002. A quick and easy reference for beginning nursing students, filled with charts, graphs, outlines, and easy-to-read tables.

Peterson's. *Peterson's Nursing Programs 2005.* 10th ed. Lawrenceville, N.J.: Peterson's, 2004. Profiles more than 2,000 undergraduate, graduate, and postdoctoral programs at more than 700 institutions in the United States and Canada.

Potter, Patricia A., and Anne Griffin Perry. *Fundamentals of Nursing.* 6th ed. St. Louis: Mosby, 2004. An important resource for nursing students that includes care plans and a CD-ROM supplement.

Rosenberg, Charles E. *The Care of Strangers: The Rise of America's Hospital System.* Baltimore: Johns Hopkins University Press, 1995. An engaging and informative history of the hospital system, from the time of Thomas Jefferson to the mid-1990s.

Smith, Sandra F., Donna Duell, and Barbara Martin. *Clinical Nursing Skills: Basic to Advanced.* 6th ed. Upper Saddle River, N.J.: Prentice Hall, 2003. This textbook is written for all levels of nursing, from new to advanced. Offers 650 new and updated skills as well as a chapter on bioterrorism.

Sorrentino, Sheila A., and Bernie Gorek. *Mosby's Essentials for Nursing Assistants.* 2nd ed. St. Louis: Mosby, 2001. Covers the fundamental skills needed to be a nursing assistant. This edition includes more than 500 color illustrations.

Sparks, Sheila M., and Cynthia M. Taylor. *Nursing Diagnosis Reference Manual.* 5th ed. Philadelphia: Lippincott Williams & Wilkins, 2001. Important guide for creating care plans—from pediatric to geriatric.

Springhouse. *Critical Care Nursing Made Incredibly Easy!* Philadelphia: Lippincott Williams & Wilkins, 2003. Illustrated, detailed book on almost 100 critical care disorders. This book also reviews steps on common nursing procedures such as interpreting results, dispensing medicine, and nursing intervention.

———. *Illustrated Handbook of Nursing Care.* Philadelphia: Lippincott Williams & Wilkins, 1998. Addresses every key nursing topic, and contains more than 500 illustrations along with charts and sample documentation forms. A comprehensive guide to the ins and outs of the nursing process.

———. *Maternal-Neonatal Nursing Made Incredibly Easy!* Los Angeles: Springhouse, 2003. Covers all aspects of maternal-neonatal nursing. CD-ROM supplement includes quizzes, exam review, and NCLEX preparation tips.

———. *Medical-Surgical Nursing Made Incredibly Easy!* Los Angeles: Springhouse, 2003. A great book for medical-surgical nursing students, including those reviewing for NCLEX exams. Includes discussion of more than 300 disorders, with quizzes, illustrations, tables, and other study guides.

———. *Nursing 2005 Drug Handbook.* 25th ed. Philadelphia: Lippincott Williams & Wilkins, 2004. Includes information on newly approved drugs, their effectiveness, interactions with other medicines, and length of effectiveness. Also features a chapter that covers Spanish-English drug translations, cross-references, and a companion mini CD.

———. *1,001 Nursing Tips & Timesavers.* 3d ed. Philadelphia: Lippincott Williams & Wilkins, 1997. Covers everything a nurse would need to know, from AIDS to computers to home health care. Includes appendices of most essential information for easy reference.

———. *Pediatric Nursing Made Incredibly Easy!* Philadelphia: Lippincott Williams & Wilkins, 2000. Covers growth and development of children. Includes step-by-step procedure instructions, quizzes, and study guides.

———. *Psychiatric Nursing Made Incredibly Easy!* Los Angeles: Springhouse, 2003. Covers more than 70 psychiatric conditions, including their diagnosis and different treatment options.

Sullivan, Eleanor J., and Phillip J. Decker. *Effective Leadership and Management in Nursing.* Upper Saddle River, N.J.: Pearson Education, 2000. Discusses nursing services, nurse administrators, nursing care, and nursing leadership. Useful and comprehensive.

Swick, Sandra, and Corrine Grimes. *Barron's How to Prepare for the Nursing School Entrance Exams.* 2nd ed. Hauppauge, N.Y.: Barron's Educational Series, 2004. Provides a great review for the exam. Gives subject reviews and a full-length model test.

Thibeault, Stephanie. *Stressed Out About Nursing School! An Insider's Guide to Success.* Orlando, Fla.: Bandido Books, 2001. What to expect before, during, and after, nursing school—all from a student's point of view.

Vallano, Annette. *Your Career In Nursing: Manage Your Future in the Changing World of Healthcare.* New York: Kaplan, 2003. This book is important reading for those interested in career mobility within the nursing field. Special chapters address the career environment for male nurses, as well as second career nurses.

Weishapple, Cynthia. *Introduction to Legal Nurse Consulting.* Stamford, Conn.: Thomson Delmar Learning, 2000. Important resource for nurses considering a career in legal consulting. Includes career profiles and advice from successful legal nurse consultants.

❑ PERIODICALS

Advance for LPNs. Published biweekly in print and online versions by Merion Publications, 2900 Horizon Drive, King of Prussia, PA 19406-2651, 800-355-5627. Provides information on issues of interest to licensed practical nurses, book reviews, job listings, and career advice. Visit http://lpn.advance-web.com to read sample articles.

Advance for Nurse Practitioners. Published monthly by Merion Publications, 2900 Horizon Drive, King of Prussia, PA 19406-2651, 800-355-5627. Provides information on clinical issues, industry developments, jobs, and salaries. View sample articles at http://www.advancefornp.com.

American Journal of Critical Care. Published bimonthly by the American Association of Critical-Care Nurses, PO Box 611, Holmes, PA 19043-9873, 800-345-8112, ajcc@aacn.org, http://ccn.aacnjournals.org. Offers clinical studies, research studies, case reports, reports on new apparatus and techniques, reviews, and guest editorials.

American Journal of Nursing. Published monthly by Lippincott Williams & Wilkins, PO Box 1620, Hagerstown, MD 21741-1620, 800-638-3030, http://www.lww.com. An important and influential magazine, containing compelling articles and editorials, photo essays, and medical essays.

The American Nurse. Published bimonthly by the American Nurses Association, 8515 Georgia Avenue, Suite 400, Silver Spring, MD 20910 800-637-0323, http://www.nursing-world.org/tan. Covers a wide variety of topics that are important to nurses in the United States, including nursing shortages and practice issues. A student discount is available to subscribers.

Critical Care Nurse. Published bimonthly by the American Association of Critical-Care Nurses, PO Box 611, Holmes, PA 19043-9873, 800-345-8112, ccn@aacn.org, http://ccn.aacn-journals.org. Seeks to provide critical care nurses with information about the bedside care of critically and acutely ill patients, as well as practice issues.

Home Healthcare Nurse. Published monthly by Lippincott Williams & Wilkins, PO Box 1620, Hagerstown, MD 21741, 800-638-3030, http://www.homehealthcarenurseonline.com. Probably the most thorough journal of home health care nursing, providing strategies for assessing the health of homebound patients, and also for dealing with terminal illness, depression, and death.

Journal of Legal Nurse Consulting. Published quarterly by the American Association of Legal Nurse Consultants, 401 North Michigan Avenue, Chicago, IL 60611, jlnc@aalnc.org, http://www.aalnc.org/edupro/journal.cfm. Offers a variety of articles about medical-legal issues, including managed care, medical and products liability issues, life care planning, and forensics, as well as business advice and networking hints.

Journal of Neuroscience Nursing. Published bimonthly by the American Association of Neuroscience Nurses, 4700 West Lake Avenue, Glenview, IL 60025-1485, http://www.aann.org/journal. One of only two journals in the world specializing in neuroscience nursing; written and reviewed by practicing nurses.

Journal of Obstetric, Gynecologic and Neonatal Nursing. Published bimonthly (on behalf of the Association of Women's Health, Obstetric and Neonatal Nurses) by Sage Science Press, 2455 Teller Road, Thousand Oaks, CA 91320, 800-818-7243, http://jognn.awhonn.org. Features articles about the latest advances in childbearing, infant development, maternal psychology, labor technique, and much more.

The Journal of Practical Nursing. Published quarterly by the National Association for Practical Nurse Education and Service, PO Box 25647, Alexandria, VA 22313-5647, http://www.napnes.org/journal.htm. Offers feature articles, editorials, educational and scholarship information, and features on licensed practical nurses.

Journal of Nursing Education. Published monthly by Slack Incorporated, 6900 Grove Road, Thorofare, NJ 08086-9447, 856-848-1000, customerservice@slackinc.com, http://www.journalofnursingeducation.com. Offers original articles and ideas for nursing educators.

Journal of the American Academy of Nurse Practitioners. Published by Blackwell, 350 Main Street, Malden, MA 02148-5020, 800-835-6770, subscrip@bos.blackwellpublishing.com, http://www.blackwellpublishing.com. The official publication of the academy, this monthly journal offers peer-reviewed articles on clinical practice, health policy, clinical management, and other issues of interest to nurse practitioners.

Medical-Surgical Nursing Journal. Published monthly by Anthony J. Jannetti, East Holly Avenue, Box 56, Pitman, NJ 08071-0056, 856-256-2300, http://www.ajj.com/services/pblshng/msnj. The official journal of the Academy of Medical-Surgical Nurses, it provides readers with useful, multidisciplinary information about providing clinically excellent patient care in various surgical settings.

Midwifery Today Magazine. Published quarterly by Midwifery Today, PO Box 2672, Eugene, OR 97402-0223, 800-743-0974, inquiries@midwiferytoday.

com, http://www.midwiferytoday. com/magazine. Offers articles about issues that are important to nurse-midwives, including multiple births, home birth, water birth, birth and disability, prenatal and postpartum care, and midwifery education.

Nurse Educator. Published bimonthly by Lippincott Williams & Wilkins, PO Box 1620, Hagerstown, MD 21741-1620, 800-638-3030, http://www. nurseeducatoronline.com. Discusses many issues of mentorship and professional role development in undergraduate and graduate nursing education. Offers a sense of what nursing educators look for in their students and peers.

NurseWeek. Published weekly by Nurse-Week Publishing, 6860 Santa Teresa Boulevard, San Jose, CA 95119-1205, 800-859-2091, ce@nursingspectrum. com. Offers interesting articles about practice issues for nurses, including job sharing, diversity, pain management, and medical developments. View sample articles at http://www. nurseweek.com/news/features.asp.

Nursing History Review. Published annually by Springer, 536 Broadway, New York, NY 10012-9904, 212-431-4370, contactus@springerpub.com, http:// www.aahn.org/nhr.html. Official journal of the American Association for the History of Nursing. Contains essays, editorials, articles, and reviews about nursing methods, theories, and movements.

Nursing Spectrum. Published online (http://www.nursingspectrum.com)

by Nursing Spectrum. Features a variety of interesting articles written by experienced nurses. Topics include practice issues, nursing careers, jobs, education, certification, and financial aid. Print issues on special topics are also available.

Nursing Standard Online. Updated weekly at http://www.nursing-standard.co.uk. Offers numerous interesting articles and abstracts from the most recent issue of *Nursing Standard*, a prominent British nursing journal.

Online Journal of Issues in Nursing. Published by the Kent State University College of Nursing and the American Nurses Association, available at http:// nursingworld.org/ojin. An excellent forum for discussing and learning about pertinent issues in nursing.

Plastic Surgical Nursing Journal. Published by the American Association of Plastic Surgical Nurses, 7794 Grow Drive, Pensacola, FL 32514, http:// www.aspsn.org. Offers information on continuing education, updates on current techniques, and information on new tools and products for plastic surgical nurses.

Practical Nursing Journal. Published quarterly by the National Federation of Licensed Practical Nurses, 605 Poole Drive, Garner, NC 27529-5203, http://www.nflpn.org. Includes articles about professional and personal issues for licensed practical nurses, health industry trends, careers, and continuing education.

RN. Published monthly by Advanstar Communications, Five Paragon Drive,

Montvale, NJ 07645-1742, 800-284-8945, RNMagazine@advanstar.com, http://www.rnweb.com/rnweb. The content of this publication is geared toward RNs working in hospital-affiliated facilities. Approximately 80 percent of the articles focus on clinical issues. Other subjects that are covered include legal issues, ethical questions, and career development.

The Student Journal of Nurse Anesthesia. Published quarterly by the American Association of Nurse Anesthetists, 222 South Prospect Avenue, Park Ridge, IL 60068-4001, http://www.aana.com. Offers case reports and abstracts about nurse anesthesia issues authored by graduate nursing students. It is distributed free of charge to all student members of the association.

Surf The Web

You must use the Internet to do research, to find out, to explore. Short of an "all nursing, all the time" channel on TV, the Internet is the closest you'll get to what's happening now all over the place. This chapter gets you started with an annotated list of Web sites related to nursing. Try a few. Follow the links. Maybe even venture as far as asking questions in a chat room. The more you read about and interact with nursing and nurses, the better prepared you'll be when you're old enough to participate as a professional.

One caveat: you probably already know that URLs change all the time. If a Web address listed below is out of date, try searching on the site's name or other key words. Chances are, if it's still out there, you'll find it. If it's not, maybe you'll find something better!

❏ THE LIST
American Association of Colleges of Nurses (AACN)
http://www.aacn.nche.edu

The AACN describes itself as the national voice for nursing education programs, and at a first glimpse this site may seem too academic. But delve into the right sections, and you'll see that it contains some precious nuggets for students con-sidering a future in nursing. In fact, one of this site's most useful tools is specifically aimed at nurses-to-be. Under a section called "Nursing Education," you'll find a lengthy, informative article that debunks some misconceptions about the field and explores the changing job market. There's also a financial aid fact sheet and a directory of AACN's more than 500 member schools.

This extremely well-organized site also includes a schedule of upcoming confer-ences and seminars. If academics is your thing, go ahead and read AACN's newslet-ter and other related publications online. The emphasis is on government affairs and college accreditation, however, top-ics that will probably be of more interest to the professional nurse.

American Red Cross
http://www.redcross.org

The Red Cross is mentioned several times in the "Get Involved" section for its blood drives, CPR and First Aid courses, and the training it provides to young people who want to educate others about various health and safety issues. At the ARC Link section if of its Web site, you'll find all of these options and many more explained in detail. There is a helpful little feature that allows you to type in your zip code and get contact information for the Red

Cross office nearest you, so you can get involved right away.

This site, which is both extensive and easy to use, also gives you an interesting history lesson via its Red Cross Museum, and puts you in touch with other humanitarian organizations that share this organization's commitment to helping others. The American Red Cross has been an integral part of the country's health and safety efforts since 1881—it has a lot to offer you as you explore the field of nursing, and its Web site deserves a look.

Association of Perioperative Registered Nurses (AORN)

http://www.aorn.org

At this well-designed, frequently updated Web site, you'll learn about the responsibilities of perioperative registered nurses and also find clear descriptions of various specialties in the field such as scrub nurse, circulating nurse, RN first assistant, and patient educator. But this site isn't for nurses only. The AORN sees itself as an advocate for patients, and they've developed a section called "Surgery Center: A Patient's Place" (http://www.aorn.org/ PATIENT), an incredibly user-friendly resource of patient-centered information relating to surgery and the surgical process. If someone among your family or friends is preparing for a surgery, point him or her here for excellent information that one might not easily find elsewhere.

As the professional organization for perioperative nurses, the AORN has more than 350 chapters in all 50 states and throughout the world. Student nurses can join for a reduced rate to be eligible for scholarships and grants and to receive the usual member perks. The site also offers several certification programs and exam reviews online.

Children's Hospital of Denver Association of Volunteers

http://www.thechildrenshospital.org/ public/helpkids/volunteer

While you can find plenty of hospitals with volunteer programs on the Web, the Children's Hospital of Denver, profiled in "Get Involved," stands out for its user-friendly home page and for the longevity and success of its program.

This site provides some background on the association, which boasts almost 1,900 volunteers who log over 160,000 hours of service a year. The volunteers work in various capacities: holding and comforting infants, offering support to parents, bringing specially trained dogs to provide animal-assisted therapy, and raising funds for a respite garden. For many of the younger volunteers (the youngest is 13), this volunteer work is a way to "test-drive" a future career in nursing or medicine. If you've been doing volunteer work for a local hospital—or would like to—this site might strike a chord.

Cybernurse.com

http://www.cybernurse.com

Founded by two nurses who also shared an interest in the Internet, Cybernurses is a fun site to visit. Not only can you find a list of accredited nursing programs nationwide—with links to many of them—but you can also find "educational moolah" via state and federal links to nursing loans and grants. Basic information is given regarding NCLEX review and testing, as well as links to job postings and nurse recruiters. Do you want a real view of the real world of nursing? Visit the Cybernurse Forum, where nurses dish it out regarding everything from the state of the profession today to the latest nurse joke. Don't forget to check out the history of "capping," complete with photos of early nurse uniforms and caps.

Discover Nursing

http://www.discovernursing.com

Get the who, what, why, and how about nursing from this Web site, which is sponsored by Johnson & Johnson Health Care Systems. Sections are headed as such and are full of useful information—all of which is well organized and accessible. In "Who," you can find profiles ranging from students to nurses with disabilities to males working in a female-dominated field. Links to specific interest organizations and books are also given. Are you still seeking a good nursing program, or perhaps unsure of how you will pay for your education? "How" can help you find scholarships or other funding choices, as well as narrow your search for the perfect nursing program. Especially useful is the Web site's listing of programs with available enrollment. Not only is Discover Nursing a great Web site for students, but second-career nurses and foreign-educated nurses will also find this site useful.

ExceptionalNurse.com

http://www.exceptionalnurse.com

This is a clearinghouse of information for nurses who have disabilities. The Web site offers a discussion board, details on scholarships, useful articles, and a wealth of other information that will be of use to nurses with disabilities.

GradSchools.com: Nursing Graduate School Directory

http://www.gradschools.com/ programs/nursing.html

This site, while somewhat rough around the edges, offers listings of nursing graduate schools searchable by state. You can use the map of the United States to narrow your school search. Listings include program info, degrees offered, school Web sites, and e-mail contacts.

HealthWeb: Nursing

http://healthweb.org/browse. cfm?subjectid=60

An impressive, collaborative effort of the Taubman Medical Library, the School of Nursing at the University of Michigan, and the HealthWeb project, this site is a heavyweight of nursing information.

Under the mantle of Career Resources, you can link to the *Occupational Outlook Handbook* in its entirety, or (if you're a rational person) just click on the nursing sections already plucked out for you, such as working conditions, employment, training, job outlook, earnings, and related occupations. You might be encouraged to read here that employment of registered nurses is expected to grow rapidly through 2014, with many of the new jobs in home health and hospital outpatient facilities.

In the Communication section, you'll find information and e-mail addresses for a number of online nursing discussion groups. If there's a particular field of nursing that piques your interest, the specialized discussion groups are a good place to gain insight into the field. The Education section has online links to international and U.S. nursing schools. Other pages will link you to nursing school newsletters and journals. If you're the kind of person who believes there's no such thing as too much information, you'll love this site.

How Stuff Works: How Emergency Rooms Work
http://people.howstuffworks.com/
emergency-room.htm

This site should also be on your short list of Web sites to explore, as it covers how "stuff," as varied and timely as tsunamis to identity theft, works. Complex concepts are carefully broken down and examined, including photos and links to current and past news items about the subject. This particular subsite of "How It Works" provides information about the inner workings of emergency rooms through detailed descriptions and photographs of emergency rooms, tools of the trade (such as stethoscopes, cardiac monitors, and suture trays), and types of workers, including emergency nurses. Best yet, the articles are written by emergency room physicians, so you're guaranteed an expert look at this sometimes confusing and scary world of emergency care.

Human Anatomy Online
http://www.innerbody.com/htm/
body.html

Whether you need a little help in your anatomy class or just want to do some exploring on your own, this site offers an interesting way to explore the systems of the human body. You have your choice of 10 systems: cardiovascular, digestive, endocrine, female reproductive, lymphatic, male reproductive, muscle, nervous, skeletal, and urinary.

Every image in every system features points on which you can click to see the name of a selected body part. Click again for a definition or description of that part. Some animation showing the parts in action is also available. This site is simple and straightforward enough for users with little background in human anatomy.

Imagine
http://www.jhu.edu/~gifted/imagine

Imagine is a bimonthly journal for the go-getter high school student with his or her eye on the future. Its tag line, "Opportunities and resources for academically talented youth," says it all.

If you're always searching for good academic programs, competitions, and internships, this publication can keep you well informed on what's available and when you need to apply. There's an entertaining College Review series in which student contributors evaluate individual colleges and universities and also a Career Options series featuring interviews with professionals.

Along with the current issue, selected portions of back issues can be read online.

Previous issues have included articles about the health and medical sciences, as well as general tips on entering academic competitions and choosing summer academic programs. For $25 a year, you can subscribe and get the printed journal delivered to your home—or for free, you can just read selected articles online.

Kaplan's Guide to Nursing and the NCLEX
http://www.kaplan.com

A commercial enterprise sponsored by Kaplan Educational Centers, this site provides some interesting information for students entering the nursing field. A great deal of the section under "Nursing" is written for students who have already earned a bachelor's degree in nursing and are preparing to take the NCLEX exam, the standardized test that evaluates for competency to practice nursing. The site offers helpful information about the NCLEX, and gives sample questions in the Strategy Sessions section. Also, in the Careers section you'll find information about using a nursing degree as a stepping-stone to advanced career paths such as nurse administrator, nurse attorney, or nurse clinician. Though you're probably still mulling over how to get through nursing school, it never hurts to plan ahead.

Men in Nursing
http://www.geocities.com/Athens/
    Forum/6011

Don't make the mistake of thinking nursing is just for women. According to this site, the world's first nursing school was in India in 250 B.C., and at that time, only men were considered "pure" enough to become nurses.

History buffs and equal opportunity enthusiasts will find some fascinating tidbits here, ranging from details about the Byzantine empire to an account of Juan de Mena, the first nurse in what was to become the United States. The table of contents is helpful when researching a particular time period. The information is presented mostly as text with some photos at the end of each section. Last updated in 1997, a new and expanded version of the site is currently under construction.

If you're intrigued by the history of nursing, this site certainly merits a visit. Even those of you who are more interested in the here and now will find modern-day factual data here, as well as contact information for the American Assembly for Men in Nursing.

My Future
http://www.myfuture.com

You want to become a nurse, but perhaps a four-year college just isn't in the cards for you. This colorful site aims to help new high school graduates "jumpstart their lives" with information about alternatives to four-year colleges, such as military opportunities and technical or vocational colleges. In the hefty military career database, you'll find dozens of job descriptions for positions such as nurse, medical care technician, physician assistant, registered nurse, and pharmacist.

While the site is divided into four main sections—Military Opportunities, Money

Matters, Beyond High School, and Career Toolbox—most of the useful stuff is in the Career section. For instance, in this section, you can learn about the hottest jobs, writing strong cover letters, or how to ace that interview. You can also take a career interest quiz to find out if you have a realistic, investigative, artistic, social, enterprising, or conventional work personality.

You'll find some good info in the Money section. In "Living On Your Own," you can learn how to set a budget and live within your means. Or visit the section called "Searching for Dollars" to get a handle on the financial aid process.

National Student Nurses' Association
http://www.nsna.org

This organization's mission is to represent and mentor nursing students, and its Web site does just that. The Career Center will assist young students, as well as older, second-career students via essays such as "Is Nursing For You?" and "Juggling Nursing School and Family." Looking for that first job is made easier with the site's listing of available internships, hospitals, and health care agencies grouped by region or magnet status. The Web site also lists available scholarship information and applications in its Foundation section.

Net Frog: The On-Line Dissection
http://curry.edschool.Virginia.EDU/go/frog

Dissect a frog online? If you've got the amphibian, a scalpel, and an Internet connection, you're ready. With color photographs and downloadable QuickTime movies, this Web site just might conjure up the aroma of formaldehyde.

The site was designed to provide a step-by-step interactive tutorial for use in high school biology classrooms. It can also be used as a preparation tool or as a substitute for an actual laboratory dissection. The complete dissection is divided into Introduction, Preparation, Skin Incisions, Muscle Incisions, and Internal Organs sections. In each section, procedures for dissection are clearly described and presented in photographs.

The creators of this site invite your feedback to make it even better. Anybody interested in anatomy will want to check it out, as will students who are thinking of authoring their own tutorial Web site.

Nurse.com
http://www.nurse.com

This Web site is pretty straightforward and easy to navigate, with the usual nurse forums and discussion boards, the latest news regarding the health care industry and first-person stories. Check out the Career section, which features a monthly profile of a specific type of nursing professional. This is a great way to learn the different specialties available in the nursing industry. Also in the Career section are job profiles of positions currently open. Hospitals nationwide are also detailed. It should be noted that most, if not all, jobs and hospitals featured in this section are part of the Tenet Services, Inc. network, which maintains and operates the Web site.

The Nursefriendly
http://jocularity.com

It takes a certain kind of person to be tickled by jokes about bodily functions. According to this site, it takes a nurse.

The Web edition of this quarterly journal for nurses is filled with satire, true stories, and cartoons written, illustrated, edited, and published entirely by nurses. And with more than 100 well-organized, easy-to-navigate online pages, you probably won't run out of laughs.

Since much of the humor at this site is derived from making fun of stressful nursing situations, you'll get a pretty accurate idea of what things stress nurses out. Recent feature articles included "The Nurse's Bladder" and "How to Irritate a Nurse." You'll also find a section devoted to true stories of student nurses in the trenches. And here's a new tongue twister that you'll see at the site—psychoneuroimmunology. Basically, what the word means is that laughing is good for your health.

Some of this humor definitely has a "you needed to be there" flavor, but it does reveal a refreshingly silly side of health care.

NurseWeek
http://www.nurseweek.com

NurseWeek, an online magazine, operates like a professional clipping service for nurses. At its home page, you can read today's medical and nursing news. Recent headlines, for example, featured a research campaign to prevent premature births, the growing shortage of nursing school instructors, and the benefits of dark chocolate. Continuing education opportunities and career fairs worldwide are also listed.

This is a comprehensive, appealing, and eclectic read for those in the nursing or health care field. One of *NurseWeek*'s regular features is an online survey where you can simply answer "yes" or "no" or submit a full letter to the editor. In subsequent editions of the magazines, readers can see the survey results online. *NurseWeek* also publishes lengthier articles about the nursing profession, and recently, a special career guide for student nurses. Students can also use this site to learn about the job market, as well as to create and post their résumés online.

And what Web site would be complete without links to other Web sites? That's right, *NurseWeek* offers many links to other nursing resources—such as education, jobs, and nursing supplies.

NursingWorld
http://www.nursingworld.org

NursingWorld, sponsored by the American Nurses Association, promises "nursing's future at your fingertips." That's a tall order, and this behemoth site doesn't always live up to it. While there's a ton of information to be found here, much of it is devoted to member information for affiliate organizations—among them the American Academy of Nursing, the American Nurses Credentialing Center, and the American Nurses Foundation.

One of the most lively sections of NursingWorld is the *Online Journal of Issues in Nursing*, published in partnership with

Kent State University's School of Nursing. A recent article dealt with the issue of nurses' safety in the workplace.

Visit NursingWorld's NursingInsider for timely health care news. NursingWorld also has a smattering of information about ethnic minority fellowships, international nursing, and legislative news. And once you're in nursing school, you'll find the searchable reading and reference rooms extremely useful.

Peterson's Education Portal
http://www.petersons.com

This site offers anything you want to know about surviving high school, getting into college, and choosing a graduate degree. Specific to nursing, check out the College and Graduate School sections, which offer school directories searchable by keyword, degree, location, tuition, size, GPA, and even sports offered. While this site is not devoted solely to nursing education, it is worth a visit for its comprehensiveness; school listings offer the usual basics plus details on financial aid, school facilities, student government, faculty, and admissions requirements.

The Pfizer Guide to Careers in Nursing
http://www.pfizercareerguides.com/default.asp?t=book&b=nursing

http://www.pfizercareerguide.com/pdfs/nursing.pdf

Nursing students will definitely be interested in this career guide prepared by the pharmaceutical giant, Pfizer. It starts with a career planning chapter, complete with résumé tips and "words of wisdom." The best part of this guide is the "Practice Areas" chapter on 31 nursing specialties. Told through the eyes of a nurse practicing in each specific specialty, you can really get a feel of what it takes, for example, to be an ER nurse, forensic nurse, or military nurse. Each article ends with a Fast Fact section that details education and certification requirements, necessary skills, and possible employment paths. This guide also devotes a chapter to the Associate Degree of Nursing (ADN), explaining some of the benefits of choosing this shorter educational path, and providing a list of possible practice areas open to nurses holding an ADN. Be warned that this guide is presented in a Portable Document Format and may be a little tedious to navigate.

The Princeton Review
http://www.princetonreview.com/home.asp

This site is everything you want in a high school guidance counselor—it's friendly, well informed, and available to you night and day. Originally a standardized test preparation company, The Princeton Review is now online, giving you frank advice on colleges, careers, and of course, SATs.

Students who've spent their summers and after-school hours volunteering at a clinic or hospital will find good tips here on how to present those extracurricular activities on college application forms. If you're looking for contact with other students who are weighing their options, too, link to one of the discussion groups on college admissions and careers.

Two of the Princeton Review's coolest tools are the Career Quiz, which creates a list of possible careers based on your interests and work style, and the Counselor-O-Matic, which reviews your grades, test scores, and extracurricular record to calculate your chances of admission at many colleges. Also helpful is the list of schools offering online programs and degrees. Get a heads up on the competition by checking out the site's Summer Program section, specifically geared toward high school students, which lists summer internships, camps, and enrichment programs.

U.S. News & World Report: America's Best Colleges

http://www.usnews.com/usnews/
    edu/college/majors/majors_index_
    brief.php

Use this free online service to search schools by national ranking, location, name, or major. (The link above will allow you to search by major.) The Health Professions and Related Clinical Sciences subsection alone lists hundreds of schools that offer nursing programs, and each school link includes contact information and details about services and facilities, campus life, mission, and extracurricular activities. Note: In order to read the full account information about each school, you must either buy the print publication or pay for the Premium Online Edition.

Yahoo!: Nursing

http://dir.yahoo.com/health/nursing

It might seem odd to include the popular search engine Yahoo! among a list of nursing Web sites, but it won't seem so after you've visited it. If you're hungry for more after visiting the sites listed in this section, pull up a chair at Yahoo!'s feast.

Yahoo! has done a tremendous amount of legwork for you. For example, if you're interested in nursing education, you can surf to one of the more than 200 sites currently included here. There are approximately 20 sites for nurse practitioners, 15 sites for nurse anesthetists, and nine sites for forensic nurses. In addition to sites about nursing education and specialties, you'll also find links to nursing events, journals, and magazines.

Ask For Money

By the time most students get around to thinking about applying for scholarships, they have already extolled their personal and academic virtues to such lengths in essays and interviews for college applications that even their own grandmothers wouldn't recognize them. The thought of filling out yet another application form fills students with dread. And why bother? Won't the same five or six kids who have been fighting over grade point averages since the fifth grade walk away with all the really good scholarships?

The truth is, most of the scholarships available to high school and college students are being offered because an organization wants to promote interest in a particular field, to encourage more students to become qualified to enter it, and finally, to help those students afford an education. Certainly, having a good grade point average is a valuable asset, and many organizations that grant scholarships request that only applicants with a minimum grade point average apply. More often than not, however, grade point averages aren't even mentioned; the focus is on the area of interest and what a student has done to distinguish him- or herself in that area. In fact, frequently the only requirement is that the scholarship applicant must be studying in a particular area.

❏ GUIDELINES

When applying for scholarships there are a few simple guidelines that can help ease the process considerably.

Plan Ahead

The absolute worst thing you can do is wait until the last minute. For one thing, obtaining recommendations or other supporting data in time to meet an application deadline is incredibly difficult. For another, no one does his or her best thinking or writing under the gun. So get off to a good start by reviewing scholarship applications as early as possible—months, even a year, in advance. If the current scholarship information isn't available, ask for a copy of last year's version. Once you have the scholarship information or application in hand, give it a thorough read. Try and determine how your experience or situation best fits into the scholarship, or even if it fits at all. Don't waste your time applying for a scholarship in literature if you couldn't finish *Great Expectations*.

If possible, research the award or scholarship, including past recipients and, where applicable, the person in whose name the scholarship is offered. Often, scholarships are established to memorialize an individual who was a religious studies major or who loved history, but in other cases, the scholarship is to memorialize the work of an individual. In those cases, try and get a feel for the spirit of the person's work. If you have any similar interests or experiences, don't hesitate to mention these.

Talk to others who received the scholarship, or to students currently studying in the same area or field of interest in which the scholarship is offered, and try to gain insight into possible applications or work related to that field. After doing your homework in this way, you'll have real answers when working on the essay about why you want this scholarship—"I would benefit from receiving this scholarship because studying geriatric nursing will help me learn about the special needs of the elderly, especially regarding dementia."

Take your time writing the essays. Make certain you are answering the question or questions on the application and not merely restating facts about yourself. Don't be afraid to get creative; try to imagine what you would think of if you had to sift through hundreds of applications: What would you want to know about the candidate? What would convince you that someone was deserving of the scholarship? Work through several drafts and have someone whose advice you respect—a parent, teacher, or guidance counselor—review the essay for grammar and content.

Finally, if you know in advance which scholarships you want to apply for, there might still be time to stack the deck in your favor by getting an internship, volunteering, or working part time. Bottom line: The more you know about a scholarship and the sooner you learn it, the better.

Follow Directions

Think of it this way—many of the organizations that offer scholarships devote 99.9 percent of their time to something other than the scholarship for which you are applying. Don't make a nuisance of yourself by pestering them for information. Follow the directions on an application, even when asking for additional materials. If the scholarship information specifies that you write for more information, write for it—don't call.

Pay close attention to whether you're applying for an award, a scholarship, a prize, or financial aid. Often these words are used interchangeably, but just as often they have different meanings. An award is usually given for something you have done: built a park or helped distribute meals to the elderly; or something you have created: a design, an essay, a short film, a screenplay, an invention. On the other hand, a scholarship is frequently a renewable sum of money that is given to a person to help defray the costs of college. Scholarships are given to candidates who meet the necessary criteria based on essays, eligibility, or grades, and sometimes all three.

Supply all the necessary documents, information, and fees, and meet the deadlines. You won't win any scholarships by forgetting to include a recommendation from your history teacher or failing to postmark the application by the deadline. Bottom line: Get it right the first time, on time.

Apply Early

Once you have the application in hand, don't dawdle. If you've requested it far enough in advance, there shouldn't be any reason for you not to submit it well in advance of the deadline. You never know, if it comes down to two candidates, the deciding factor just might be who was more on the ball. Bottom line: Don't wait, don't hesitate.

Be Yourself

Don't make promises you can't keep. There are plenty of hefty scholarships available, but if they all require you to study something that you don't enjoy, you'll be miserable in college. And the side effects from switching majors after you've accepted a scholarship could be even worse. Bottom line: Be yourself.

Don't Limit Yourself

There are many sources for scholarships, beginning with your guidance counselor and ending with the Internet. All of the search engines have education categories. Start there and search by keywords, such as "financial aid," "scholarship," "award." Don't be limited to the scholarships listed in these pages.

If you know of an organization related to or involved with the field of your choice, write a letter asking if they offer scholarships. If they don't offer scholarships, don't let that stop you. Write them another letter, or better yet, schedule a meeting with the president or someone in the public relations office and ask them if they would be willing to sponsor a scholarship for you. Of course, you'll need to prepare yourself well for such a meeting because you're selling a priceless commodity—yourself. Don't be shy, be confident. Tell them all about yourself, what you want to study and why, and let them know what you would be willing to do in exchange—volunteer at their favorite charity, write up reports on your progress in school, or work part time during school breaks or full time during the summer. Explain why you're a wise investment. Bottom line: The sky's the limit.

❏ THE LIST

Air Force ROTC

Scholarship Actions Branch
551 East Maxwell Boulevard
Maxwell AFB, AL 36112-5917
866-423-7682
http://www.afrotc.com

The Air Force ROTC provides a wide range of four-year scholarships (ranging to partial or full tuition) to high school students planning to study nursing or other majors in college. Scholarships are also available to college and enlisted students. Visit the Air Force ROTC Web site to apply.

Alpha Tau Delta

Scholarship Chair
11252 Camarillo Street
Toluca Lake, CA 91602-1259
http://www.atdnursing.org

Alpha Tau Delta is a national fraternity for professional nurses. Undergraduate and graduate members of an Alpha Tau Delta chapter are eligible for grants to help finance nursing training. Applicants must have strong academic records and demonstrate financial need. Amounts vary; contact ATD for more information.

American Academy of Nurse Practitioners Foundation Scholarship and Grant Program

PO Box 10729
Glendale, AZ 85318-0729
623-376-9467
foundation@aanp.org
http://www.aanpfoundation.org

The foundation offers a variety of scholarships and grants to undergraduate and graduate nurse practitioner students. Contact the foundation for more information.

American Assembly for Men in Nursing Foundation

Attn: Jim Raper, DSN, CFNP, JD.
1108 Fern Street
Birmingham, AL 35209-7010
jimraper@aamn.org
http://www.aamn.org/
    aamnfoundationscholarships.htm

The foundation, in cooperation with Johnson & Johnson's Campaign for Nursing's Future, offers $1,000 scholarships to male students who are currently enrolled in nursing education programs. Applicants must have a GPA of at least 2.75 and submit an essay that answers the following questions: Why do you want to be a nurse? How might you contribute to the nursing profession as a nurse? What are your current career plans? Visit the foundation's Web site to download an application.

American Association of Colleges of Nursing (AACN)

CampusRN/AACN Scholarship Fund
1 Dupont Circle NW, Suite 530
Washington, DC 20036-1135
202-463-6930
http://www.aacn.nche.edu/
    Education/financialaid.htm

The association awards six $2,500 scholarships to students who are seeking baccalaureate, master's, or doctoral degrees in nursing. Preference will be given to students who are enrolled in a master's or doctoral program and plan to pursue a nursing faculty career; completing an RN-to-baccalaureate program; or enrolled in an accelerated baccalaureate or master's degree nursing program. Contact the AACN for more information.

American Association of Critical-Care Nurses (AACN)

Attn: Scholarships
101 Columbia
Aliso Viejo, CA 92656-4109
800-899-2226
info@aacn.org
http://www.aacn.org/AACN/Memship.
    nsf/vwdoc/mainawards

Educational Advancement Scholarships of $1,500 annually are open to current members or those enrolled full or part time in a nursing education program. Applicants must be in their junior year of college and have at least one year of experience working in a critical care unit. Twenty percent of the awards will be allocated to qualified ethnic minority applicants. Visit the association's Web site for more information and to apply online.

American Association of Neuroscience Nurses

Neuroscience Nursing Foundation
4700 West Lake Avenue
Glenview, IL 60025-1468
888-557-2266
info@aann.org
http://www.aann.org/nnf

The foundation offers a $1,500 annual award to registered nurses who are pursuing studies to advance a career in neuroscience nursing at the undergraduate or graduate level. Contact the foundation for more information.

American Association of Nurse Anesthetists (AANA) Foundation

Student Scholarship Application
Attn: Mary Collins
222 South Prospect Avenue
Park Ridge, IL 60068-4001
http://www.aana.com/foundation/
    applications

Students who are currently studying to become nurse anesthetists at an accredited program can apply for a variety of scholarships ranging from $1,000 to $5,000 from the foundation and affiliated organizations. Applicants must be AANA members and have completed a specific level of coursework depending on their grade level. Visit the foundation's Web site for more information.

American Health Care Association (AHCA)

1201 L Street NW
Washington, DC 20005
202-898-9352

http://www.ahca.org/about/
    scholarship.htm

Applicants who work at a long-term-care facility that is a member of the AHCA or the National Center for Assisted Living and are enrolled in or accepted to an accredited LPN or RN school of nursing program may be eligible for Durante Nurse Scholarships. Contact the association for more information.

American Holistic Nurses' Association (AHNA)

PO Box 2130
Flagstaff, AZ 86003-2130
800-278-2462
info@ahna.org
http://www.ahna.org

The Charlotte McGuire Scholarship is offered to nurses undertaking a holistic nursing program; applicants must be members of the AHNA for at least six months and have a minimum 3.0 GPA. The amount of the award varies; contact the association for more information.

American Indian Science and Engineering Society (AISES)

PO Box 9828
Albuquerque, NM 87119-9828
505-765-1052
http://www.aises.org/highered/
    scholarships

The AISES offers a variety of scholarships to Native American students at the undergraduate and graduate levels. Applicants must be student members. Contact the society for more information and to download applications.

American Legion Auxiliary

777 North Meridian Street, 3rd Floor
Indianapolis, IN 46204
317-955-3845
alahq@legion-aux.org
http://www.legion-aux.org/
    scholarships/index.aspx

Various state auxiliaries of the American Legion offer scholarships to help students prepare for nursing careers. Most require that candidates be associated with the organization in some way, whether as a child, spouse, etc., of a military veteran. Interested students should contact the American Legion Auxiliary for further information.

American Psychiatric Nurses Association

1555 Wilson Boulevard, Suite 515
Arlington, VA 22209-2429
703-243-2443
inform@apna.org
http://www.apna.org/foundation/
    scholarships.html

The association offers scholarships to students who are currently studying psychiatric nursing. Visit its Web site for more information.

Army ROTC

800-USA-ROTC
http://www.goarmy.com/rotc/
    scholarships.jsp

Students planning to or currently pursuing a bachelor's degree in nursing may apply for scholarships that pay tuition and some living expenses; recipients must agree to accept a commission and serve in the army on Active Duty or in a Reserve Component (U.S. Army Reserve or Army National Guard).

Association of Perioperative Registered Nurses (AORN)

2170 South Parker Road, Suite 300
Denver, CO 80231-5711
800-755-2676, ext. 328
ibendzsa@aorn.org
http://www.aorn.org/foundation/
    scholarships.asp

Undergraduate, graduate, and doctoral students who are active or associate members of the association are eligible for scholarships covering tuition and fees. Guidelines vary by scholarship; contact the AORN for further details.

Association on American Indian Affairs

Scholarship Coordinator
966 Hungerford Drive, Suite 12B
Rockville, MD 20850-1743
240-314-7155
general.aaia@verizon.net
http://www.indian-affairs.org

Undergraduate and graduate Native American students who are pursuing a wide variety of college majors (including nursing) can apply for several different scholarships ranging from $500 to $1,500. All applicants must provide proof of Native American heritage. Visit the association's Web site for more information.

Business and Professional Women's Foundation

1900 M Street NW, Suite 310
Washington, DC 20036-3554

202-293-1100

http://www.bpwusa.org

The foundation's Career Advancement Scholarship Program awards scholarships to women in health-related professions. Applicants must be at least 25 years old, accepted by or attending an accredited university program, plan to graduate within 12 to 24 months of the awarding of the grant, demonstrate financial need, and be U.S. citizens. Visit the foundation's Web site for deadlines and to download an application.

Chi Eta Phi Sorority

3029 13th Street NW

Washington, DC 20009-5303

202-232-3858

chietaphi@erols.com

http://www.chietaphi.com/scholar. html

The sorority offers scholarships to minority students currently enrolled in a program of study leading to the baccalaureate, master's, or doctoral degree in an accredited school of nursing. Visit its Web site for further details.

Collegeboard.com

http://apps.collegeboard.com/ cbsearch_ss/welcome.jsp

This testing service (PSAT, SAT, etc.) offers scholarship search engines that feature scholarships in various fields worth more than $3 billion. You can search by specific major and a variety of other criteria.

CollegeNET

http://mach25.collegenet.com/cgi-bin/M25/index

CollegeNET features 600,000 scholarships (not all nursing related) worth more than $1.6 billion. You can search by keyword (such as "nursing") or by creating a personality profile of your interests.

Daughters of the American Revolution (DAR)

Scholarship Committee

1776 D Street NW

Washington, DC 20006-5303

202-628-1776

http://www.dar.org

Caroline Holt Nursing Scholarships are available to students who have been accepted or who are currently enrolled in a nursing program in the United States. Selection criteria include academic standing, financial need, and letters of recommendation; applicants need not be affiliated with DAR. The Mildred Nutting Nursing Scholarship is also available; preference for this scholarships will be given to candidates from the Greater Lowell, Massachusetts, area. Contact DAR for more information.

Discover Nursing

http://www.discovernursing.com/ scholarship_search.aspx

This Web site, sponsored by Johnson & Johnson, offers a nursing scholarship search engine (as well as extensive career information). You can search by scholarship, keyword, state GPA, ethnicity, and grade level.

Emergency Nurses Association

915 Lee Street

Des Plaines, IL 60016-6569

800-900-9659, ext. 4100
foundation@ena.org
http://www.ena.org/foundation/
    grants

The association offers scholarships ranging from $2,000 to $10,000 to undergraduate and graduate students who are currently enrolled in nursing programs. Visit its Web site to download an application.

ExceptionalNurse.com
Scholarship Committee
13019 Coastal Circle
Palm Beach Gardens, FL 33410-1344
http://www.exceptionalnurse.com/
    scholarship.html

Nursing students with disabilities may apply for scholarships of $250 or $500. Preference is given to undergraduates. Visit ExceptionalNurse.com to download an application.

FastWeb
http://fastweb.monster.com

FastWeb is one of the largest scholarship search engines around. It features 600,000 scholarships (not all nursing related) worth more than $1 billion. To use this resource, you will need to register (free).

Foundation for the Carolinas
PO Box 34769
Charlotte, NC 28234-4769
704-973-4500
infor@fftc.org
http://www.fftc.org

The foundation administers more than 70 scholarship funds that offer awards to undergraduate and graduate students pursuing study in nursing and other disciplines. Visit its Web site for a searchable list of awards.

Golden Key International Honor Society
PO Box 23737
Nashville, TN 37202-3737
800-377-2401
http://www.goldenkey.org

Golden Key is an academic honor society that offers its members "opportunities for individual growth through leadership, career development, networking, and service." It awards more than $400,000 in scholarships annually through 17 different award programs. Membership in the society is selective; only the top 15 percent of college juniors and seniors—who may be pursuing education in any college major—are considered for membership by the organization. There is a onetime membership fee of $60 to $65. Contact the society for more information.

GuaranteedScholarships.com
http://www.guaranteed-scholarships.
    com

This Web site offers lists (by college) of scholarships, grants, and financial aid (not all nursing related) that "require no interview, essay, portfolio, audition, competition, or other secondary requirement."

Hawaii Community Foundation
1164 Bishop Street, Suite 800
Honolulu, HI 968132817
scholarships@hcf-hawaii.org
http://www.
    hawaiicommunityfoundation.
    org/scholar/scholar.php

The foundation offers a variety of scholarships for high school seniors and college students planning to study or currently studying nursing and other majors in college. Applicants must be residents of Hawaii, demonstrate financial need, and plan to attend a two- or four-year college. Visit the foundation's Web site for more information and to apply online.

Health Occupations Students of America (HOSA)

6021 Morriss Road, Suite 111
Flower Mound, TX 75028-3764
800-321-HOSA
http://www.hosa.org

HOSA works with schools "to promote career opportunities in the health care industry and to enhance the delivery of quality health care to all people." It teams up with the following organizations to offer more than $40,000 in scholarships to students interested in health care careers: Delmar, Hobsons, Hospital Corporation of America, Kaiser Permanente Healthcare, National Honor Roll, National Technical Honor Society, Nursing Spectrum, and Who's Who Among American High School Students. Contact HOSA for more information.

Health Resources and Services Administration (HRSA)

U.S. Department of Health and
    Human Services
Nursing Scholarship Program
Parklawn Building
5600 Fishers Lane
Rockville, MD 20857

http://bhpr.hrsa.gov/nursing/
    scholarship

The HRSA's Nursing Scholarship Program pays tuition, required fees, reasonable costs, and a monthly stipend to applicants who are willing, upon graduation, to serve two years at a health care facility that has a critical shortage of nurses. Applicants must be U.S. citizens or nationals and be accepted or enrolled as full- or part-time students in an accredited school of nursing in a professional registered nurse program (baccalaureate, graduate, associate degree, or diploma). Registered nurses preparing for teaching careers also are eligible for scholarships toward graduate study. Apply through the attending institution. Contact the HRSA for more information.

Illinois Career Resource Network

http://www.ilworkinfo.com/icrn.htm

Created by the Illinois Department of Employment Security, this useful site offers a great scholarship search engine, as well as detailed information on careers (including nursing). You can search for nursing scholarships based on specialty. This site is available to everyone, not just Illinois residents; you can get a password by simply visiting the site. The Illinois Career Information System is just one example of sites created by state departments of employment security (or departments of labor) to assist students with financial- and career-related issues. After checking out this site, visit your state's department of labor Web site to see what they offer.

International Order of the King's Daughters and Sons

Health Careers Scholarship
   Department
PO Box 1040
Chautauqua, NY 14722-1040
http://www.iokds.org

Health Careers Scholarships of up to $1,000 are awarded to students who have completed at least one year of study in nursing, medicine, dentistry, pharmacy, physical or occupational therapy, and medical technologies. Applicants must be U.S. or Canadian citizens and enrolled full time in an accredited institution. Contact the International Order for deadlines and more information.

John D. Archbold Memorial Hospital

Education and Training Department
PO Box 1018
Thomasville, GA 31799-1018
229-228-2795
http://www.archbold.org/AboutUs/
   scholarships.htm

Scholarships are available to students who are planning to study or are currently studying nursing, physical therapy, or another health field; recipients must agree to work for up to three years at the hospital following graduation. Contact the hospital's Education and Training Department for more information.

March of Dimes

Office of Fellowships and Awards
1275 Mamaroneck Avenue
White Plains, NY 10605-5201
202-659-1800
profedu@marchofdimes.com
http://www.marchofdimes.com

Registered nurses who are enrolled in graduate programs of maternal-child nursing are eligible to apply for several $5,000 scholarships. Visit the organization's Web site to learn more and download an application.

Marine Corps Scholarship Foundation

PO Box 3008
Princeton, NJ 08543-3008
800-292-7777
mcsf@marine-scholars.org
http://www.mcsf.com/site/
   c.ivKVLaMTIuG/b.1677655/k.BEA8/
   Home.htm

The foundation helps children of marines and former marines with scholarships of up to $5,000 for study in nursing and other health fields. To be eligible, you must be a high school graduate or registered as an undergraduate student at an accredited college or vocational/technical institute. Additionally, your total family gross income may not exceed $61,000. Contact the foundation for further details.

Maryland Higher Education Commission

Maryland State Nursing Scholarship
839 Bestgate Road, Suite 400
Annapolis, MD 21401-3013
800-974-1024
http://www.mhec.state.md.us/
   financialAid/ProgramDescriptions/
   prog_nurse.asp

High school seniors and undergraduate and graduate students who are Maryland residents and planning to pursue or currently pursuing nursing education can apply for $3,000 Maryland State Nursing Scholarships. Applicants must have a GPA of at least 3.0, enroll or be enrolled at a two-year or four-year Maryland college or university, and agree to serve as a full-time nurse in an eligible Maryland health care organization one year for each year of aid received. Visit the commission's Web site to download an application.

National Alaska Native American Indian Nurses Association (NANAINA)

Attn: Dr. Better Keltner, NANAINA Treasurer
3700 Reservoir Road NW
Washington, DC 20057-1107
888-566-8773
http://www.nanainanurses.org/Main_Pages/scholarships.html

Undergraduate and graduate students who are currently enrolled in a nursing program are eligible to apply for Merit Awards of $750. Applicants must be enrolled in a U.S. federally or state-recognized tribe, members of the NANAINA, and full-time students. Visit the association's Web site to download an application.

National Association of Hispanic Nurses (NAHN)

NAHN Awards and Scholarship Committee Chair
1501 16th Street NW
Washington, DC 20036-1401
202-387-2477
info@thehispanicnurses.org
http://www.thehispanicnurses.org

Hispanic nursing students who are currently enrolled in a nursing program may apply for $1,000 National Scholarship Awards. Applicants must be members of the association, have a GPA of at least 3.0, demonstrate financial need, and show potential for leadership in nursing. Visit the NAHN's Web site to download an application.

National Association of School Nurses (NASN)

PO Box 1300
Scarborough, ME 04070-1300
877-627-6476
nasn@nasn.org
http://www.nasn.org/Default.aspx?tabid=71

The association awards two $1,500 scholarships to members who are registered nurses who are interested in pursuing education beyond a bachelor's degree. Visit its Web site to download an application.

National Black Nurses Association (NBNA)

8630 Fenton Street, Suite 330
Silver Spring, MD 20910-3803
800-575-6298
http://www.nbna.org/scholarship.htm

The association offers a variety of scholarships ranging from $500 to $2,000 to students who are currently enrolled in nursing programs. Applicants must be members of the NBNA. Visit its Web site for further details and to download an application.

National Federation of the Blind
Scholarship Committee
805 Fifth Avenue
Grinnell, IA 50112-1653
641-236-3366
http://www.nfb.org/sch_intro.htm

Scholarships are available to blind high school seniors and undergraduates who are interested in or currently studying medicine or general studies. Contact the federation for further details. Visit the federation's Web site for an application.

National Health Service Corps
Scholarship Coordinator
5600 Fishers Lane
Rockville, MD 20857
800-221-9393
http://nhsc.bhpr.hrsa.gov/join_us/
    scholarships.asp

National Health Service Corps Scholarships paying tuition and a monthly stipend are available for students training at the graduate level to become family nurse practitioners and nurse-midwives. Recipients must practice one year in an underserved area for each year of aid received. Request an application by phone. Scholarships for other health specialties—such as physicians, physician assistants, and dentists—are also available.

National Student Nurses'
Association Foundation
45 Main Street, Suite 606
Brooklyn, NY 11201-1099
718-210-0705
nsna@nsna.org
http://www.nsna.org

Career Mobility Scholarships of up to $2,500 are available to students who are currently enrolled in nursing programs; high school seniors are not eligible. Promise of Nursing Scholarships are also available to nursing students in selected regions. Visit the foundation's Web site for more information and to download scholarship applications.

Navy: Careers: Healthcare:
Nursing
http://www.navy.com/healthcare/
    nursing

The Nurse Candidate Program provides financial support for students enrolled in a four-year nursing program; recipients must later serve on active duty with the Navy. This is one of several financial aid programs the Navy offers for nurses. Contact your local recruiter for details.

Oncology Nursing Society
Foundation
125 Enterprise Drive
RIDC Park West
Pittsburgh, PA 15275-1214
412-859-6100
http://onsfoundation.org

Registered nurses enrolled in an undergraduate or graduate program who are interested in oncology nursing may apply for $2,000, $3,000, and $5,000 scholarships. Contact the foundation for further information.

Pilot International Foundation
PO Box 4844
Macon, GA 31208-4844

478-743-2245
pifinfo@pilothq.org
http://www.pilotinternational.org/
html/foundation/scholar.shtml

Undergraduate students preparing for careers working with people with disabilities or brain-related disorders are eligible for scholarships; applicants must be members of a local Pilot Club. Contact the foundation for details.

Sallie Mae
http://www.collegeanswer.com

This Web site offers a scholarship database of more than 2.4 million awards (not all computer-related) worth more than $14 billion. You must register (free) to use the database.

Scholarship America
1 Scholarship Way
St. Peter, MN 56082-1693
800-537-4180
http://www.scholarshipamerica.org

This organization works through its local Dollars for Scholars chapters in 41 states and the District of Columbia. In 2003, it awarded more than $29 million in scholarships to students. Visit Scholarship America's Web site for more information.

Scholarships.com
http://www.scholarships.com

Scholarships.com offers a free college scholarship search engine (although you must register to use it) and financial aid information.

United Negro College Fund (UNCF)
http://www.uncf.org/scholarships

Visitors to the UNCF Web site can search for thousands of scholarships and grants, many of which are administered by the UNCF. High school seniors and undergraduate and graduate students who are interested in nursing and other careers are eligible. The search engine allows you to search by state, scholarship title, grade level, and achievement score.

U.S. Public Health Service
Division of Health Professions
    Support
Indian Health Service Scholarship
    Program (IHSSP)
801 Thompson Avenue, Suite 120
Rockville, MD 20852-1627
301-443-6197
bmiller@na.ihs.gov
http://www.ihs.gov/JobsCareerDevelop/
    DHPS/Scholarships/Scholarship_
    index.asp

The Health Professions Preparatory Scholarship Program provides awards to students who are preparing for entry into a Bachelor of Science in Nursing Program. Recipients must serve one year in an Indian health facility for each year of aid received. Visit the IHSSP Web site for more information.

Look To The Pros

The following professional organizations offer a variety of materials, from career brochures to lists of accredited schools to salary surveys. Many of them also publish journals and newsletters that you should become familiar with. Many also have annual conferences that you might be able to attend. (Although you may not be able to attend a conference as a participant, it may be possible to "cover" one for your school or even your local paper, especially if your school has a related club.)

When contacting professional organizations, keep in mind that they all exist primarily to serve their members, be it through continuing education, professional licensure, political lobbying, or just "keeping up with the profession." While many are strongly interested in promoting their profession and passing information about it to the general public, these busy professional organizations are not there solely to provide you with information. Whether you call or write, be courteous and to the point. Know what you need and ask for it. If the organization has a Web site, check it out first: what you're looking for may be available there for downloading, or you may find a list of prices or instructions (to send a self-addressed, stamped envelope with your request, for example). Finally, be aware that organizations, like people, move. To save time when writing, first confirm the address, preferably with a quick phone call to the organization itself: "Hello, I'm calling to confirm your address. . . ."

❑ THE SOURCES

Alpha Tau Delta
Scholarship Chair
11252 Camarillo Street
Toluca Lake, CA 91602-1259
http://www.atdnursing.org

Alpha Tau Delta is a national fraternity for professional nurses. It offers financial aid to its members, as well as a nursing job search engine at its Web site.

American Academy of Nurse Practitioners (AANP)
PO Box 12846
Austin, TX 78711-2846
512-442-4262
admin@aanp.org
http://www.aanp.org

The AANP offers information on national certification, scholarships, professional competencies, and employment opportunities; membership for nursing students; and a searchable database of nurse practitioner programs in the United States and throughout the world. You can also visit its Web site to read *A Nurse Practitioner Is Your Partner in Health*.

American Assembly for Men in Nursing Foundation

11 Cornell Road
Latham, NY 12110-1499
518-782-9400, ext. 346
aamn@aamn.org
http://www.aamn.org

The assembly is a support organization for male nurses. It offers scholarships, an on-line discussion forum, and membership to male and female nurses, nursing students, and the general public.

American Association of Colleges of Nursing

1 Dupont Circle, NW, Suite 530
Washington, DC 20036-1135
202-463-6930
http://www.aacn.nche.edu

The association offers information for nursing students and educators, including a nurse educator career summary, on-line courses, job listings, information on scholarships for currently enrolled nursing students, and online publications for nurses, such as *Your Nursing Career: A Look at the Facts and What Nursing Grads Should Consider When Seeking Employment.*

American Association of Critical-Care Nurses

101 Columbia
Aliso Viejo, CA 92656-4109
800-899-2226
info@aacn.org
http://www.aacn.org

This organization offers information on certification, job listings, and professional and consumer (non-nurses who are interested in the field of critical care nursing) membership. It also offers the following useful career publications at its Web site: *About Critical Care Nursing, Areas of Expertise,* and *Tap Into a Career in Critical Care Nursing.*

American Association of Legal Nurse Consultants

401 North Michigan Avenue
Chicago, IL 60611
877-402-2562
info@aalnc.org
http://www.aalnc.org

The association offers information on careers (via online publications such as *What is a LNC?* and *Getting Started in Legal Nurse Consulting*) and certification. It also offers publications, books, and an annual conference.

American Association of Neuroscience Nurses

4700 West Lake Avenue
Glenview, IL 60025
888-557-2266
info@aann.org
http://www.aann.org

The association offers information on certification, scholarships, and employment opportunities at its Web site.

American Association of Nurse Anesthetists (AANA)

222 South Prospect Avenue
Park Ridge, IL 60068-4001
847-692-7050
info@aana.com
http://www.aana.com

The AANA offers a variety of useful career information in the Students section of its Web site, including Questions and Answers about a Career in Nurse Anesthesia, which answers the most frequently asked questions about the profession. The Web site also includes information on the history of nurse anesthetist practice, accredited programs, jobs, scholarships, and the qualifications and scope of practice of nurse anesthetists. Students may also be interested in learning more about AANA-sponsored writing contests and its Anesthesia College Bowl.

American Association of Occupational Health Nurses

2920 Brandywine Road, Suite 100
Atlanta, GA 30341-5539
770-455-7757
aaohn@aaohn.org
http://www.aaohn.org

Visit the association's Web site to read an occupational and environmental health nursing profession fact sheet.

American College of Nurse-Midwives (ACNM)

8403 Colesville Road, Suite 1550
Silver Spring, MD 20910-6374
240-485-1800
http://www.acnm.org

Visit the ACNM's Web site to read *A Career in Midwifery*, which presents a basic overview of the field, educational requirements, and sources of financial aid. Its Web site includes lists of education programs and information on core competencies, financial aid, credential-

ing and licensure, history and philosophy of nurse-midwifery, and FAQs for students.

American Holistic Nurses' Association

PO Box 2130
Flagstaff, AZ 86003-2130
800-278-2462
info@ahna.org
http://www.ahna.org

The association provides information on careers in holistic nursing, educational programs, scholarships, and certification at its Web site.

American Hospital Association

One North Franklin
Chicago, IL 60606-3421
312-422-3000
http://www.aha.org

Contact the association for information on hospital-based nursing careers.

American Nurses Association

8515 Georgia Avenue, Suite 400
Silver Spring, MD 20910-3492
800-274-4ANA
http://www.nursingworld.org

This organization provides information on careers, an online journal about issues in nursing, a publications catalog, and links to state nursing associations.

American Organization of Nurse Executives (AONE)

Liberty Place
325 Seventh Street NW
Washington, DC 20004

202-626-2240
aone@aha.org
http://www.aone.org

Contact the AONE for information on careers and continuing education.

American Psychiatric Nurses Association

1555 Wilson Boulevard, Suite 515
Arlington, VA 22209-2429
703-243-2443
inform@apna.org
http://www.apna.org

Visit the association's Web site for answers to frequently asked questions about careers in psychiatric nursing, a list of graduate programs in psychiatric nursing, and information on membership for nursing students and scholarships.

American Society of PeriAnesthesia Nurses

10 Melrose Avenue, Suite 110
Cherry Hill, NJ 08003-3696
877-737-9696
aspan@aspan.org
http://www.aspan.org

The society offers information on nurse anesthetist careers, scholarships for undergraduate and graduate nursing students, membership options, and information on continuing education.

Association for Gerontology in Higher Education (AGHE)

1030 15th Street NW, Suite 240
Washington, DC 20005-1527
202-289-9806
http://www.aghe.org

Visit the AGHE's Web site to read *Careers in Aging: Consider the Possibilities*, which discusses the field of gerontology, careers available, how to select a program, and how to find jobs in aging. Also available online is scholarship information, special resources for students, and a searchable database of more than 750 gerontology programs.

Association of Perioperative Registered Nurses

2170 South Parker Road, Suite 300
Denver, CO 80231-5711
800-755-2676
custserv@aorn.org
http://www.aorn.org

Visit the association's Web site to read *What is Perioperative Nursing?* which details career options in the field. Its Web site also includes information on scholarships and grants, a Perioperative Nursing Program Online Directory, and a list of questions to ask about perioperative nursing courses.

Association of Women's Health, Obstetric and Neonatal Nurses

2000 L Street NW, Suite 740
Washington, DC 20036-4912
800-673-8499
http://www.awhonn.org

This organization represents nurses who specialize in the care of women and newborns. Its members include neonatal nurses, OB/GYN and labor and delivery nurses, women's health nurses, nurse scientists, nurse executives and managers, childbirth educators, and nurse practitioners. It offers membership to nursing students and associate membership status for non-nurses who are "involved or interested in women's health, obstetric, or neonatal specialty."

Commission on Graduates of Foreign Nursing Schools (CGFNS)

3600 Market Street, Suite 400
Philadelphia, PA 19104-2651
info@cgfns.org
http://www.cgfns.org

The CGFNS offers support to foreign nurses who are interested in coming to the United States to work. Its Web site offers tips on finding a job, relocating to the United States, and selecting a recruiter. The organization also offers hospital location guides for a nominal fee.

Emergency Nurses Association (ENA)

915 Lee Street
Des Plaines, IL 60016-6569
800-900-9659
enainfo@ena.org
http://www.ena.org

Contact the ENA for information on careers, certification, and scholarships.

Midwives Alliance of North America

375 Rockbridge Road, Suite 172–313
Lilburn, GA 30047-5870
888-923-6262
info@mana.org
http://www.mana.org

Contact the alliance for information on the career of nurse-midwife.

National Association for Practical Nurse Education and Service

PO Box 25647
Alexandria, VA 22313-5647
703-933-1003
napnes@bellatlantic.net
http://www.napnes.org

This organization offers a certification program, information on continuing education, a professional journal, job listings, and membership to nursing students. It also hosts an annual convention.

National Association of Clinical Nurse Specialists

2090 Linglestown Road, Suite 107
Harrisburg, PA 17110-9428
717-234-6799
http://www.nacns.org

Contact the organization for information on clinical nurse specialists careers, education programs, and membership for nursing students.

National Association of Geriatric Nursing Assistants

2709 West 13th Street
Joplin, MO 64801-3647
http://www.nagna.org

Visit the association's Web site for information on certification and employment opportunities and to participate in an online discussion forum.

National Association of Hispanic Nurses (NAHN)

1501 16th Street NW
Washington, DC 20036-1401

202-387-2477
info@thehispanicnurses.org
http://www.thehispanicnurses.org

Contact NAHN for education and career information of particular interest to Hispanic nursing students, including scholarships, financial aid, and student services.

National Association of Neonatal Nurses

4700 West Lake Avenue
Glenview, IL 60025-1485
800-451-3795
info@nann.org
http://www.nann.org

The association provides information about neonatal nursing careers, employment, membership for nursing students, and publications at its Web site.

National Association of Nurse Practitioners in Women's Health

503 Capitol Court NE, Suite 300
Washington, DC 20002-7707
202-543-9693
info@npwh.org
http://www.npwh.org

Contact this organization to learn more about opportunities for nurse practitioners who specialize in women's health.

National Association of Pediatric Nurse Practitioners (NAPNAP)

20 Brace Road, Suite 200
Cherry Hill, NJ 08034-2634
856-857-9700
info@napnap.org
http://www.napnap.org

The NAPNAP's Web site provides information on the career of pediatric nurse practitioners and a list of educational programs.

National Association of School Nurses

PO Box 1300
Scarborough, ME 04070-1300
877-627-6476
nasn@nasn.org
http://www.nasn.org

Visit the association's Web site for more information on school nurse careers, certification, and membership for nursing students.

National Black Nurses Association (NBNA)

8630 Fenton Street, Suite 330
Silver Spring, MD 20910-3803
800-575-6298
NBNA@erols.com
http://www.nbna.org

Contact the NBNA for education and career information of particular interest to African-American nursing students. The organization also offers information on membership for nursing students, scholarships, and job listings at its Web site.

National Conference of Gerontological Nurse Practitioners

4824 Edgemoor Lane
Bethesda, MD 20814-5306
301-654-3776
admin@ncgnp.org
http://www.ncgnp.org

Visit the National Conference's Web site for a list of gerontological nurse practitioner educational programs.

National Council of State Boards of Nursing
111 East Wacker Drive, Suite 2900
Chicago, IL 60601-4277
312-525-3600
info@ncsbn.org
http://www.ncsbn.org

Contact the council for information on licensing and a list of state boards of nursing.

National Federation of Licensed Practical Nurses (NFLPN)
605 Poole Drive
Garner, NC 27529-5203
919-779-0046
http://www.nflpn.com

The NFLPN offers a national certification program, publications (including a professional journal), membership for nursing students and supporters of the federation, job listings, an on-line forum, and a list of state practical nursing associations.

National Gerontological Nursing Association
7794 Grow Drive
Pensacola, FL 32514-7072
850-473-1174
ngna@puetzamc.com
http://www.ngna.org

Contact this organization for information on gerontological nursing and certification.

National Health Council
1730 M Street NW, Suite 500
Washington, DC 20036-4505
202-785-3910
http://www.nationalhealthcouncil.org

The council offers *300 Ways to Put Your Talent to Work in the Health Field* ($18), which lists job descriptions and education requirements for health professions ranging from art therapists and clinical chemists to nurse practitioners and physicians. It also lists sources of information on training schools and financial aid programs for health professions.

National League for Nursing (NLN)
61 Broadway, 33rd Floor
New York, NY 10006
212-363-5555
generalinfo@nln.org
http://www.nln.org

The NLN's goal is to "advance quality nursing education that prepares the nursing workforce to meet the needs of diverse populations in an ever-changing health care environment." Visit the NLN's Web site for career guidance materials (such as *A Career as a Nurse Educator*), information on approved schools of nursing, and links to other nursing organizations.

National League for Nursing Accrediting Commission
61 Broadway, 33rd Floor
New York, NY 10006-2800
http://www.nlnac.org/Forms/
    directory_search.htm

The commission accredits all levels of nursing educational programs in the United States (including Puerto Rico), Guam, Scotland, and the Virgin Islands. Visit its Web site for a searchable database of these programs.

National Network of Career Nursing Assistants

3577 Easton Road
Norton, OH 44203-5661
330-825-9342
cnajeni@aol.com
http://www.cna-network.org

At its Web site, this organization offers a discussion board and information on state agencies that offer nurse aide training programs.

National Organization for Associate Degree Nursing

PO Box 3188
Dublin, OH 43016-0088
614-451-1515
http://www.noadn.org

Contact the organization for information on associate degree nursing programs.

National Student Nurses' Association (NSNA)

45 Main Street, Suite 606
Brooklyn, NY 11201-1099
718-210-0705
nsna@nsna.org
http://www.nsna.org

The NSNA's goal is to *"organize, represent, and mentor students preparing for initial licensure as registered nurses, as well as those enrolled in baccalaureate completion programs."* Its Web site provides information on nursing careers, surviving nursing school, scholarships, and résumé writing and job hunting.

Oncology Nursing Society (ONS)

125 Enterprise Drive
RIDC Park West
Pittsburgh, PA 15275-1214
866-257-4ONS
customer.service@ons.org
http://www.ons.org

Contact the ONS for information on oncology nursing and certification. The Society also offers scholarships to undergraduate and graduate oncology nursing students.

U.S. Department of Health and Human Services

Bureau of Health Professions,
    Division of Nursing
5600 Fishers Lane, Room 9–35
Rockville, MD 20857
301-443-5688
http://bhpr.hrsa.gov/nursing

The USDHHS offers a variety of information on health professions student loans at its Web site, including scholarships and loans for disadvantaged students.

Index

Entries and page numbers in bold indicate major treatment of a topic.

O